Changing Positions

Changing Positions

WOMEN SPEAK OUT ON SEX AND DESIRE

JOANNE MARROW, PH.D.

Adams Media Corporation
Holbrook, Massachusetts

Published by Adams Media Corporation
260 Center Street, Holbrook, MA 02343

ISBN: 1-55850-760-4
Printed in the United States of America.

First Edition
J I H G F E D C B A

Library of Congress Cataloging-in-Publication Data
Marrow, Joanne.
Changing positions: women speak out on sex and desire / by Joanne Marrow.—1st ed.
Includes index.
ISBN 1-55850-760-4 (pbk.: alk. paper)
1. Women—United States—Sexual behavior. 2. Women—United States—Psychology. 3. Women—United
States—Attitudes. 4. Interpersonal relations—United States. I. Title.
HQ29.M38 1997
306.7'082—dc21

The names of the participants have been changed to protect their anonymity.

This publication is designed to provide accurate and authoritative information with regard to the subject
matter covered. It is sold with the understanding that the publisher is not engaged in rendering professional
advice. If expert assistance is required, the services of a competent professional person should be sought.

This book is available at quantity discounts for bulk purchases.
For information, call 1-800-872-5627 (in Massachusetts, 617-767-8100).

Visit our home page at http://www.adamsmedia.com

CONTENTS

ACKNOWLEDGMENTS

I gratefully thank all the women who participated in the interviews for this book. All freely shared their deepest sexual selves so that our conversations were enlightening for us both. I also thank Mike Kellermann, my statistician. His ease in discussing all levels of sexuality as well as his expertise in his field made our many consultations fun and intellectually exciting. I thank the women who were instrumental in leading me into and through the publishing world. Theresa Corrigan sent me to the American Booksellers Convention where I met my agent, Helen McGrath. Anne Weaver, my editor, recognized the importance of this manuscript. She understood the concepts and creatively and enthusiastically led me through the revisions. The meticulous eye of Merry Post, copyeditor, improved the book.

Finally, I thank my mother, Genevieve Marrow, who taught me intuitive, direct, and open communication skills. And I am grateful to my sisters, Claudia Marrow and Madeline Marrow, who from childhood to adulthood have shared with me their sexual stories. Our conversations taught me that talking about sex is important to our sexual development and is informative, playful, funny, and a delightful continuation of our unique intimacy as sisters.

— JOANNE MARROW, PH.D.

INTRODUCTION

WOMEN TODAY

Sometime in the 1970s a sexual revolution was said to have occurred. Sexuality was liberated. Women and men could now shamelessly and without guilt experience and explore their sexuality without the constraints of marriage, monogamy, and other social rules of conventional morality and sex. Yet in my interviews with 213 women, there is little evidence that a sexual revolution has shaped their sexuality.

There has been a revolution in reproduction: Women can separate pregnancy and sexuality. When "the pill" became widely available as effective contraception, women could engage in sexual activity without the dread of an undesired pregnancy. Sexual partners did not have to be evaluated in terms of their ability or willingness to be fathers.

During the same historical moment, more women chose to live with men without getting married. There was a time when those who lived together kept it secret from their families by having one partner temporarily move out when parents came for a visit. Those who cohabited were considered radical in the 1960s and early 1970s. But the phenomenon became so common that it was no longer remarkable. Now "living together" has its place. For some it is an economical arrangement for those who choose to be lovers with no fixed time commitment. For others it is an experiment in compatibility as preparation for marriage. For many women this has been a freeing experience as they explored partner sex without the constraints of committed relationships, marriage, and reproduction.

But the word *revolution* implies a drastic restructuring of an institution, and these small changes do not constitute a revolution. A true sexual revolution cannot be imagined by most American women. It would mean a freeing up of sexuality in all its forms. A sexual revolution would require a profound change in sexual morality. The United States in its diversity entertains many different sexual moralities. The most visible one is the one that enforces heterosexual marriage as the correct place for sexual expression for women. The "double standard" for men and women means that men incur less censure for sexual activity outside of marriage. Another feature of this form of scruples about sex is that sexuality should not be discussed. This means that few parents discuss sexuality with their children; lovers find it difficult to talk openly about sex; and it is uncommon for women to share their sexual experiences candidly with one another.

The policy of silence around sexuality extends into the educational system. Sex education is incomplete, and teachers are themselves embarrassed to discuss the topic. There are serious attempts by conservative groups to force school boards to limit all levels of sexual education. Teachers are instructed to tell young people to just say "no" to sex and to become celibate. Teens ignore the adults and, denied honest counseling and information, continue to experiment with sex in ways that endanger their health. Consequently, the incidence of teens with unplanned pregnancies in the United States is the highest of any industrialized country. Teen pregnancies are high-risk pregnancies. Twenty percent of teens contract a sexually transmitted disease. Teenage girls are also a high-risk group for date rape.

Despite the fact that gay and lesbian activist groups have significant presence in the media, during interpersonal conversations lesbians and bisexual women maintain silence in the discussions with heterosexuals about sexual orientation. Americans live with a presumption that everyone they know is heterosexual. Many lesbians and bisexual women tell of listening in silence to a heterosexual remark, "I can always tell who is gay!" Since the speaker usually follows such an observation with an antigay comment, she does not risk disclosing her orientation. Heterosexuals who are not overtly hostile are often uncomfortable with the topic of lesbianism and bisexuality. This stifles open communication from bisexual and lesbian women about their lives.

When silence about sexuality prevails, it is difficult for women to enjoy sexual activities without emotional tussle. Masturbation, a never-discussed and secretly performed activity, is not seen as a simple pleasure; instead, it is a source of conflict for many women. When a woman enjoys partnered sexual activities that are different from the so-called "missionary position" (man lying on top of the woman) of sexual intercourse, she may feel awkward in initiating novel sexual interactions with her partner. Given the silence about sexuality, it is difficult for her to explain what she really wants to happen in a sexual interlude. In addition, women are reluctant to point out to men that they are sexually inept. Fear of harming a man's ego is another justification for women to hush their talk about sexuality.

Although there is this personal silence about sexuality, the media are sexualized. TV talk shows, films, advertising, and music are all saturated with sexual themes. Most of these are full of sexual misinformation, sexual shaming, the objectification of women, female models who do not look like average women, and the biases of the maker of the product. Few women are able to sort through these stimuli and obtain information that is personally useful. Many women are made angry by the sexual images in the media that exploit women's bodies. Yet, in spite of their hatred of how women are depicted, millions of women aspire to physically resemble advertising models. Few can achieve this goal. Unable to look like the cultural fantasy of "woman," some women feel that they will not be seen as sexually desirable. Only a stroke of luck will allow them to find a compatible sexual partner.

Many women in the contemporary world are divided selves in their sexual experiences. Cultural conditions have created a situation in which women alienate their minds and spirits from the physical event of a sexual exchange. If a woman experiences shame, guilt, trepidation, fear, embarrassment, uncertainty, or disrespect from her partner when she is aroused in the sexual embrace, she is torn apart from her personal identity. She places her body in a circumstance that is sexual, yet her mind and spirit are not fully participating with pleasure in the experience. Later, she has to find the means to reestablish herself into a whole being. Being torn apart and then reconstructing the self is a painful process that no one should have to endure. Yet this is a common occurrence for women who are not completely free in their sexual expression.

But it is possible for a woman to transform herself sexually from the divided self who cannot completely enter and embrace her sexual activities to one who claims her wholeness and full capacity for erotic delight. This transformation is the joyous journey of a woman's path of passion.

A REAL SEXUAL REVOLUTION

After a sexual revolution, women's sexual expeditions will be safe, comfortable, and an open, spontaneous, joyful, and continuously transformative adventure. Women and men will engage in sexual practices without shame, but instead with ecstatic mutual pleasuring. People will have the capacity to openly discuss sexuality with the same understanding and complexity with which they can discuss politics and religion. Sexual education in the schools will be age-appropriate, explicit, direct, and unembarrassed. Everyone will understand the cause and prevention of sexually transmitted diseases (STDs). The use of condoms for safe sex will be a matter of course. The art of sexuality and its psychological and emotional components will be taught as part of sexual education.

Ageism, in the sense that the young and the old are presumed nonsexual, will disappear. The assumption that fat people and those judged physically unattractive do not deserve to be sexual will be gone. Women and men will not be criticized for dating more than one sexual partner. As long as they practice safe sex, they will not be judged for their number of lovers. People who pair up for a sexual exchange will first discuss prevention of STDs and contraception. Then they will confer about their favorite sexual activities or the sexual practices that they would like to share with each other. Sexual identities like bisexual and lesbian might become irrelevant because the gender of the partners would not be a matter of concern to anyone but the couple. The culture will be healed of homophobia. All of this would happen in the absence of shame, guilt, embarrassment, confusion, judgmental attitudes, blaming, shock, and disgust.

More profoundly, violence will never be paired with sexuality. Rape will not occur. Children's sexuality will be cherished and protected. Childhood sexual abuse will disappear. Battering will not happen between spouses, as the sexual bond would be understood to be a kind and nurturing connection, not a license to "only hurt the one you love." As these elements vanish, so will the many victims disappear. New generations will not have members who have experienced sexual violence. Women of this post-revolutionary period will be free to exercise their sexuality without the dilemma of simultaneously recovering from the trauma of sexual assault.

Bodies will not be defined as property. The sale of human bodies in the industry of prostitution will end. If the norm for sexual exchange is full sharing of mind, body, emotions, and spirit, it could not be performed in exchange for economic gain. In the personal arena women and men will enjoy sexuality in full, whole interactions worthwhile in and of themselves.

Exploitation of women's (and men's) bodies in advertising will cease to exist. It will be seen as a symptom of a sexually dysfunctional culture. Only in a culture that conceals sexuality in real-life exchanges can sexual images be used in a titillating manner to advertise goods that are unrelated to sexual activities. In the post-revolutionary society that is truly open and unembarrassed by sexuality, this advertising will be evaluated as inane and silly.

Drug use will not be associated with sexuality. Today, many thousands of people do not engage in a sexual exchange without the "facilitation" of alcohol, cocaine, "poppers," nicotine, or marijuana. They need drugs to allow themselves to relax and to open up physically and sexually to another person. Those who openly and clearly communicate about pleasuring each other and themselves want a natural high for the experience. A healthy drug-free body and an aware consciousness that can perceive all the nuances of the sexual interaction are essential to shared sexuality.

A revolution is a radical change, and there has been no radical change in how American women relate to themselves as sexual beings nor in what they expect from their partners. It is clear that

American society is still very far from a sexual revolution. The changes I have described are just beginning to enter the awareness of the public consciousness. Public policy about sexuality still promotes silence instead of education. The social mores still withhold from women the full expression of their sexuality.

WOMEN SEXUAL REVOLUTIONARIES

Why haven't the feminist revolutionaries of the 1970s made the revolution about sexuality? The answer lies in the prioritizing of issues. For themselves, these women want free, egalitarian, and independent relationships; nonjealous lovers; the opportunity to explore all aspects of their sexuality; freedom from childbearing; economic independence; the right to pursue higher education; and political power. When these goals were translated into political work, the focus on sexuality soon concentrated on rescuing the victims of sexual violence. The reason was obvious. Women who are in trauma from sexual abuse cannot be freely expressive of their own sexuality until they are healed. In addition, often the rest of their lives became a shambles. Some of the revolutionaries recognized their own sexual victimization and set out to heal themselves and other women. These revolutionaries are the women who broke the silence about sexual assault and who started rape crisis centers. Further consciousness-raising led to the creation of shelters for battered women. In the 1980s, women began publicly revealing their traumatic experiences with child sexual assault. When pornography was defined as propaganda that celebrates sexual violence, some feminists took on the task of limiting or changing pornography through education, social pressure, and legal restrictions on it. The result of this work is that sexual violence and victimization are now acknowledged as major social problems. One turn of the sexual revolution has been made by these activist feminists. This push brought into the light the magnitude of the sexual damage that many women endure.

The other side of the sexual revolution is the creation of good, free, healthy, and fun-filled sexuality. This quest has been left for women to pursue in private. Women protect themselves from sexual objectification and from punishing social judgments by keeping their sexual experiences secret except for sharing this part of their lives with a few close friends. But it is freeing to vocalize, share, and receive reactions about one's experience. With communication, a woman's isolation is broken, and she finds she has a commonality with other women. This liberation of spirit has healed women in terms of their victimization by rape and sexual violence. But we have not heard the voices of women on how they have celebrated, enjoyed, and cultivated their sexuality. Few women are willing to publicly admit that sexual satisfaction is as important to them as their work or family.

Women are keeping their silence about their successful sexual experiences because the culture still labels the sexual woman as immoral. Instead of challenging the social judgment of being labelled immoral, lacking values, evil, or sinful, women keep silent about their sexual adventures. There is no space for women to share and celebrate their sexual experiences. This means that there is no place where women can be taught what is necessary to make a celebratory sexual experience occur. Just as women suffered in silence about their pain of being raped, women are quietly silent about their failed sexual attempts. In isolation they think something is wrong with themselves. They settle for unsatisfying sexual experiences or they wait for a new partner who may be knowledgeable and who may provide them with a better experience. Women protect their sexual partners from the awareness of their sexual dissatisfaction. They do not want to be labelled by their partners as having a sexual problem, so they fake orgasm and convince themselves that sexuality is not so important. The women who do have fulfilled and creative sexual lives have no place where they can teach and share their experiences. Their sexuality is their happy but very private secret.

Few feminist sexual revolutionaries have sustained the goal to practice free and open sexual expression, or to design forums in which women share their sexual adventures, failures, and successes. One platform may be the college classroom in women's studies. Another is the confidential group therapy session. The public social atmosphere is still one of sexual repression, especially for women. Despite the ongoing work of the sexual revolutionaries, the climate of women's sexual expeditions is one in which sexuality is discussed in a humorous and superficial way. Feminist sexual revolutionaries function in a small niche in academia, the art world, and in lesbian and bisexual subcultures. They have had little influence on the public representation of sexuality that is sexualized with masculine fantasies. Most women are not influenced by this discourse on female sexuality. In the normal context of a woman's life, there is no conversation about sexuality with her mother, limited and indirect discussion with women friends, and only hesitant and difficult talk with a lover.

Unable to adopt the masculinist detachment of sexual exchange as a purely physical event, women are left to wonder, "Why isn't it so easy and simple for me?" Women can open themselves to a deep experience of intimacy when being sexual with a partner. It holds the potential of exquisite pleasure when found, as well as dreadful pain when lost. The potential for emotional pain, and the fears of pregnancy, STDs, sexual ineptness of herself as a partner, and the inability to achieve orgasm all add to the intensity and seriousness of sexual arousal for women.

Most women do not see sexuality as terrain to be traversed alone. They are not independent explorers, seeking sexual journeys for the value of the adventure itself. Sexuality is a companionate road. Most women want a monogamous and, therefore, a safe partner for the trek. The women who do want the adventure of more than one sexual partner and who desire sexual experiences for their intrinsic value receive no support for their ability to take a more perilous route.

Silence about their sexual hopes and dreams is the greatest enemy for women who would begin to discover their sexual selves. Silence from parents creates a mystery around sexuality. It can foster an unrealistic romantic notion that speechlessly and spontaneously two people can come together and create joyous sexual play. A woman with this idea can only hope that the right person appears in front of her some day soon. When a woman takes the risk of a sexual encounter and discovers it lacking, she often blames herself. Today a woman would not characterize herself as frigid; instead she can initiate a complicated analysis of herself and her partner to try to explain "what went wrong." Sometimes the simplest explanation is never made: They did not talk about what they like to experience sexually.

For years I have broken the silence around sexuality by asking women to describe their lives as sexual beings. Each woman's story has elements of joy, confusion, pain, sadness, revolution, and transformation. Sexuality is not a drive that women direct at any available object. Women consciously consider their sexual choices and adventures. As a woman matures and broadens her erotic consciousness, her serenity and security in her sensual identity deepens. A woman's sexuality is the physical presentation of her core self. This core self is developed as the woman expresses her passion and so learns from experience who she is as a sexual being.

SEXUAL TRANSFORMATIONS

Open talk about sexuality can create the possibility in a woman to live a joyous and creative sexual life. This transformation can happen when she learns how other women were able to achieve it. But popular culture presents women with faulty maps of the sexual journey that leads to transformation. The most accessible social map of women's sexuality illustrates a freeway to heterosexual marriage, penile-vaginal intercourse, the bearing and rearing of children, and an old age wherein sexuality loses its importance. This cartography includes instructions on how to become sexually pleasing and accessible to men, how to define one's appearance, and simultaneously how to remain sexually modest and discreet. Another chart (labelled "bad girl" or "slut") marks the trail for the female sexual rebel who defies sexual restrictions by brazen clothing, risqué conversation, and sexual libertinism. Although the woman who uses this alternate chart may think that she is expressing independence, she has merely adopted the dominant social path that is the mirror opposite of the conformist woman. These maps are respectively labelled the virgin/mother and the whore paths.

Women are conditioned to be receptive and to be concerned with social approval and social relationships. We take these maps naively as though they were the true reflection of our sexuality. Women use these public charts for sexuality as the guideline for their sexual explorations. It is not long before most women discover that there is a conflict between the map and their own sexual experiences. Trained to blame themselves and to accept guilt, many women become confused. "Is the map faulty or is something wrong with me?" they ask themselves. Since open discussion about sexuality is silenced, many women become trapped with a sense that there is something different and wrong about their sexual responses and interests. They accept the cultural map as a perfect chart. Other women find a new pathway into their sexuality by acknowledging that the social maps are missing some parts, lacking in detail, and often are simply erroneous.

Women who trailblaze their own sexuality start from a perspective that their own experience is valuable and is the true compass against which to test the social cartography. Assuming this stance requires strong self-esteem, confidence, the mastery to discuss sexuality openly, and, often, the competence to find sexual information that is scientifically accurate and unbiased by moral judgments. These qualities are not merely the starting point. The very act of trailblazing, of using one's own inner compass as a measure of one's own sexuality, will develop and foster these characteristics. The necessary condition for a woman to uncover and cultivate her individual sexual life is the willingness to embrace the fact that she is the expert who can measure the quality of her own sexual experience.

When a woman acknowledges that her own feelings and perceptions are the milestone of the value of her sexual life, she discovers that the nature of her sexual-

ity is extremely private, though often shared with a partner. Each woman is a unique sexual being. While women do share many commonalities, they individually have distinctive sexual histories, personal fantasies, singular physical responses, and unique desires from a partner. Every woman must come to an understanding that her sexual path is her own. She must take her own survey of her pleasure and chart a singular course based on the pursuit of her own bliss.

The experience of personal transformation is a mysterious and potent elemental evolution into a new and stronger being. Life is a process of the availability of transformative experiences. Some women ignore, dodge, repress, and flee the opportunities for sexual transformation that arise in their lives. Fear prevents them from embracing the challenge of movement into greater sexual awareness and self-possession. Their erotic timidity offers the illusion of safety, but the cost is a sensuality that is like a giant redwood pruned into a bonsai.

The progress of women's sexual development is best understood as a continuous transformation of awareness, education, and experience. These three processes operate in a cycle. When a woman becomes aware of some aspect of her own erotic self, she obtains information about it from the world. The information stimulates her curiosity and interest, and she is impelled to enter a sexual experience. The woman who fears her own passion will deny herself the opportunity to use the experience transformatively. She will not examine the changes and shifts within herself that the experience has set in motion. But the woman who is on her sexual journey of awareness processes the experience in self-reflection. If the event validates the education or information that propelled her into the activity, the woman integrates the event and moves on to create similar experiences. If the event contradicts the data that was the source of the impetus, the woman encounters conflict. This struggle can be resolved in a number of ways. She can change her perception of herself or her perception of her partner. She can alter her perception of the situation or of the experience.

For example, a teenage virgin becomes aware of her own sexual feelings. She receives information that sexual intercourse is the epitome of pleasure. She experiences sexual intercourse for the first time, and, as many women report, "It was no big deal." This contradicts the information that she would experience sexual ecstacy. The teenager, depending on her self-awareness and her breadth of information, may resolve the conflict in different ways. If she evaluates herself and her partner, she may say, "Neither of us knew what we were doing." She may place the responsibility for the sexual failure on her partner: "He didn't know what he was doing." Or, "A more experienced, older man will be a better lover." She may assess herself in a number of different ways: "There is something wrong with me." "It will be better if I'm in love." "It will be better after I get used to it." "I don't like sex with men." She may explain the problem as the result of an aspect of the situation: "We were high."

The manner in which these struggles are resolved will determine the course and direction of the teenager's next sexual move. Unfortunately, the prohibition against honest communication about sexual experiences will not allow her the opportunity to validate the accuracy of her conclusions. Her journey into her subsequent step of transformation is unaided by the experiences of women who have traversed the same path. Instead of a strong, sure movement forward, she will hesitatingly totter toward her next sexual event. Uninformed, and unconscious of her true sexual feelings, she will meander into and through sexual activities that may be potentially dangerous. If she is fortunate, she may have been educated into a sense of self-protection, caution, and self-care. These strengths will enable her to pursue her next move with confidence and vulnerability.

This book is a travelog through the land of women's sexuality. It is a documentation of the transformations that women experience as they dare to journey into the mysterious countries of their sexual selves. Women have described a diverse country. The heterosexual plains are well explored. There is a veritable freeway through the heterosexual lands. For many women the freeway of heterosexuality is the only discovered territory. They never see the exit lane marked "bisexual" or "lesbian." The information that there are different sexual places to explore can be exciting or terrifying. Most heterosexual women overlook these crossroads.

The women who are interested in scaling the lesbian alps discover the ascent arduous and alarming. Homophobia warns them that the lesbian landscape is dangerous. When she does persist on this road she may discover the difficulty in finding other lesbians. Lesbian culture is at one and the same time evident and hidden. Entering this realm may require passwords at the crossroads. Even lesbians struggle with finding the path to the lesbian community and becoming accepted as a part of it. While the society of women exists in every vicinity, it is well concealed. Many lesbians seek safety in quietly withdrawn alliances. They practice invisibility.

The bisexual lanes crisscross and meander across the entire range. Some bisexual women may appear to settle in heterosexual or lesbian lands, but they carry within themselves the ability to traverse all of the sexual domain. Bisexual women may explore the lesbian alps and come to love them with the same passion that lesbians hold. But within themselves they also appreciate the wonder of sexuality and companionship with men. The travels of their lives are marked by periods of apparent settling in various geographies. Most often the choice is made when a particular companion offers a rewarding period of time.

Wherever a woman settles in the sexual territory, she can find similarities with women of different sexual orientations. There is a common ground of the female sexual experience. This book is a guide through those realms.

CHILDHOOD

EXPLORING THE BODIES OF OTHER CHILDREN

When young girls are curious about others' bodies, it is an innocent interest in the unknown. They know that the world is divided into girls and boys, but they do not know exactly what that means from experience. How are boys' bodies different from their own? They are also curious about individual differences in bodies. Do all boys look the same? Do other girls look like their own bodies? What happens to the girls who set out to answer these questions?

Twenty-nine percent of the women I interviewed stated that they never looked at the bodies of other children. They were simply not interested. As Kristie said, "It never occurred to me to do." Since it was not an issue for them, they did not have a sense if it was wrong or right. It simply did not exist. Parents never warned them not to look at other children. These were not obedient little girls whose parents told them "Don't!" They were nonsexual girls, and they were never in contact with children who suggested that they look at one another.

Seventy-one percent of the women explored the bodies of other children when they were younger than eight years old. Of these, 44 percent had the opportunity to study the bodies of both girls and boys. Eleven percent investigated other girls, and 16 percent looked at boys only. There is no relationship between which gender was studied and adult sexual orientation. Children looked at the other children with whom they were allowed to play. The girls who studied only girls simply did not have the opportunity to look at boys. Heterosexuals, bisexuals, and lesbians were equally as likely to explore both boys and girls as children. These girls were inquisitive about the appearance of other children's bodies, or they were happily cooperating with the investigations of children who were eager to learn about how bodies are constructed.

Crystal, who is 20, was a California 5 year old who had an innocent curiosity about a neighbor boy. In his room they played "hot tub." They were acting out the one situation where they knew people took off their clothes together. Beverly, 47, has a vague memory of playing doctor with her brother and "being silly about it." The doctor is the one person who can closely examine bodies and for whom it is good and right. The doctor asks questions about bodies. In this game children get their curiosity about physical appearance satisfied by acting out a respected adult role.

Children who help attend to younger siblings or relatives are able to make natural observations. Beverly says, "I helped change diapers of infants and toddlers. We brothers and sisters closely examined each other, and none of the adults said anything about it." Nina says she had no desire to explore neighbor children, "I saw my little brother bathe so I knew what boys looked like." Beverly's and Nina's parents were matter-of-fact about exposure of children's bodies during their care. This allowed them to satisfy innocent curiosity without creating an extraordinary situation. Still, the silence about sexuality was maintained. These parents did not discuss the differences between male and female bodies.

Sex-Positive Parents

Did their parents provide guides or maps for these girls as they took their first innocent steps into the sexual realm? A few did, to a limited degree. Seventeen percent of the women interviewed remembered that their parents took their play at "doctor" in stride and did not punish them. These parents gave their daughters the impression that their glance into the mysterious territory of the bodies of others was right and natural. Hope, 40, recalls: "My mom would say, 'Just don't hurt yourself, honey,' when she found us." Recollections of this childish sex play were pleasant and held a sense of fascination and wonder. Amity, 18, recalls: "Theodore and I used to run around the backyard naked, watering the plants. My mother made me feel it was okay."

Paula remembers that her parents never gave her the impression that there was anything wrong with her sex play. "My parents were not inhibited. They, especially my mom, were open, liberal, and comfortable with themselves. They were demonstrative with each other." Hoshi, 37, also recalls: "My mom was good. She never instilled bad things about sex in my mind. I always felt it was okay to look at boys and girls." Leotie's parents were also "very comfortable with their own sexuality. Bodies were treated as nothing very special; bodies were okay; no big deal."

Some women had parents who were nudists. The appearance of the human body was a simple fact. For them, there was no secret mystery to uncover.

Charlene, 48, says: "In my family it was natural to not wear clothes, so I didn't have a lot of curiosity about bodies." Roseann, 22, states: "I'd seen my dad naked. My family was very open. My parents just walked around naked when I was a child. My whole family, the kids walked around naked, too." When parents are relaxed about sexual issues, they can bring this attitude to their daughter's awakening sexual interest. These daughters learned that sexuality and bodies are good, interesting, and not mysterious.

PARENTAL PROSCRIPTIONS

Some parents do talk to their children about sexual games. Their message is that it is wrong and "don't do it." Most parents gave their daughters the message, "Don't do that!" Sixty-four percent of the women stated that their parents clearly instructed them that looking at their friends' bodies was wrong. Nineteen percent of the parents never talked about looking at other children. Yet somehow their daughters learned the concept that it was wrong to examine the genitals of playmates. In sum, 83 percent of the women received the communication from their parents that it was wrong to look at their friends. These parents were trying to prevent their daughters from beginning their sexual paths. Were they successful? No. Carmen, 42, is typical. She remembers: "I was told by my mother not to look at other children without clothes. I did it anyway."

Now 41, Leanne remembers: "My parents told me it was bad to see another's sexual parts. 'Keep your dress down so no one can see it.' Other kids said it was wrong. Their parents told them. So we snuck in the first grade, in kindergarten." These youngsters learned not to let their parents know what they were doing.

Some parents create a household where every reference to sexuality rings with the message that it is sinful. These parents pretend to be nonsexual. They do not touch each other or the children with affection. Daughters with parents like this still found a way to satisfy their curiosity about bodies. Kate is now 31, and her parents behaved this way. She explains: "My parents' attitude was that anything that had to do with bodies and sexuality was bad and wrong. So when we looked at each other, we did it in secret, knowing they wouldn't approve." Eileen, 30, had a Catholic upbringing and remembers thinking that examining other kids was wrong: "Little was said. And there was very little outward physical contact in the family. Physical touch didn't happen among the unmarried. But I still played 'doctor' with boys and girls." Doris is 50 and says, "I was raised with Catholic moral values. But I looked at Tony, feeling it was okay. I was told that it was wrong. It was a hidden thing, but it wasn't wrong. It was a curiosity. I never saw my father. My cousin was the first nude boy I'd seen."

PARENTAL SILENCE

Parents who don't talk about sexuality leave their children to their own devices when the opportunity to explore other children's bodies arises. Children learn that this topic is never raised in the household. Julia is 38 and remembers investigating her 5-year-old girlfriend: "It was okay with us, the participants. But I kind of knew adults wouldn't be okay. I'd never heard anyone say anything, so I assumed it was a taboo subject." Parental silence was not an emptiness or an absence of information for Julia. Instead it was a real message that some things are unspeakable. Julia was doing something that is never discussed. Therefore she would not reveal this behavior to adults. She could be punished for talking about it as well as for doing it.

The pattern of thinking that if parents do not talk about it, it is best to keep it from them is expressed by Kyoko, who is 36: "I don't think my parents said anything outright about sexual show and tell. Genitals were supposed to be private, so showing it was naughty. I took baths with my brothers, but that was different. We were related. When we played 'I'll show you mine, you show me yours' it was wrong because it was someone not related, my brother's friend being there. My parents never talked about sex. There were no verbal instructions about it."

Nadia got the point that researching other bodies was wrong despite the fact that her parents were silent about sexuality: "I knew that looking at other kids was something you had to sneak at. We used different bathrooms at home. You weren't supposed to be naked in front of the other sex. The different bathrooms taught me that we weren't supposed to see others' bodies."

GETTING CAUGHT

Women recall that as little girls they reacted to adults out of an "us" versus "them" mentality. Even before the age of 8, they determined that they had one way of looking at things and adults another. Jennifer, 21, recalls: "I was playing with a boy, and his mom caught us. We got in trouble. His mom talked to my mom. She came into my room later to talk with me, and was she mad! So after that we always hid." A generation older than Jennifer, Julie, at 58, remembers what happened when she got caught: "I looked at both boys and girls, and I thought it was okay until my mother caught us. She said it was not nice, not to do it. She smelled my hands and said I was naughty. Then I didn't let her catch me, I was still curious." Ellen is 57: "I played doctor with a neighbor boy, and we thought it was all right to do until his mother caught us and punished us both. She told us we were terrible, and then my mother punished me. She told me I couldn't play with him for a month and told me I was bad and told me not to do it again." These women are typical. Even as adults, they use the childish terms "got caught," "got in trouble." These expressions denote the dual morality that children establish. What they are doing is okay as long as adults do not discover them. It is being found out, getting caught, that is the problem, not the activity itself.

Cath, a 45-year-old lesbian, develops this theme: "I had to have been around 7 or 8 at that point. I remember playing 'doctor' with Margie. We went over to her house. She had one of those nurse's kits. I think we just looked at each other. And we gave each other shots and things. I have some kind of a vague memory of telling my parents that I and my female friends were playing doctor, and my mother's reaction was 'Don't do that with her.' I generalized that to mean that it was not okay to do it with anybody. I got a clear message from Mom that it was not okay to do. I felt like I got caught doing something I shouldn't do, and I knew I shouldn't talk about it. I don't think I stopped doing it, I just stopped talking about it. With the onslaught of sexual feelings, you conceal it and lie." Cath regards her sexual secrets as a kind of lie. As we shall see, many little girls keep a secret falsehood.

Women have vivid memories of what happened when parents "caught" them. Kenya is 25 and heterosexual. She played "house" with boys and girls and felt it was a fun and positive experience with the other children. Playing house meant husband and wife and the ability to be naked in the bedroom. She played house with girls, taking turns with the male and female roles, and none of the adults knew. But "I was caught by my mom with boys and she was very angry and told me not to kiss boys. After that Gramma and Mom started to watch me more."

Spring remembers a complex game that involved sex play: "I liked to play with the boys when I was 5. If I took off my clothes and let the boys look at me, I could go in the boys' tree or ride their bikes. This was their idea and sounded fine to me. When Mom found out, I was told I couldn't play with boys, and she was angry. She yelled at us." At the time, Spring did not mind undressing for the boys, so she did not understand why her mother did not like the game.

Daphne is 29 and recalls what happened when her parents caught her with boys and girls. "I knew what we were doing was wrong when my parents caught us. They were embarrassed, stiff, formal, and uncomfortable. My parents said, 'Don't do it again.' They didn't punish us. That made it strange and bad. Because they were quick to punish. So such a measured reaction was a crisis." Here the fact of not being punished, yet at the same time being told that it was something she was not to do, created a situation that was extraordinary. Daphne knew that her innocent childish game was somehow a crossover into a mysterious and hazardous region. But she had no explanation about why this game was so dangerous.

Children need some kind of explanation for modesty, however simple, to make sense of a rule that prohibits nudity. An example of a simple explanation is, "Grown-ups wear clothes all the time, and you are starting to grow up. Only babies go without clothes." Children have no shame about their bodies until their parents teach them shame by violently reacting to nudity. Later in life women will need to unlearn shame so that they can have a fully satisfying sexual life.

Sometimes the consequences of getting caught were severe. Rene, 39, was abused for exploring boys and girls: "Mom caught me and beat me for it. She told me it was the wrong thing to do. For us kids it was a secret, but it was okay. It was fun until then." Rene took the beating in stride, as do many children who are raised in abusive households. But her parent destroyed the innocence of the play among the children. The beating cast an unexplained shadow over an ingenuous game. Having fun looking at bodies was now, for an unknown reason, a bad thing to do. As an adult Rene had to consciously shed this childhood specter that lingered over her nudity with a lover.

Sanura

Sanura, 32, tells her stories with an insightful awareness of the negative repercussions on her formative sexual self and her ideas of how the adults could have more appropriately responded to her. "When I was 5 years old, I had a lot of confidence. Raymond was five also and a neighbor. He wanted to play on the swing set, and I told him he could if he showed us his hot dog. He did it and was nonchalant. He reached in and pulled it out. It was okay.

"I lived in a small town just outside New York City. When I was 6 and in school, a boy said, 'Show me yours, I'll show you mine.' I said, 'No,' lots of times. Once during naptime in the darkened room we were supposed to put our heads down on the desk. Wayne sat next to me and said, 'Sanura, look.' His genitals looked like a pile of dark something. He was dark-skinned, and the room was dark. I started to tell the teacher, 'Wayne showed me . . .' But the teacher stopped

me and said, 'Sanura, put your head down on your desk. Sanura, put your head down.' I tried to keep saying it, but she stopped me. I felt that I did something wrong when she cut me off. I felt she was protecting him. She should have asked me to step aside to discuss it with me to see how I felt about it. But her way was not to deal with it. The message was: 'Don't bring it up, don't tell.'

"Other sexual things happened in school. In the first grade there was a couple. They were boyfriend and girlfriend. They exposed their genitals to each other all the time, and all the kids knew. We knew because they were open about it. I had a boyfriend, and every time the teacher left we would kiss and these kids exposed themselves. Bruce and I would go behind the drinking fountain. It offered more privacy in case an adult walked in. We knelt behind the sink area and kissed. We'd tell the class they could come and watch. They did, and they encouraged us, 'Come on, kiss.' We never got caught, and it was fun to do. There was always something going on when the teacher left the room. The privacy was almost like it is a secret, but a shared secret from adults.

"My feelings of fun and confidence changed on my ninth birthday. We were playing 'truth or dare' and we did a lot of kissing. In a 'truth or dare' the kids asked us to kiss for one minute or some period of time. Jesse was sweet and nice and we were kissing. I looked up, and I saw that my mom and my two oldest sisters had been peeking out the window watching. My older sisters were laughing hysterically. My mother gave me a very sharp, stern look of disapproval and disgust and stopped me dead in my tracks. I went inside to find out what was up. But all she said was, 'I can't believe you would do something like that in front of all the neighbors. You don't know who could have been watching!' I was devastated. I broke up with the boy, and I never talked to him again. He cried and he cried every time I saw him. I see that as a pivotal point. Prior to my ninth birthday I had a lot of sexual curiosity. This incident put a stop on that for me. The strong disapproval and disgust from my mother was enough to dampen significantly my sexual development.

"What would've been better would have been for my mother not to be intrusive and not to allow my sisters to participate and make it a shame ritual. What would have been healthier, if she had concerns, was to talk to me about it and ask me how I was feeling. To let me know that I was healthy, but to help me set parameters of what was healthy. And if I had any questions that she would be there to answer them for me. Obviously she had concerns, but she wasn't able to offer me this."

Sanura remembers her childhood experiences as innocent explorations. Her cogent analysis of her experiences is a result of her processing of her significant sexual transformations as an adult. She has claimed her right to a powerful, sensual adult sexuality and knows that she overcame the negative messages of her childhood.

SECRECY

Many children never got "caught" because they intuitively kept these activities secret. Vanessa, age 24, vividly recalls: "When I was 7 there was Debbie across the street who was 5 years old. She had this deck in the backyard and once we were there. There were me, my brother, and about eight neighborhood kids. We were on the deck. All of us circled around Debbie and she pulled down her pants and showed us her vagina. The boys looked really closely. And she took off her underwear and passed it around to everybody. It was like a show. We were really interested in seeing it. The boys' noses were almost against her vagina. She didn't allow anyone to touch it. I didn't understand the underwear part of it. But the boys were interested in it. It was safe and a good thing. We were laughing. It was fun. No one was home at her house, so it was a secret from the grown-ups."

Ryfka, a 47-year-old lesbian, recalls a similar situation: "When I was 10 I played with the boys next door who were the same age. We played 'doctor' in the basement playrooms of our houses. I don't remember who started it, me or the boys. I looked at the boys, and they looked at me. We didn't touch each other. It had to be secret, because the message you get is: 'You're not sexual, and don't mess with anybody.' No one said this, so I don't know how I got that message."

If their parents never mentioned that it was wrong, how did these girls know to conceal these experiments from their parents? It may be that they were imitating the secrecy of their parents. Most parents were never naked in front of their children. Some never kissed or touched one another in front of these daughters. Sexual activities were also private and quiet. These things were never discussed. So, when they were little girls, these women followed the same pattern.

Brandy indicates an understanding of the parental attitude as well as a stance of separation from it: "I really can't explain how I knew studying the other kids was wrong. I don't remember any one thing, or things, that happened. I just remember that we were always sneaking, and I never told my parents what we did. I'm sure my parents would have been shocked if they knew what we were doing. They were very uptight."

When women say that as children they thought that sex play was wrong, they mean that they knew their parents thought it was wrong. They themselves did not experience guilt. Robin says: "I didn't have any sense of it being wrong. But I thought my parents would find it wrong. It mostly struck me as funny." Eve, 33, has a slightly different take on secrecy: "I felt that what we were doing was okay. But it was always done in secret, and my parents made me feel that secrets were bad."

Little girls found private places for their explorations. Under the table seemed to be a favorite place. Tina says: "We did it under a card table in a basement. It had a long tablecloth. Dougie and I were quiet, secretive, used flashlights, and wanted to keep it from the adults." At 28, Nokomis recalls: "When I was 5 we played

"doctor." I organized it. I made the other kids go in the closet and take their clothes off, but we didn't really look at each other. One would be naked and someone would peek in, but you couldn't see anything." Lakeisha, 32, found a similar hiding place: "When I was 8, a boy next door had a table in the backyard with a tarp on it. We sat under the table with another girl. We were touching and looking. Then my brother, who is five years older, came under the cloth and said, 'I'm telling. Mom and Dad will be mad, and think you're bad. You're nasty.' I never again explored kids after that." Lakeisha's hiding place was not secret enough, but her brother did not tell her parents. Still, being found out traumatized her and ruined the game.

MORE THAN LOOKING

Some of the younger women were exposed to more explicit sexual images at a young age. Their sex play took on characteristics that were more than satisfying curiosity about appearances. Lily, now 20, experienced sex play at the age of 6 that was more than the simple examination of genitals. "When we were about 6 we played 'truth or dare.' The dare was to run around naked and to hump the ground, or follow the jogger and take off your clothes. We got caught by Tommy's mother. She scolded us, 'It's bad. It's dirty. Don't do that.' But my parents never said anything to me, and I always thought it was all right." Sharisse is the same age as Lily, but when she was 6 she knew she was doing something wrong because Brad's parents both spanked him. "His mother told my mother, and I got in trouble. We were trying to figure out how to have sex. I thought it went in my navel." Lacking instructions from adults, they were experimenting with behavior that they thought adults performed. If they tried these things out, they would know why adults did them.

Some children experienced play that moved into behavior that was more actively sexual. When she was 8, Lily's girlfriend, who was one year older, said, "'I want to show you how boys kiss,' and she practiced on a pillow. She showed me what a boy would do. She kissed me and went down on me. I was shocked. I didn't know anything. I thought, 'It's good to know.'" This lesson in sexuality was more than Lily was prepared for. But she accepted it as information, surprising though it was. Lily did not interpret this experience as offensive. Some adults might regard this event as Lily being sexually molested by a 9 year old. Yet, Lily does not see it that way. Her friend was teaching her something. She does not remember coercion or fear, just astonishment.

Even now, at age 35, Molly, a bisexual, does not recall the following recollection as one in which she could have been harmed: "When I was 8, three brothers lived down the street. They invited me to their basement and asked me to pull down my pants so they could look at me. I was frightened. I remember being tied up to the bedpost in their mother's bedroom. It was a game. I think they were all off somewhere consulting as to what they'd do next. Then I heard their mother walking down the hall looking for them. I was afraid of getting caught. It would've been fun had it not been for fear." This situation had the potential for gang rape. But at the age of eight and with no instruction about sexuality, Molly could not have known this. Parental silence and the secrecy about children's sex play created a perilous situation. Molly's parents did not talk to her about rape or about sexual abuse. She experienced this event only as another day as a child playing with the neighbors. Some little girls are raped in exactly this sort of scenario.

PRE-LESBIAN EXPERIENCES

With the onset of puberty and the novel and unrecognized sexual feelings that accompany it, some girls stepped into lesbian territory at a young age. Molly had a special girlhood friend. "I had a friend when I was 8 and she was 11. I used to go spend the night at her house. We would take off our clothes and rub each other's breasts. I don't know if she started it or not, but I was the one who wanted to do it again and again. I was having a good time. We stopped when she moved away." Star is also bisexual and recalls: "When I was 10, my friend Linda undressed for me and modeled bathing suits. It was very erotic without touching. It was exhibitionism and voyeurism. I got very turned on." At 36, Shawna is heterosexual: "I was 12. My girlfriend and I used to touch each other, and we both liked it. It was fun. We instinctively kept it a secret. Then she started to feel it was bad because she heard about lesbians, and she wanted to stop. I was sorry about stopping." Ryfka, a 47-year-old lesbian, carried sex play into her adolescence. "In high school I was 15 playing strip poker in the house in the den with my girlfriends and making sure the blinds were pulled 'cause the high school boys would come around and ask, 'What are you doing inside?' My parents were working. So the game went that if you lost and were naked and lost again, someone got to touch you. The winner did. She patted you on the breasts, basically. It was my idea. I've always been a breast woman. We were laughing and probably drinking, too. Everyone but me turned out to be heterosexual. I had no sense of myself as a lesbian at that time."

This type of close play with same-age girlfriends was safe, mutually agreed upon, and comfortable for all the girls. As young girls, it was a secret and exciting game. Only from their adult perspective do women identify this kind of play as sexual.

SEXUAL TRANSFORMATIONS

Few parents provided their curious daughters with information and directions about their bodies. Those who did created an atmosphere in which the appearance of the body is natural and unsurprising. These daughters learned an early appreciation of their bodies and an awareness of the differences between male and female anatomy. They understood that boys and girls, men and women are interestingly but predictably different. They entered the sexual arena with a foundation of confidence and self-assurance.

Parents who order their daughters not to look at other children do not prevent them from continuing these explorations. Instead they cast a negative and shameful aura over what is essentially an innocent curiosity that children feel they have a right to satisfy among themselves. Daughters learn to be secretive and private about their sexual interests. They learn that parents and adults are not a resource and that they are on their own in their sexual trek.

When adults are not helpful and only admonish, "Don't," young girls set up a separate morality. They secretly pursue their explorations into the mysteries of the body. They feel that what they are doing is all right, but they know that adults think otherwise. At a young age, girls learn that adults think that their sexuality is bad. Daughters do not seem to wonder if or when sexuality will be permissible—they know that they have a dirty little secret.

Without a map, these girls are left to their own devices as they walk into the land of sexuality. Parents lose their value as a reasonable resource for sexual data. These daughters learn that they are on their own as they move into the erotic realm. There remain many mysteries about sexuality, but they will solve these with their peers. They prepare for travel into the vast plains of sensuality with a sense of isolation.

Girls who experience some uneasiness about their sexual explorations do not have a guide with which to evaluate or explain the discomfort. Unequal power dynamics, attempts by other children at too much physical intimacy, and the punishing attitudes of parents, can all create a sense that sensuality and bodies are both frightening and shameful. In later years, these attitudes will inhibit these women in the full and joyful expression of their core sexual selves.

THE MYSTERY OF SEX

After the mystery of genital differences is uncovered, curiosity is aroused about the next great mystery that adults keep from children. Sex is seen as a private adult preserve, which makes the unearthing of it all the more tantalizing.

Although sex can mean a variety of activities, for most Americans sex means sexual intercourse between a man and a woman. Most women learned about sexual intercourse in the context of information about reproduction. They were told, "This is how babies are made." Very few grasped the idea that sexual intercourse is pleasurable for women. By the age of 7, 24 percent of the women had learned about sexual intercourse. By age 10, 64 percent had learned; and by age 14, 90 percent knew. Four women performed sexual intercourse before they knew what it was. They were aged 5, 13, 14, and 18 years old, respectively. Their stories will be discussed later.

Who Explained Sexual Intercourse

Parents

Fourteen percent of the women recalled that their mother (in two cases both parents) explained the facts of sexual intercourse to them. The average age when they were told was 7 years old. Many people believe that parents are the most appropriate ones to discuss sexuality with the young. But parents are not skilled in talking about sexuality, nor do they necessarily have both accurate facts and a sex-positive outlook. Therefore, their efforts do not always produce a response in the daughter that experiencing sexuality with another person is good, pleasurable, nurturing, fun, and loving.

Some parents took a scientific approach. This consisted of a lecture on reproduction, often supplemented by children's books written for this purpose. Women remember these books in a very good way. Now 36, Shawna recalls that when she was 4 years old: "My parents had a book called *Peter and Caroline*. It was an excellent book. They read it to me, and I would ask them to read it to me. They didn't make a big deal out of it. I remember it clearly. The story is about a little boy who comes to his mother and says his friend is going to have a baby brother and that the stork brought it. The mother explains about sperm and egg, draws a picture, and the details are realistic. I remember not being embarrassed about it. I loved the story."

But using books is not a guarantee that the daughter's attitude will be positive. Cindy, who is now 21 years old, remembers that when she was 9: "My mother went through some books with me. I tried to picture my parents together, but it was hard to picture. You don't want to think of your parents that way. I didn't really think of it beyond 'That's where babies come from.'"

A scientific approach needs to be simplified to correspond with the developmental age of the child. Nokomis is 28 years old: "I remember being little and trying to figure out how a baby comes out. How does cell miosis make a baby? I couldn't relate to how intercourse made a baby. I kept it in perspective of my mother and father." Nokomis was 4 years old when her highly educated parents explained cell miosis. They were talking about reproduction. But Nokomis was wondering about sexual behavior. She was asking, "What is it that adults are doing together and why?" This is the question that was unanswered.

Shelley's mother tried to do the right thing, but she did not pay attention to her daughter's emotional reaction. "My mom read a book, *The Stork Didn't Bring You*. I was 6 and I felt bored. My parents would lock their bedroom door for privacy, and I hated it that they hid." For Shelley, what her parents were doing behind closed doors was more important than the discourse on childbearing. Her parents could have explained to her that they needed to be alone for special time to be close to only each other. And they could have arranged to make special time for her later.

On the other hand, Maureen, who is 38, was trying to understand reproduction when she was 7: "I read a chicken and egg type book with eggs and sperms and I went to my mom to ask how they got mixed together. I remember being completely and totally stunned. It was gross. It didn't seem like a neat thing to do." As we will see, disgust is a common reaction to learning about sexual intercourse. Maureen's mother did not reassure her daughter that the sexual exchange is pleasant, not disgusting, and that when she was older she would understand. Jody, 25 years old and bisexual, had an experience remarkably similar to Maureen's: "My mom used to read a book to us called *Where Babies Come From*. I remember starting to understand when I was 5, but I was read the book earlier. I remember trying to understand 'when a man lies on a woman and puts his penis in her vagina.' When I visualized what it would be like, I was disgusted. It was too close to be to a man." Like Maureen, Jody was left to deal with this feeling on her own.

An event like a relative's or neighbor's pregnancy was often the reason for the sex talk. Spring, lesbian and 43 years old, recalls that when she was 10: "The mother of a friend was pregnant. I said to my mom, 'Wouldn't it be nice if so-and-so had a baby?' Mom and Dad told me what you do to have babies. I thought it was disgusting. What I hated the most was the thought that my swim coach and his wife would do that, or that my parents would do that."

When she was 4 years old, Rebecca, bisexual and 25, remembers "asking my mother about how babies were born. We were sitting at the kitchen table, but I learned more about physiology and reproduction than about sex and pleasure. I didn't know a lot about sex until I had it. Mom explained it in such nonsexual terms that I didn't identify with it." Rebecca is relating the central problem of this issue: explanations of reproduction must include a discussion of the human relationship and the physical interaction. Without this combination, the daughter is confused. Later, the information is not available for use when the woman begins her sexual trek with a partner.

Two mothers explained to their daughters the sounds they heard from the bedroom while the parents were making love. The girls' reactions were different. Leotie, 40, a lesbian, says: "My mother explained the noises I'd been hearing from their bedroom by giving me a book with human figures in it performing intercourse. I wasn't interested in it for myself. I didn't think I'd ever want to do it." Ashley, 29 years old: "My mother told me about intercourse when I heard sounds from their room and I thought he was hurting her. I knocked, and I was told to go away. My mother later came and told me what was going on. I thought, 'Gross, ugh. That doesn't sound good at all.'" Ashley's mother allayed her concern about physical violence, but she failed to depict the sexual embrace as inviting.

Jolene, 40, was frightened by the thought of intercourse as a young girl. Her reason was different from Ashley's. "My mom sat me down and told me where babies came from. I was interested and curious. Mom said I asked a lot of questions. She explained using the example of horses since I had seen them mate, and she transferred it to her and Dad. She drew pictures. It scared me when I wondered if Dad were that big." Jolene's mother failed to account for the difference in size between species. With modesty in the home, Jolene had no way of knowing what a man looked like, that human penises are smaller than horses' penises. She did not mention her fear to her mother, so her mother did not know to clarify.

Some mothers did not give explanations until unfortunate circumstances of abuse occurred. Vicki, 35 years old, recalls that when she was 8: "A guy tried to get me into his car. He had a hard-on. I told my mother, and she gave a rational story of birds, bees, and contraception, a diaphragm. I thought it sounded kind of icky." Vicki's mother probably was uncomfortable talking about sexuality, but felt she had to say something to protect her daughter. She should have talked about how molesters abuse children, since what had occurred was visual molestion. She should have told Vicki that she did the right thing by escaping him and by telling her mother. She should have talked to her about self-defense. Her talk on reproduction did not deal with the event. Instead, her mother linked child abuse and reproduction, which are completely separate issues. On another day, at another time, her mother could have taken up the topic of reproduction and sexuality. Dialog about sexuality should happen in a context that is pleasant and relaxed, a time when sexuality is talked about for its own sake.

Alana's mother did not explain sex until after she had been molested. She remembers that when she was 5 and her sisters were 7 and 3 years old, "Some teenage neighbor boys took us into the basement of a house. They fondled us. We told Mother, and she told us about sex, intercourse, when it was appropriate and when not. It was a positive talk. There was no judgment. She was concerned about us."

Thirty-nine years ago there was not the same awareness about child sexual abuse as there is today. Alana's mother made an attempt to inform her daughters without frightening them. But she failed to make a distinction between molestation and loving, sexual contact between willing adults. Alana and her sisters were not doing a sexual act. They were being victimized and objectified. Girls need to know that when they grow up and want to be sexual, their experience will have no resemblance to sexual assault or molestation. Alana's mother should have saved the discussion of sexuality for another time. Instead, she should have told her daughters that they have a right not to be touched and that what the boys did was wrong. She should have reassured them that it would never happen again. She could have followed up on the promise by notifying the boys' parents as well as the police.

Today we know that it is important to draw a clearer line between sexual activity and sexual abuse. Abusive situations are best named as molestion, attempted rape, or rape. These situations are not sexual for the victim. Alana did not have a sexual exchange at the age of five. She was molested. For Vicki and Alana, these explanations came after the fact and too late. Children need to have information about sexual abuse at an early age if abuse is to be prevented. Many people wonder at what age children should be given sexual information. We are seeing that they need age-appropriate explanations by age three.

Sometimes mothers transfer information about intercourse in improper and untimely ways. Kameko, now 21, recalls: "When I was five, my mother showed me a porn film, and I thought it was gross, the whole thing. My parents, especially my mother, were very open about sexuality and intercourse. But, in a sense, I felt the film was negative because of the situation. My mother, my brother, and I were in an apartment while my dad was in London, and we were hunched up at a wall looking at the stag film, doing something bad, secretive from my dad." No sex educator would recommend showing pornography to five year olds. In addition, there seemed to be no interaction between the mother and Kameko to explain the purpose of watching the film together and why the people in the movie were behaving as they did. Kameko had an adverse reaction to both the content of the film and the situation in which it was shown. This was a detrimental initiation into the mysteries of sexuality.

A better way to handle sexual content in media is described by Dale, 21 years old: "I watched soap operas with my mom on TV. We saw people having sexual relations. I told her it made my crotch feel funny, and she told me that was normal. It allayed any fears. I thought, 'There's more to life.' Later, when I was 9, she gave me a book that included pictures of intercourse in it. I looked at the pictures, and I thought it was neat." Dale's mother normalized her physiological arousal to the soap opera and later offered more explicit information as Dale matured. Early on, Dale developed a positive outlook toward sexuality. But she adds, "I got negative feelings about sex from my peers in junior high school, that it was dirty and bad. They called girls 'sluts.' " Dale could not be protected from the widespread cultural condemnation of women's sexuality.

Chloe

Chloe, 22 years old, learned about sexuality from her father and her mother in a wholesome way, yet she was still embarrassed. "I was an only child. One day when I was 9 years old, Dad was driving me to San Francisco for an excursion. It was just the two of us, and he told me about sexual intercourse. I knew he planned this opportunity because I was trapped in the car. It was one of those Dad things. I couldn't walk away from the conversation. He said men and women had certain feelings about each other, and it led to sex and intercourse. He told me about how the penis is inserted into the vagina and that it was pleasurable for the man and the woman. That it was done often to have children. That's how I came about. But people did not necessarily have sex just to have children. He was very clear that sex was an enjoyable thing and that that is mostly the reason why people did it. He explained about oral sex, too. He said that there were many ways that people gave each other the good feeling. It was politely put. When I was 8, I heard about a blow job and I thought it had to do with a man's penis and a blow dryer. I asked my dad about blow jobs, and he cleared that up for me. That's why he told me about oral sex.

"I was stressed because I was trapped in the car, and I had no option. I was going to hear it whether I liked it or not. I was not comfortable about it at age 9. I would have rather avoided it, but later I was glad I knew. It answered my questions, and cleared up my thinking about men and women. It came at the right time for me. Dad stressed the fact that it was making love, and you should do it with someone you loved. My dad never told my mom about the conversation because a month later my mom brought out all these books about sex. And I had to go through the books with her. Hearing it from Dad was enough, but hearing it from both parents separately was awful! It was uncomfortable to discuss the whole subject over again. The book was visual and it had people in the act of intercourse. I was embarrassed at seeing the pictures."

This event happened in 1980. Chloe's parents model for us an excellent way to discuss sexuality with their daughter. Each parent gave her accurate information in a private, straightforward, and relaxed manner. Chloe supposes that her parents did not know that the other was providing sexual education. She may be wrong about this. They may have decided together to share the task. Chloe received her father's perspective about sexuality. He also provided an introduction to the topic. Her mother expanded on the subject and provided the visual materials to supplement her explanation. Together, they gave her a comprehensive view of sexuality from both the male and female perspectives. Even so, Chloe was embarrassed. But after the fact, she was comfortable and was prepared to experience her sexuality as shared pleasure when she became an adult.

Evie's mother is another example of a parent who provided accurate sexual information to her daughter when she was developmentally ready for the information. When Evie, now 21, was 10, she remembers: "We were in the car driving home from church. They said 'virgin' on the *Love Boat* show the night before, and I asked Mom what it meant. She wouldn't say because my younger sister was there, so I asked her the next day. She explained the whole bit about intercourse. I remember thinking it would have been adequate to say, 'It's somebody who never had sex.' But I'm glad she explained because I don't know when I would have found out about it." Like Chloe's parents, Evie's mother talked to her alone and gave her reliable information in a comfortable way.

We have seen that most mothers do not do well in presenting sexual information to their daughters. Even some well thought out attempts at education fell through because the parents could not comfortably discuss the human interaction of sexuality.

Sex Education Classes

Six percent of the women first learned about sexual intercourse during sexual health classes in school. The average age for girls in these classes was 11 years old, but the range was 9 to 16 years old. This was new knowledge for these girls, but not for the majority of girls in the classes. As we have seen, by age 10, 64 percent of the girls had learned about sexual intercourse. For them these classes came too late.

There is a range of reactions to the sex education classes. The girls did receive the basic information about reproduction, but no one had a supportive classroom situation that dealt with their responses. Carla remembers that when she was 8: "Our teacher in elementary school tried to describe intercourse nervously. The teacher was embarrassed. We thought it was funny that she was embarrassed. I wondered, 'Why is she so nervous?'" Carla's reaction was to her teacher's emotional state, not to the material she was learning. Tina, 36, states: "I learned about sex in sexuality class in fourth grade. I was incredulous. I didn't believe it. I felt fearful, reticent, and apprehensive with a tinge of fear." Tina, as a 9 year old, had no assistance from the teacher in overcoming these feelings. Her learning experience was one of being left alone to sort out her reaction. Maggie, 35, was in a sexuality class when she was 10. She also felt no support when she found the information "repulsive, shocking, and revolting."

In sex education classes the scientific context, while accurate, did not present a human relations perspective. Glenda is 37, and was 11 "when the school had a program on the menstrual cycle and reproduction. Being a curious kid, I was interested in what they would say. They stayed scientific, so you didn't know what they were talking about." Glenda's perception is that "they are telling us something, but they're not telling us." The "science" left out human beings. Crystal's experience was similar. Now 20, she was 10 when she saw a health film in school. "The penis enters the vagina. I thought it was funny; we were all giggling. I don't think we associated it with people." Guadalupe is 29 and a lesbian. She recalls, "We had sex-ed. It didn't impact on me. Kids laughed—no one took it seriously. They could have deleted that class from our education altogether. I learned nothing from it that I could recall. No one's behavior changed due to the class." The topic that children discuss among themselves secretly is openly presented to them, and they are shocked and embarrassed. No one tells them that this is a simple human behavior, and there is nothing to be embarrassed about. When the teacher is herself embarrassed, the children are simply following the adult's example.

The sex education provided by the schools was not adequate for most of the girls who experienced it. The teachers were directed to keep the topic scientific, with indirect allusions to human behavior. Yet the girls needed sensitive, realistic, and holistic applications to the behavior in which they might soon be engaging. Today, with the danger of transmission of deadly sexually transmitted diseases like AIDS, girls require a complete picture of female sexual behavior, including how to use condoms as well as how to make the choice of a sexual partner.

Reading Pornography

Eight young women (4 percent) learned about sexual intercourse from reading pornography. All of this reading was unsupervised by adults. These girls thirsted for information. The quality of their sex education depended on the nature of the reading material that fell into their hands.

Some girls found pornography in the home. Marla, 44, was 8 "when I first got hold of a pornographic book of my dad's. There were no pictures, but it was very explicit. I thought it was funny, but I also felt guilty because I knew it was wrong to read the book. I told my brothers, and they told my dad, and he tore it up. It was funny because it seemed weird. Why anyone would do that I couldn't imagine." When her father tore up the book, Marla knew that she was guilty of doing something wrong. But she was left without any explanation about why anyone would perform intercourse and why she should feel guilty.

Some children who find pornography share it with classmates. Lakeisha, 32, remembers that when she was 9, "on the school bus someone had a dirty book. In it were pictures of people having sex with each other and with vibrators and with animals. It interested me and sexually excited me. However, I thought it was wrong to look at the book, and that everything in it was wrong. Those people were nasty and bad." Lakeisha had had prior experiences when she was caught masturbating and looking at other children's nude bodies. At those times she was told that doing those things was "nasty." She thus believed that looking at the book must also be wrong.

Maybelle, 50, a lesbian, had no basis to think that her discovery of sexual activities could be wrong. When she was 12, she was able to find what interested her in "a book called *Queenie* that was passed around school. It was about cunnilingus. I was physically interested."

Other girls who were unsupervised by adults made their own judgments about the knowledge of sexual intercourse based solely on their own emotional reactions. Glynis, 37, was 10 when she remembers "hearing my parents making love and then reading my dad's porno novels. I thought it was intriguing, and I got a feeling in the pit of my stomach, which I've come to realize is sexual desire." Glynis's exploration was a secret, so she had no negative repercussions for it. Ryfka, 47, saw pornographic material provided by other children. "One girlfriend was a fountain of information. She found a deck of cards her father had. It had pictures of women fucking dogs, horses, and men. It was the 'Eee . . . ooo' factor. I thought it was disgusting in terms of the animals, but not the men."

Other children found reading material on their own. Their reactions reflect their personalities. Molly, 35, recalls: "I got all my information when I was 12 from reading books, the 'bodice rippers.' Until then, I thought intercourse was penis on the breasts. I don't recall them being sexually explicit, but they gave me more information than anyone else did. I was a loner even as a teenager, so I got no information from peers. My parents let me read any book in the house. I had access to a variety of reading material. I spent my entire teenage years involved in sexual fantasies based on the books I read. But I didn't know how to mastur-

bate, so I had some frustration." When she was 11, Eileen, 30, read about intercourse in X. Hollander's, *The Happy Hooker*. "I was fascinated and maybe a little turned on." While Molly and Eileen were secretly feeling the first tugs of sexual excitement, Amy, 25, had a different reaction. "I was 13 when I read about sexual intercourse in dirty books. It was disgusting. The act seemed like your parents couldn't have possibly done it, that two bodies shouldn't go together like that." Amy's feelings were very much like those of girls who learned about intercourse from other children.

Other Children

About 80 percent of girls learned about sexual intercourse from other children. Just as children have their secret morality and games about examining each other's genitals, they have their secret sex talk. Children can have only limited understanding about sexual activity, something that most of them have never done. They have no access to sophisticated sex information, much less the simple facts of sexual arousal and physiology. Searching for information, children are left with the crude, false, and strange sketches invented by other children.

Susie, 33, had a matter-of-fact attitude about intercourse. She said, "I always knew. I saw my sister fucking when I was 2 years old. She was 18 and in bed with her boyfriend. They laughed and talked to me when I walked in on them. They didn't think I knew what was going on. She'd be embarrassed now if I told her I remember it. So I'd seen sex. But I'd never seen an erect penis, and I didn't know what was so exciting about a flaccid one." Camille, 40, was 14 when her girlfriends talked together. "It was no shocking revelation. I thought, 'Oh, that's what this all means.' It was a positive reaction. I probably felt relief. I didn't want anybody to know that I didn't know anything about it."

Many girls reacted with a neutral feeling of interest and curiosity. Lima remembers, "I heard whispering. It seemed like it was fun." Yvette is 25 and first learned of intercourse when she was 8. "In elementary school a girl told us. I wondered what sperm was. When I was 15 my sister explained it to me. It was interesting. She told me of her preferences, like the 69 position. It was positive. I felt more at ease. Until then, I was frightened about moving into sexual activities in my relationship with my boyfriend. My mother was ill, so my sister assumed the maternal role in my upbringing."

Doris, 50, learned about intercourse when she was 12. "I had no particular feeling about it. I had a curiosity to experience it, but I had no desire for it." Concepcion, 37, was 6. "I was curious about it. But it did sound to me like something that was wrong. My older sister told me, and her language made it seem dirty; her delivery implied that it was wrong." Daphne, 29, was 10 when she was walking down the street with a "school friend and we saw the word 'fuck' written in the street. My friend told me what it was, how men and women made babies. I thought it was fascinating, and I looked forward to when I could do

it. I thought it was neat. My friend saw it the same way."

Lily is 20, and when she was 10 a friend told her about intercourse. "I didn't think about the act of intercourse; I seemed to take on an observer attitude. I couldn't picture it or think about it even when told." Shaniqua is 25 and recalls that when she was 8 years old "one of the girls told me how she found out about sex: 'my big sister told me that a boy will stick his wee wee in a girl's kootchie to get a baby.' She was learning stuff from her older sibling. I had heard the names before, so I wasn't shocked. I was surprised she had a sister who told her all this. My sisters and I didn't talk about it." Shaniqua's reaction was more to the breaking of the silence around sexuality than to the information. Audrey, 42 and lesbian, thinks she knew about intercourse by the time she was 6. "It's the weirdest thing; it's like I always knew. I wasn't interested in it. I saw myself as male and engaging in that kind of behavior with women. I didn't like the idea of them on top me. I didn't like men physically close to me."

Many girls' reaction to the information was simply disbelief. Wendy, 37, learned when she was 4. "I couldn't believe it. I was incredulous. My brother told me he saw Mom and Dad: 'Dad peepees into Mom's tinkle.' " Kyoko, 36, heard when she was 8. "I thought, 'Oh, you're kidding.' I couldn't imagine it. Someone putting their body into you. It was a shock." Bonnie, 52, was 11. "My reaction to learning about intercourse was disbelief. I didn't think it sounded too great. My family was not physical, and close body contact didn't sound right. A cousin who was the same age told me. She felt the same, not fear, but disbelief." Denise, 39, was 11 years old: "The girls my age were telling dirty jokes. I couldn't believe my parents would do that. It was a shock. I always tried to be a good girl. I thought a good girl wouldn't do it. I didn't like the idea that I'd have to do that to have kids." Bea, 43, was 12: "It was animalistic, surprising. I thought human beings would do it more refined."

Fear was a common response, and it spanned the age groups. Leanne, 41, was 8 and remembers: "It sounded scary, and it didn't sound like it would feel good or pleasurable." Sharon is 34 and was 11 when her friends told her. "I was really scared to think that a man with a big cock would put it inside me. I thought about my father and mother, and it made me feel kind of sick." Koren, 28, was 14 when friends told her. "I thought it was repulsive and unbelievable. It was scary that a man could put a penis into a vagina. I didn't know what my vagina was or how this would work."

Some girls were told that intercourse is painful for women. Kenya was 8 when she overheard a cousin's conversation: "It was nasty. Not something I wanted to do." Carolyn, 29, was 12 when "I was told that it would be terribly painful. I would bleed, and my vagina would feel like it was being torn." Merry, 37, was 14 when peers told her about intercourse: "I was frightened about it because it sounded painful and unpleasant."

When she was 10, Jennifer learned that sex was gross: "A guy puts a thing in her and pees in her and that makes babies." Lynette, 21, "was totally disgusted. My younger sister and a friend said what happens when people fuck: 'a man sticks his wiener into the vagina and pees in there.' It made me sick. I believed it for a while."

Sanura, 32, vividly recalls an all-girl slumber party when she was 7 years old. "A 9-year-old girl who was well informed described to us what sex was: 'When a man and a woman stand on opposite sides of a beach naked and run toward each other and throw their arms around each other and fall down on top of each other and press their bodies together.' I thought, 'Wow, I'm getting the scoop!' It was a big deal. It was something that grown-ups talk about, and it was on a par with saying a swear word. It seems to me we thought it was disgusting—maybe because we thought they were naked. I was never around naked people. I don't know how I got the true story of sexual intercourse. By the time I had sex education in the fifth grade, I knew the penis went inside, not exactly where, but I knew a lot by then."

Some girls felt discomfort at the thought of such physical intimacy. Emily, 32, was 6 years old and remembers: "I was told by girlfriends. I don't remember specifically what they said. It was not presented as a loving, happy experience. It was how babies were made and that women had to do it, but don't enjoy it. I didn't believe it. I was standing around with a bunch of girls, thinking 'no way!' I refused to believe it. It was the first time that I realized that men and women get together physically. I remember feeling it was dirty or nasty and only for the purpose of having babies. People wouldn't do it voluntarily. It was repugnant."

Mitzi, now 37, remembers: "When I was 11, my dad had a dirty book that had sex in it. I found the book in his drawer, my sister showed me where it was. I learned a little more about sex, and it gave me a weird feeling in my vagina. I thought I had to pee, but actually the feeling was one of getting turned on. But this was before I knew what that was. In a way, I thought it was bizarre and disgusting, because at that point I didn't like boys. Gross! I'll never do that!"

An explanation from her parent didn't improve Blythe's feelings. She recalls: "I was in fifth grade walking home from school, and kids told me 'fuck' means a man puts his penis in a woman. I didn't believe it and asked Mom what fuck meant. She validated what the kids said. It sounded awful, dirty, degrading, or humiliating."

Confused feelings and thoughts left some girls planning to simply evade intercourse. When Mary, 23, learned of intercourse at age 10, "I thought it sounded weird. I heard it from a girl in the neighborhood, and I decided she was lying. I asked my mom, and she said it was true. After that I decided I would never let a boy touch me." Mary's first reaction was one of avoidance of the experience, starting with the initial approach a male could make.

Some women recall that they felt a range of emotions. Brandy, 24, learned about intercourse when she was 6. "I thought it sounded funny, mysterious, exciting." Claire is 37 and bisexual. She remembers, " My friend's older brother told us a silly joke. There was a mother and a father sitting at a glass table, and they didn't have clothes on. A child asks Daddy, 'What's that?' He says, 'It's my pink banana.' 'Mommy, what's that?' 'It's my gorilla.' 'Oh no, Daddy! Mommy's gorilla is eating Daddy's pink banana!' It eased me into the weird idea of it. It was surprising, not shocking. I thought it was naughty and exciting." Rachel, also bisexual, was 7 when "I heard from a boy in the neighborhood. I was somewhat disgusted, and I laughed. But it didn't upset me. It didn't seem like that big of a secret." She was disgusted, amused, and embarrassed, yet not upset.

Hope, 40, was 10 and her image of sex was comedic. "I thought it was hysterically fun, silly. I'd never seen a penis. I was laughing about it for weeks and weeks."

Some girls were immediately indoctrinated with the thought that sex is evil. Tamika, 29, did not learn about intercourse until some friends told her when she was 16. "I was taught by my parents that sex before marriage was nasty. The church taught me that the body was a temple, and sex before marriage would be like destroying the temple." She had learned a moral attitude about sexuality before she knew what the behavior was. Penny, 49, didn't remember how old she was, but the message she received was that "intercourse is a nasty thing that women do because it is their duty."

Girls who are attracted to females don't know what to make of this definition of sex. They do not want contact with men, but they do not know what would be sex with another woman. Lindsay, 22, is a lesbian and was 13 when her sister told her about intercourse. "She told me about how many guys she had been to bed with. Later I heard about it from my peer group. I had uneasy feelings, because all I heard about was male and female, and I knew that was not what I wanted."

Some girls performed sexual intercourse with no idea what they were doing. Rene, 39, is a lesbian. She was 6 when she experienced intercourse: "I was screwing around with kids at age 6. I was curious. I didn't hear it talked about. A 12-year-old boy was the son of my mom's friend. This was his idea of playing. I wasn't uncomfortable. It seemed okay. I had intercourse with him later through to the end of high school." Due to the age difference, which creates a power imbalance, therapists would see this as a case of child sexual abuse. Rene does not interpret it that way. As an adult, she expresses a neutrality about the experience. She does not remember coercion as a factor, and she sees it as unrelated to her current lesbian identity.

Rosalie, 46, now a lesbian, was 14 when she "heard of it from a boyfriend who talked me into testing it out. There was a gradual build-up over a year. We got into heavier petting. He said, 'This is a sign of how I love.' I wasn't that impressed with it. I thought there were more important things in life, such as going dancing or talking." Today Rosalie is angry about this experience. She feels that her ignorance about sexuality set her up for this sexual interaction that she now labels as sexual abuse. She had no idea that intercourse was related to reproduction. At 14, she became pregnant and was forced to put her baby up for adoption. This traumatic event would never have happened if she had known what sex was.

Beverly, 47, recalls that she "experienced intercourse at age 13. I never heard it described. I was in love with a sophomore in high school. I enjoyed him holding my breasts. We played at having sex in Dad's car in the garage." Some young women learned what sex was on their wedding night. Trudy, 49, had no sex education. "I'd never seen a penis until age 18 when I got married. I had an idea from reading books, but it was a vague notion. I never knew what an erection was. I just accepted it. I had no emotional connection. It was an attitude that was scientific." Carmen, 42 and heterosexual, recalls that at 18 "I never knew about sex until I actually did it. I was amazed. I was dating the man who became my husband. He got me drunk, performed intercourse, and I got pregnant. I didn't particularly enjoy it. No one ever talked about sex. I was raised in South America. My parents did not sleep in the same room, and they did not kiss or touch."

With the exception of Rosalie, the women who performed sexual intercourse before they understood what it was were behaving in a context of interaction with their peers. While there is a tone of male coercion in their stories, the women do not recall this intimidation as hostile. As adults, they have a context that males initiate sexual activity. This sexual role may serve to normalize their memory of these youthful experiences.

But a woman's sexuality should be an expression of her inner awareness of her own erotic energy flowing outward toward a partner. Her sexual growth is a slow, gradual awakening to her desires. When a woman moves into her sexuality from an inner confidence of her passion, she is an active, self-assured, erotic person. These girls were pushed into sexual activity before they wanted it. Before their own maturation, they participated in sexual activity. This unfortunate start gave them the mistaken understanding that sexual activity is done to appease men. It will be a challenge for them to overcome the passivity that this role demands of them.

A SEXUAL REVOLUTION

If there had been a complete sexual revolution, girls would not be introduced to the bodies of other children and to the concepts of sexual intercourse in the ways in which women describe their experience. As girls, they were immersed in a sexualized culture where sexuality was never discussed. They were naturally curious to discover what it was. The way in which this curiosity was satisfied sets

another pattern for the girl's emerging sexual self. A few fortunate girls learned about intercourse from their parents in an atmosphere that was natural, matter-of-fact, and that satisfied their curiosity. Elements that aroused fear and disgust were not present in their learning experience. These girls were prepared to enter this adventure with an openness that it would be a normal step when they reached maturity.

Secret discussion of sexuality among peers is how most girls learn about sexual intercourse. This continues a pattern of keeping sexual secrets from parents. Adults are not a resource. Even when adults offer the information as parents and teachers, their embarrassment and awkwardness ensure that girls will not seek their guidance.

Most girls learned about reproduction, not sexual pleasure. Peers, parents, and teachers talked about how to make babies. Discussions of sexuality in terms of reproduction alone do not leave room for a dialogue about the real experience that the couple shares. Furthermore, most girls heard the message that sexual intercourse is when "the man sticks his penis in the woman's vagina." This depicts an act that is one step further than nudity. This is not a description of affectionate touch. One body penetrates the woman's body. The depth of this intimacy is shocking and disgusting to many girls. Education about reproduction alone can leave the girl believing that she must participate in this strange and uncomfortable act solely in the service of the species. Rarely were girls told that sexual activity feels good. Sexual feelings were not mentioned.

Girls are trained in modesty. They are punished for looking at naked bodies. They are usually touched affectionately only while fully dressed. This context of bodily concealment creates a startling contrast to the physical intimacy of sexual intercourse as penetration of the male body into the female body. Most girls were disgusted, shocked, fearful, and disbelieving when they learned about penetration. Many promised themselves never to engage in it. So, for most girls, sexual intercourse is perceived as a very negative activity. This experience warns the girl that her sexual travel will be within a fearful, perhaps painful, environment.

What is it about the message of sexual intercourse that is so disturbing to girls? One aspect is that of nudity, the display of one's naked body to another person. Girls have already learned the importance of covering and concealing the body. It is presented to them as a necessity. There is rarely a safe place for nudity within the home or elsewhere. Therefore simple nudity is perceived to be appalling, too intimate, and uncomfortable. Another feature is the intense physical closeness. Girls do not understand how having a part of a man's body inside them can be a good experience.

But there is another element of this language that goes beyond the physical intimacy. The terminology of sexual intercourse, "a man puts his penis in a woman's vagina," portrays the woman as a passive receptacle. She is acted upon.

Something is done to her. She is not portrayed as welcoming this act; she merely accepts it. This message may be the first time that the girl learns that her role as a female is to be a sex object. She is a thing, available for a man. Some girls actively resist this hated role and say that they will never do it.

The language that describes sexual intercourse can be altered so that these negative elements are removed. Sex with a partner can be described it as an active behavior for the woman. This eliminates the deep objectification imposed on the female role. The girl can be told that when a woman is grown up, she sometimes has a feeling in her body, mind, and heart that she wants to put the man's penis inside her vagina. She wants to be so close to him that she embraces the man and his penis by taking his penis into her body, her vagina. In this description as an active participant, the woman loses the status of an object. The concept of the sexual embrace as a special kind of hug tells the girl that she will enjoy doing it when she has these feelings. The girl can be confident that if she does not have these feelings she should not perform intercourse. As the girl matures and is ready for further explanations, she can be told that the feeling the woman has in her body is sexual arousal to a heightened degree, that in her mind she knows the man very well and trusts him, and that in her heart she has affection and caring for him and feels the same from him. Women who enjoy sex with men state that this combination of these elements is what is important to their best sexual exchanges. Parents who listen to their daughters can be confidantes to them later. The teenage woman would be able to discuss with her parent when she thinks she has the body, mind, and heart feelings that mean she wants to perform intercourse. Parents can also explain that some women have these feelings for other women and that when they do, they touch one another's genitals.

Sex education for girls needs to go further. For only a few women (30 percent) does the act of penetration produce orgasm. Intercourse is only one part of sexual activity. To say that sex is intercourse ignores the fact that sexual pleasure for women means stimulation of the clitoris. For women, sex is clitoral stimulation, not intercourse (albeit that most heterosexual women enjoy intercourse). Not one woman said that as a child she learned that sex is clitoral stimulation. Most men achieve orgasm through intercourse. When girls learn that sex is intercourse, they are learning about male sexuality. They do not learn how women achieve orgasm. Girls are learning what will satisfy men, but not necessarily what will satisfy themselves. In addition, to say that sex is intercourse is to ignore the fact that women have sex with other women. The imagination does not allow for a sex act without a penis. For the girls who will grow up to be lesbians and bisexuals, the standard definition of sex does not describe what they will be doing when they perform sex. This omission can leave them confused. They do not plan to have sex with men, but they do not know what they will be doing with other females.

Some girls have already discovered the pleasures of their clitoris when they masturbate, but for them, masturbation is not sex, not the real thing. They expect intercourse to offer some new, strange delight. With no information about female sexuality, girls grow into women who discover sexual pleasure with a partner only through trial and error. Some never do achieve orgasms, though they are sexual with partners.

When there is a sexual revolution, real sexual education will go beyond the information about reproduction. In cases where the interpersonal exchange and pleasure are included in the instruction, girls are still learning only about pleasure for men. Girls learn about how men achieve sexual pleasure, but not about how women do. It is a sad fact that they are not taught about their own bodies before they learn about the other gender's sexual response. It is not surprising, then, that adolescent girls become further confused about their sexuality when they experience intercourse and find that it is unsatisfying.

After a sexual revolution, parents will be at ease about talking about sexual issues with their children. They will be comfortable with giving their daughters the correct names for their anatomy, including the labia, clitoris, and vagina. They will find a way, by letting young children observe each other's bodies or by showing them children's books about sexuality, to allow children to observe the anatomy of the other gender. Other children will not be the first informants about sexual intercourse; the parents will be the best resource for the child. With open and relaxed communication about all things sexual, girls will find that their parents will give them information that is accurate and age appropriate. Parents will have the skill to respond to a girl's emotional reaction to the concepts of adult sexuality. Intercourse and other sexual activities will be presented to a girl in a way that she learns that she is an active person in the sexual encounter. She can look within herself and decide when she is fully prepared to be sexually active with a partner.

chapter two
ADOLESCENCE: PROGRESSING WITHOUT A MAP

High school society can be pivotal for the direction of sexual expression with a partner. While some women say they became interested in boys "when the hormones kicked in," the context of the active peer pressure is just as significant. Socializing is probably the most important activity for teenagers. High school is the experimental testing ground for interactions with the other gender; for dating and formulating sexual patterns and values; and for the discovery of lesbianism. Young women approach these milestones with willingness and adventure. But they are not aware of the extent of their conditioning to be compliant with men, to defer to the male ego, and to silence themselves from articulating their sexual needs and disappointments. Young women who are fortunate to have a best female friend may obtain supportive and commiserative feedback from her. Others keep their sexual

misadventures a secret as they have been trained to do.

High school women are attempting to exercise their will as adults. They will date a young man for all of one month, yet maintain that it was truly a "relationship." They claim social competence, assurance, and responsibility without the experience necessary to actually secure these skills. Their need to maintain this modeled behavior drives most young women to be silent regarding their sexual adventures. In reality, they are operating reactively to male sexuality and to the sexual mandate prevalent in social situations. Many women continue to model this behavior into their twenties.

As the young girls in Chapter 1 grew into adolescence, many of them experienced changes in their attitudes toward sexual intercourse. The disgust and fear many had felt as girls was now transformed into curiosity and interest. However, when this transformation took place varied according to each woman's initial reaction to sex. Many girls were shocked and disgusted upon learning of the reality of sexual intercourse. These women became more favorable toward it after their first experience of intercourse. Even if it was not pleasurable, experiencing intercourse was the most common explanation expressed for developing an improved attitude toward intercourse. Other women said that it was their curiosity about intercourse that made it seem more favorable. Some women's education in college human sexuality classes improved their attitudes. For others, the addition of the concept of love and romance was the incentive. Women who had strong religious backgrounds found that their formation of a personal value system was the turning point. These women discarded their fundementalist religious beliefs in favor of a secular belief that as women they had a right to sexual expression and freedom. The majority of lesbians stated that after they came to terms with their lesbianism they became indifferent to heterosexual intercourse and realized that they did not have to participate in it. Some women describe their changing attitudes toward sexual intercourse as an ongoing process that they can trace throughout their adult experiences.

EXPERIENCES OF FIRST INTERCOURSE

The change toward a more positive attitude about sexual intercourse occurred in tandem with the desire to try it and to perform it. At age 13, 7 percent of the women had voluntarily experienced intercourse. By age 16, 40 percent had tried intercourse. By this age, 47 percent of the women thought about intercourse in a more positive way. Developing a positive attitude toward intercourse is closely associated with performing it. Even if the women were not orgasmic, most of them were neutral or affirmative in their stance regarding intercourse. It was no longer gross or disgusting. By age 20, 92 percent had experienced sexual intercourse and 88 percent had a more positive attitude about it. The 4 percent difference is due to the fact that some women experienced intercourse and did not like the experience. Therefore their attitude about it remained negative.

There is a significant difference of age at first intercourse among the age groups of women. Women in the age group of 18 to 25 experienced first intercourse on the average at the age of 16. For the age group of 26 to 35 it was age 17. And for the group of women over age 35 it was 18 years. There is a significant difference between the youngest group and the oldest group. The trend in recent years is toward an earlier age at first intercourse.

Teenage women who voluntarily became sexually active with a male peer discovered that in the context of sexual arousal, petting, and a romantic atmosphere, the act was not disgusting or extremely painful or frightening. Most established some level of trust in their partners before making the decision to lose their virginity. In spite of this, many describe their first experience as unsatisfying and sometimes coercive. The young man talked them into the activity before they were fully comfortable. Or, in the context of necking, he refused to stop before penetration. Some young women clearly were victims of date rape. The term 'date rape' is a modern phrase. When mature women described their experiences of 20 or so years ago, they brought along with the memory the ideas they had at that time: that men initiate sex, that a woman should not be a "tease," and that once started, sexual activity should finish with intercourse. These women did not articulate these as their own chosen values. In fact, they wished that they had been given the control to stop the event. However, they perceived that "this is just the way it is." Men manage the sexual experience. The inability to appreciate that these are created values that reflect the male control of women's sexuality is one example of how heterosexual women are reactive to male sexuality and do not express their own sexuality. In retrospect, some women older than 35 now analyze their first experience of intercourse as rape. However, most do not. They may describe the event as coercive and even scary, but they do not apply the word *rape* to the experience.

Evie

When two inexperienced teenagers fumble with each other's bodies, can they have a successful interchange? Evie is now 21. "In my sophomore year, I thought about having sex, but it was not something I was going to do. I never considered sex an option, maybe because how I was raised. When I cared about my first boyfriend, we

didn't have a problem forgetting that we should be married.

"With my second boyfriend, I decided that I cared about him a lot. It took us no time to start doing everything. Maybe I never thought about it being sexual. Maybe because if I let myself think that this was my sexuality, it would come out straight against my religion and everything I'd been taught to believe. I never felt guilty about it, but I decided that 'this is okay.' It took a couple of months to decide that what I was doing was all right.

"It was great the first time. I was 17. We had fooled around before this. One romantic day Jarred came over to my house. I was sleeping, and everyone else was gone. He brought me a rose and breakfast and woke me up. Then we had sex in my room. We kissed and petted, felt each other everywhere, and had intercourse. It was romantic and tender and sweet, not a passionate, throwing-clothes-everywhere sex. We kissed a long time. I was sexually aroused. He wore a condom. It didn't hurt, and it was enjoyable to have intercourse."

Evie's first time was enjoyable, private, in her own bed, tender, and comfortable. She had prepared herself for it by resolving her moral dilemma when she decided that premarital sex was okay. Her lover used a condom for birth control. Finally, it was a complete sexual exchange. It involved all the activities called "outercourse": talking, relaxing together, caressing, foreplay, and afterplay, not simply intercourse. At the time of the interview she had not yet experienced orgasm so that she was uncritical of the fact that her sexual arousal cycle was not carried through to orgasm and resolution phases.

Dale, who is 21, had a very different experience with her first intercourse at age 13. She says: "I did it on a dare with a neighbor boy who was 14. He said he'd make me chicken enchiladas if I did it. I was scared. It didn't hurt so bad. We took a shower. I thought the shower was better. I was barely aroused. I wanted to be like my girlfriend, who was sexually active." Dale's approach to this life passage was childish. The behavior did not originate with herself. Dale had no adult guidance to prepare her for this experience. She had no way to judge that perhaps the boy was using her. Her brief summary of the interaction indicates that it held no meaning for her, except that now she had something in common with her girlfriend. She passed a sexual milestone, but she was not involved in sexual intercourse as a female evolving from her sexual self.

Trina

Trina is 24, in the same age group as Evie, but her story is traumatic. She was not prepared for intercourse and she did it to "get it over with." "I was masturbating, and I was curious. I wondered how a boy would feel with me. Some kids talked like they were having sex, and I wondered what it was like. It was fun and adult. A girl became a woman once she had sex. I had a lot of pressure in school because I was a virgin. I only had sex the first time because I didn't want to be a virgin.

"His name was Paul, and he was someone I was dating for two months. He was older, 19. It was my 17th birthday night, and we went to his apartment. And I made the choice to have sex with him. I didn't love him, and I didn't like him a whole lot. It was painful. It hurt, and he didn't seem like he cared how I was feeling. He wasn't interested in pleasing me. He wasn't concerned about what felt good to me. We didn't neck very much. He didn't play with me. We kissed, but I don't think I was aroused. It was short, maybe ten minutes. I wanted it to be quick at that point. I was disappointed. I went home and started crying and told my younger brother. He was the first to know. I wanted a hug, and he didn't know how to take it. He just looked at me. He didn't give me the hug. He didn't know how to react. He was stunned. I never saw Paul again. I will never forget him."

Trina's experience was traumatic due to the selfish and inconsiderate attitude of her partner. While she wanted to be sexually active, she lacked the personal skills to be assertive and to guide her partner to her needs. In fact, her lack of information was so complete that she was unaware of her needs. Sexual intercourse was to her the act of penis in vagina. She did not fully understand what she would need to make this a sexual experience for herself. She turned to her younger brother for comfort. But he did not understand her distress, since he was a virgin, naive, and held romantic illusions about sexuality. Trina could not articulate her disquiet, so she was alone in her sadness. Today Trina observes that she has gone through the process of healing from this unfortunate initiation into sex with a partner. When her sexuality entered the context of true friendship with a man, it began to flower.

Devorah

Devorah is 25 and bisexual. "I was more asexual than heterosexual before I came out as bi. This goes back to me growing up fat. I started losing weight at age 22. I lost 100 pounds. That was the age at which I first started being sexual with another person. I didn't believe that people would be attracted to me in the body I had.

"One reason I decided to lose weight was that I was looking for a relationship. I was 21, and I weighed 320 pounds. I had graduated from college and I wanted a real relationship. That was something I wanted to explore. It was not the only reason I lost weight, but it's been one of the terrifying things about losing weight, losing that shell. Terrifying, because it makes me vulnerable if I allow myself to be sexual. Emotionally, it's difficult for me to open up sexually. I force myself to do it when I want to. It's similar to when I go to the gym and take off my clothes. I weigh 220 pounds now, and it doesn't feel

natural and comfortable to disrobe. It's the same thing I felt when I began to be sexual. I'm terrified of rejection.

"I had a job at a college in southern California, and while I was working there, I posted a personal ad on a computer network. I started corresponding with a man. The first time I had intercourse was with him. I thought, 'Oh, this is what all the fuss is about!' He was not a talented lover. He was not interested in what would please me. He just wanted to fuck. The fact that I hadn't had sex before was a turn-on to him. He looked at it in the context of the pleasure it could give him. I dumped him a few days later. It took me a while to raise my expectation level and then learn to communicate what I want and need to a lover."

Devorah's experience was much like Trina's. She found a man to give her the experience of intercourse, but his definition of the experience was the fulfillment of his own pleasure and not hers. Like Trina, she became immediately aware of the imbalance and left him.

Shaniqua

When Shaniqua was 15, she decided that she was ready for intercourse. She recalls: "It was horrible. My boyfriend and I went to the beach. I grew up in Monterey. My first instinct was, 'It will be perfect. The perfect setting. How romantic!' As we got down to it, I pulled my pants off and he tried to enter me. All I remember is pain. I wasn't ready. I was stiff, and I was nervous. We never had intercourse. I said, 'No, this hurts. Leave me alone.' I thought that it was not anything that the media portrays it to be. I watched soap operas and she's always happy afterward and smiling. I was disappointed. I was ready to explore and I wanted to try this. He seemed disappointed when I told him, 'I can't do this. It hurts.' Later he was apologetic for not making it as comfortable as it could have been.

"About two months later it was better. I think with the first attempt, my hymen broke. The second time was at his house. His parents were gone. We were in his room, relaxed and comfortable. He used a lubricated condom and he took his time. I think that is what made the difference. I enjoyed it, but wasn't orgasmic. I enjoyed the sensation, the closeness, the sensing of how it would feel, not having had the experience before."

Shaniqua's experience was mixed. She was mentally engaged in the activity. She had made the decision for herself that she was ready to explore intercourse. However, she was with a caring, but ignorant partner, in a semipublic place and without the benefit of a long and relaxed petting session. Later, in the privacy of his home, tranquil, and with birth control, the experience was more positive. Since both partners were uneducated about female sexuality, Shaniqua was inorgasmic.

May

May went to a private college on the east coast. In this atmosphere, she began to come to terms with the opportunities to become sexually active. "I got intrigued with the idea of intercourse. I was 18 and Jay was two years older than I. We dated my freshman year in college. Before Jay, I had it in my mind that I shouldn't have sex with someone I wasn't married to or not in love with. We went on dates and he immediately pressured me to have sex. I said, 'No,' and he said he would not ask again but would wait until I decided. After a month, I decided to. Why? I was curious and attracted to him, and I really wanted to go ahead and start having sex. But I had to work myself up to a sizable infatuation with him before it was all right. After Thanksgiving break, we returned to school together, necking in the back seat of a car. I told him I loved him, and he talked me into coming into his room to spend the night as I had done in the past, nonsexually. But this time I said, 'OK, let's have sex.' At one in the morning he couldn't get an erection, so we slept. He woke me at 3 A.M., and we had intercourse. He probably knew less what he was doing than I did. He was a virgin and hadn't dated anyone before, and I didn't know how to tell him to make me enjoy it. It was awkward. I was tired and not lubricated. It was, 'OK, so that's what it's about.' He had an orgasm. I thought, 'Gosh, this is what the fuss is about?' "

May's narrative reflects her current understanding of sexual dynamics. She says she had to "work up a sizable infatuation" in order to justify sexual expression outside of marriage. She no longer believes that she needs to be in love with a sexual partner. Like so many other women, May wondered, "Is that all there is to sex?" She experienced the sexual event, but she was unimpressed with its value. Now she can see that mutual sexual ignorance contributed to the failure of this exchange.

Sanura

Sanura relates, "I was 16 and it was the evening of the junior prom. I had a year-long boyfriend. We'd been petting and decided this would be the big night. We went to a park with another couple at midnight and laid a blanket under a tree. We took off our clothes. I was nervous but felt ready for the experience. Unfortunately all the heavy petting we normally did, we didn't do. I wasn't lubricated. All of a sudden intercourse was the focus, not the heavy petting. Intercourse and male ejaculation, once part of the experience, became the whole experience. It was so painful we didn't complete it all the way. He put it in part way and I yelled in pain. I remember looking up at the stars. I was enjoying it, and it was painful at same time. Just as we were warming up, a police car put its headlights on us. We jumped up and put on our clothes. I lost my panty-hose, a shoe, and his class ring, which did not go over very well when we got home. I felt it was a wonderful experience and I looked forward to completing it. I felt much closer to him, thinking, 'This has really brought us together.'"

Even though this experience was awkward, incomplete, interrupted, and painful, Sanura still evaluated it in a positive way. She had made a decision to perform intercourse, and she believed it was an event that drew two people together. For these reasons, her teenage self was satisfied with the experience. Today, a fully expressive sexual woman, Sanura regards her first experience with wry humor. It is not so highly rated now that she has had truly erotic sexual exchanges.

Mitzi

Mitzi's story is familiar, but she has the added fear of pregnancy due to her refusal to use birth control. "I was 15 years old. We'd talked about it and we'd done a lot of heavy petting before and decided that we were ready. He was my boyfriend I'd dated for two months. I didn't have birth control yet. But right after, I asked my mom for it, and she took me to get a diaphragm. We were at his house on his waterbed. It only lasted a couple of minutes. I had an orgasm, just a little. He was 16. The second time is when he popped my cherry and that time it hurt. He prematurely ejaculated and I was thrilled because it hurt so bad, and I wanted it to be over. I guess I got over it because from then on every time we got together we had sex. We didn't have oral sex. I thought it was disgusting. (I don't think it's disgusting anymore!) He wanted to give me head, and he tried it, and I didn't like it at all. Every time we had sex, I got off.

"My parents were divorced. Mom was cool and got me a diaphragm, which I rarely used. It was a pain to have to stop and put it in. I didn't get pregnant until I was 21, and I hardly used birth control for seven or eight years. But I worried about it every month."

Mitzi is one of the approximately 30 percent of women who can achieve orgasm through intercourse alone. Her first experience was with another young virgin, yet she managed to pursue the specific sexual activities that excited her. Mitzi is unusually free and assertive. She managed the sexual exchange in a way that would provide her with the stimulation she needed to achieve orgasm. She had been masturbating since childhood and had received clear and realistic sexual education from her mother. She credits her single mother, who gave her excellent sexual information, as a force who helped her to make her sexuality satisfying. But it was Mitzi's assertive personality and self-directed sexuality that allowed her to experience satisfying sex shortly after the initial awkwardness of the first time.

Claire

Claire describes the process that led to her first experience of intercourse. "Over a period of almost a year I thought about intercourse and I felt I had a built-in veto against it because of my religious upbringing. It took me that long to change my mind. When I finally did, it was with a Muslim man who had a double standard. He saw women as all good or all bad, and his goal was to make them bad. When I decided I wanted to have sex, he didn't try to seduce me anymore. He was lousy in bed and I instructed him on foreplay. He had difficulty with an erection. Then he didn't want to spend the night with me, and that hurt my feelings."

Like Trina, Claire's first experience was with a man who had a misogynistic attitude toward women. But she was already in her twenties and had given serious thought to her decision to become sexually active. She had enough self-esteem to understand that he was sexist and negative toward her because she is was woman. And she was assertive enough to confront him. Still, she was unable to take the initiative to end the relationship. After him, Claire went on to choose her partners more wisely.

Annie

Annie was 20 at the time of her first intercourse. As appears to be a common experience, she felt she was old enough to try intercourse, and she was trying to find a partner to achieve this end. "It was the beginning of January, my sophomore year in college. I was trying to lose my virginity. One guy said he wanted it to be a special thing for me, and he wasn't in love with me. The guys who would've done it were too intense. They were trying to seduce me, and I knew they didn't care about me. I wanted somebody I liked, at least.

"I met a beautiful guy. I had seen him a year earlier. He was pretty like Mel Gibson: neat eyes, not too tall, nice complexion. My roommate and I both saw him and admired him. We built up a fantasy about him, and we hoped he would like one of us. One night I was riding my bike alone. I saw him walking, and I stopped and talked to him. We walked around and talked for a couple hours. We started dating. I fell in love with him. That was the first time I ever had strong feelings for a guy. I think he told me that he loved me. We were alone the night we decided to do it. He had a roommate and shared a bedroom. We went to his apartment, and we were necking, and we decided I'd spend the night. By then I knew I wanted sex with him, and I had gone to a birth control clinic to get on the pill. His roommate didn't come home. I told him I was a virgin. He had the tiniest penis you have ever seen! He was 22 years old, but his penis looked like a boy's.

"He told me, 'I'll be gentle with you.' It was so anticlimactic: one, two, three! (laughs). I felt so grown-up sleeping with him, but I was wondering, 'Was that the way it was supposed to be?' I could hardly feel him inside of me. I think he did do it because I felt the goo. We didn't do much foreplay except just kissing. One, two, three, and he fell asleep and, I lay there thinking, 'This is strange.' Sometime later I heard his roommate and his girlfriend having sex and making all kinds of noises. I wondered what was going on with them that wasn't going on for us. I wasn't making noise, and it wasn't lasting as long as they were. He stopped seeing me after we talked about our lovemaking and he said, 'And then when you came . . .' I said, 'I never came.' And it blew his mind. He stopped calling me, and he avoided me. He made a speech that we had to break up. But I found out from friends that he was gay and was sleeping with a college professor and was moving in with him. It was totally traumatic. That was the worst pain. I felt a lot of love for him. I wondered if I pushed him over the edge to be gay because I said I didn't come."

Annie's story has the same element of Sanura's: when the focus of sexuality became intercourse and male ejaculation, it was not satisfying. She also experienced her sexuality in a semipublic way. Another couple shared the same room at the same time. However, her story has the added feature that her lover was gay, pretending to be heterosexual. Now she can look back at it and know that social pressure forced him to try to relate sexually to women. His homosexuality could be one part of the reason that the sexual exchange was unfulfilling. Unlike Sanura, Annie had already experienced orgasm through masturbation. She knew that she was missing something in the exchange, but she had no idea why this was so.

Leah

Leah was searching for the opportunity to become an adult by becoming sexually active. She places her first discovery of partnered sex in the context of her picture of herself as a credulous, emotionally abused, and starved-for-affection teenager. As her story illustrates, in her early sexual meanderings she was compliant and unaware of what it was that she was seeking.

"It was 1968, the summer of love, I was 18 and living in Marin county (outside of San Francisco) as a live-in babysitter for a woman who was a mother figure for me. I was shy, depressed, studious, anxious, worried, and lonely. I was 18 when I went on my first date. I naively said, 'Let's go to a drive-in movie.' Once there he quickly kissed me, and I cried. His touch showed me I needed closeness, and until that moment I didn't know it. He felt my breasts, and as he started to put his hand in my girdle, I asked him to stop, and he did. Then I went home, and my makeup was smeared. I told Susan what happened. I said, 'I'm a lesbian, I didn't respond to him.' I had no boyfriends, and this was my explanation for it. Susan got angry at the guy and said he pushed me too far.

"I hitchhiked to San Francisco to Haight Street on the weekends to visit a girlfriend who lived in a communal house. This was the first time I was away from my family. I became a hippy overnight. Then I found out about the House of Love and Prayer, a real warm and nice healthy community. I met a man there. Later,

when I was visiting his sister at his house, he came in and asked me if I wanted to go to bed with him. So I did. There was blood, and I figured that was it. It hurt, but I liked it. I wasn't orgasmic. He didn't want to have a relationship, and it was disappointing. I was turned on somewhat. Now I knew I wasn't a virgin. And I was glad I did it."

Leah took her step into adulthood when she performed intercourse. Her partner was pleasant, but disinterested in furthering the friendship. He assisted her in meeting her goal of having a sexual experience. It was impersonal, but Leah recognizes that she was compliant and accepted what was given to her unquestioningly. In retrospect, she carries a great deal of sadness about these first ventures into partnered sexuality. She remembers her emotional desperation, her yearning for mature adulthood and her unsatisfied desire for love and affection. She was attempting to meet these needs through a sexual exchange. Her needs went unmet, and she was as lonely as before. It has taken years of therapy for Leah to sort through the complex set of emotions that she associated with partnered sexuality.

Rudy

Rudy is a 44-year-old lesbian who began her partnered sexual career as a heterosexual. Her story is unusual in that she extensively directed her first voluntary sexual encounter. She had been sexually abused as a child and was wary of male sexuality. "I was 18, and it was near the end of my first year in college. I had met a man during the first semester in college, Jeff. He was 19, and we started out being good friends. Then he wanted to take our friendship a little further. He invited me to stay over at his house, and so I started sleeping over. But I said we couldn't have sex, including kissing. I slept in bed with him fully clothed on top of the covers. He said, 'Okay, whatever you want.' And he said he was attracted to me. Then I slept under the covers clothed. Then I took pajamas over. Then I slept with underwear on and I made him keep his underwear on. I had never seen him naked. We weren't sexual, but we hung around together.

"Then I went on a trip, and while I was away he got involved with one of my roommates. He said he loved me, but he had sexual needs. It hurt me a lot. I felt pressure to have sex with him or he would marry her and leave. So I thought I should. One day I said, 'I was ready the other night when we were stoned, but I'm not ready now.' He said, 'Let's try.' And finally I said, 'Okay. But first tell me everything you want to do before we do anything.' So we kissed for the first time, and we ended up having sexual intercourse. He was slow, patient, and true to his word. He told me everything first. It was like I wasn't there, but that I was in my mind watching, seeing what the technique was. Studying it as though I was reading a book. I wasn't emotionally or sensually there. It was

something I needed and wanted to do for this relationship.

"Our relationship was so much about talking that I expected that we'd talk. But he rolled over and went to sleep, so I went to the living room. I wept and thought, 'This is what makes people jump off cliffs, get excited about each other.' And it felt like nothing to me. After a half hour, Jeff came out. I felt empty. There is an anticipation that sex will change your life. You'll feel something you never felt before. Sometimes that is true. It wasn't true for me that night, and I assumed there was something wrong with me. Just before that I had tried to drive my car into the river. I felt I was incapable of ever feeling anything. I knew feelings were important, and I could not feel. I didn't acknowledge pain as a feeling.

"So Jeff and I talked, and I said I didn't like it and didn't want to do it anymore. He said it was okay and that he loved me and he'd stay with me. He was the perfect person for me to enter the world of sexuality. He was a wonderful guy. I couldn't have done that with someone who wasn't as patient. He never made me feel that there was something wrong with me. In that context I could explore who I was. But I never had an orgasm with him."

Rudy approached her initiation into heterosexuality with reluctance, but an acceptance that it was a necessary part of a lover relationship. She was wary, self-contained, and assertive enough to direct the physical contact in a way that made her feel comfortable. She was fortunate to have a partner who was sensitive to her needs and who was not coercive. But she was not fully present to the situation. She says, "I was in my mind watching, seeing what the technique was." Sex therapists call this "spectatoring." It reflects a woman who is not fully present in her body to experience her full sensuality. After Jeff, Rudy pursued more mutually fulling sexual relationships with men before she came out as a lesbian.

Barbara

Barbara did not plan to perform intercourse when she was 18. "I didn't know the first time we performed intercourse. He always used his finger from the back. It was from the back so I didn't even know until I asked him. We would make out for hours and he would use his finger. I was lying on my stomach, and he would lie on top of my back, and I didn't know if it was his finger or not until he told me afterwards. I can't remember whether I wanted him to or didn't want him to. But I knew it was the thing that was the next step so I asked him. My thought was, 'Wow, so that was it! Do I look different? Could anybody tell?' It made me feel more like a woman; more grown up, like a member of the tribe. I was not orgasmic. I didn't think about it. We never did it facing each other until we were married. I thought that the face-to-face position was going to make the difference. The whole time we were going together he entered me from the back. I almost felt that we were saving something for the marriage.

"When we finally did it face to face there was nothing. Then I was disappointed and he would ask me, 'Did you come? Did you come?' Even before that he would ask me that. I said, 'I don't think so.' I don't think I told him about my personal adventures with masturbation. One time he touched my clitoris, and I came. That was the only time, and he never did it again. I was very passive. We rarely did it face to face. I tried to suggest things, but he would get mad.

"He never pushed for missionary style because that wasn't what he wanted anyway. I was disappointed with the missionary position. It wasn't a big deal, and it wasn't any better than it had been. I didn't have any orgasms. I think I might have told him I was disappointed, and he probably said it would get better and to trust him. But it didn't."

In the early 1960s Barbara was of the mind that she should save her sexuality for marriage, but that sex play was all right with her fiancé. Barbara had been masturbating regularly, and she expected an orgasm, but with her husband she never learned how partnered sexuality could produce an orgasm. He was controlling and selfish and never discussed with her the possibilities of how to make her sexual experiences with him more thrilling. Barbara was not permitted to initiate any sexual variations. It was her husband's responsibility to know about sexuality. Barbara's sexuality flowered after she left the marriage.

Cheryl Jean

Cheryl Jean is 43 years old. She recalls, "I was seeing a guy when I was 17. I liked him a lot. We spent time together. We worked on cars together. We necked. We went to his brother's house. He put a condom on. Guys carried them around to be cool, and for pregnancy protection. And it was his first time, too. It was over before it started. He said, 'That is not such a big deal. I could have done that by myself!' At first I was taken aback. I felt I did something wrong. Then I realized I didn't do anything wrong. Then I thought, 'The hell with it!' I brushed it off. It was over so fast I didn't get excited about it. It was like it didn't happen. I think he was interested in getting laid once. In a week he broke up with me. I was trying to please him. It confused me."

Cheryl Jean suffered the same disappointment as Trina, Annie, Claire, Devorah, Shaniqua, and May. Ineffectual male partners and uncomfortable settings and situations produce a failure of the romantic fantasy of sexual intercourse. Feeling used, most of these women found that the first time of sexual intercourse, which is supposed to be a magical moment of mysterious ecstacy, was instead an initiation into male-focused immature sexuality. They were present in the sexual exchange only as a receptacle to produce a male orgasm.

Ryfka

Ryfka felt more in control of her first sexual experience. It went exactly the way she wanted. "I was a sophomore in college, and I went on a student/faculty conference. It was hot, and when I was swimming my history professor came onto me. He said, 'Leave your door unlocked. I'll come by and see you tonight at 11 P.M.' He came to see me. It was pretty exciting. I was attracted to him. He was 27 and had seven children. The youngest was three weeks old. His wife didn't have time for him. I can't believe I fell for that shit!

"He came into my room. I was dating another student and he was in my room from 8 to 10:30 P.M. making out with me. I said, 'You have to leave.' He left at 10:45. At 11 P.M. the professor came to my room. He brought rubbers, and he had a difficult time getting hard. He told me to use my mouth on his penis. I wasn't into doing it. He had me use my hand to get him hard. He showed me. It was exciting. We both had been drinking. He brought hard liquor. He played with my breasts. I got very excited. I have sensitive breasts. I had an orgasm from nipple stimulation.

"I knew it was illicit. He was married, and it was adultery. None of that bothered me. It was not a big deal except in the sense that he was my professor. I didn't go to his class for two days, and he called me to see if I was okay. He told me to come to class. He wanted to see me again. He arranged a couple more times at a friend's apartment, one of his colleagues who was single. I started to feel guilty about him being married. It was inappropriate for a professor and a student. I transferred colleges. I wanted to go to a bigger school. His friend came up to me and said, 'Don't leave him. He needs you.' I wrote him a letter that I wouldn't see him again. I didn't talk about it to anyone at school. There would be trouble if anyone there knew.

"I think I was taken advantage of— young coed, enthralled with the attention of the professor. But it was consensual to a certain degree. Under those circumstances if I said, 'No,' I'm sure he would have respected it. The transgression was part of the sexual charge."

Ryfka achieved her purpose when she became sexually active with her professor. Like other young women, she did not want to be a virgin anymore. She was with someone she liked and respected. She was not immediately bothered by the fact that he was married. She was not looking for a long-term relationship, and she left him without regrets.

Peggy

Peggy recalls with pleasant nostalgia her first intercourse. "My first lover was one of the best relationships I have had. I was 24 and had never dated. I was opposed to the Vietnam War, and I went to a peace march. I started at the front of the march and started walking and looking at everyone, wondering, 'Who will I walk with?' I came to three men who were together. One was tall, dark, handsome with a great body, lithe, yet muscular. He gave me a brilliant, yet shy, smile and said, 'Hi!' He was it.

"We dated for five months. Every date we did something special, exploring another part of the city: eating at ethnic restaurants, going to hear the blues, theater, dance. I started sleeping with him, but I kept my underwear on. We gently discovered one another. He always said, 'You're in charge. What do you want to do?' I was perfectly comfortable and safe with him. He was two years younger than I.

"Then I decided I was ready. I got birth control. I waited to do it on Valentine's day. My roommates were out, and I made an exotic four-course dinner for the two of us. Then we went over to his place to sleep. There wasn't enough privacy at my place. We had a very psychic connection. I think he knew this would be it. I took off all my clothes, and he asked me to stand, and he admired my body.

"In bed we did all the gentle touching, kissing, and arousing that we always did. I pulled his penis to me so he'd know I was ready. But it hurt when he tried to enter me, so we stopped. He was fine about stopping. He wanted me to be enjoying myself. So we cuddled and slept. Then in the morning we started again, and that time it was so wonderful and erotic. I had my first orgasm ever, and I saw stars! Literally! I dissolved into the cosmic bliss! Yes, it was one of the best moments of my life. I thought, 'Oh, my God! This is why people like sex so much!' I'll never forget his smile after my orgasm. It was such a wonderful shared moment. I still love him, and I feel so grateful for that communion with him."

Peggy was older than average at the time of her first intercourse. This proved to be to her advantage. She had developed a strong personality and had good self-esteem from her success at work and at school. She found a lover who was physically attractive, and they developed a relationship that involved mutual respect, caring, and shared interests. She was confident in her decision and created an emotionally romantic, safe, sensuous, and private place for this erotic experience. Because of all this planning, her first time was completely fulfilling. Peggy was fortunate to begin her sexual journey from a starting place of the maturing of her own erotic self. Her subsequent sexual adventures were entered into with foreknowledge, erotic desire, and the expectation that she could set the stage to meet her own needs. Peggy's story is the rare exception.

A number of cultural situations contribute to the fact that for most young women the first time with intercourse is unfulfilling. There is no information given to young women about their own sexual response. Sexual education, as we have seen, is about reproduction and the fact of penile-vaginal penetration. If women have heard about female orgasm, they think it will automatically happen during intercourse. When intercourse fails to produce this effect, they are taken aback. "Is this all there is?" The silence around sexuality does not allow them to find a way to answer this question. Only those women who masturbated to orgasm prior to intercourse were likely to know that some part of the act failed them.

TRANSFORMATIONS

As these women took their steps into partnered sexuality, they brought with them the history of their early sexual information or misinformation. Some of them had explored other children's bodies, others had not. If they had not, this first intense emersion into another's body had an even stronger emotional impact. Some of the women had masturbated to orgasm and brought the expectation of orgasm to sexual intercourse. When their own sexual response was not carried through its full cycle to orgasm, these women still were happy with the exchange because it provided an experience of being close to a man.

Evie, Sanura, Leah, Shaniqua, and Rudy had not experienced orgasm prior to sexual intercourse. They were all hoping to have this exhilarated response when they did the "real thing." Yet, when they did not experience orgasm they were not disappointed. They defined the exchange as satisfying because the man was satisfied, pleased with them as a partner, and (except for Leah) willing to continue the relationship. The affection and arousing aspect of the physical experience was defined as satisfying enough. These women did not know what they were missing, and they settled for the experience as it was. Their self-esteem and womanhood was validated by a man who was content with the exchange. They were valued as a sexual being, even if their own sexuality was unfulfilled. These young women were unable to express their own eroticism with a man because they were unaware of their own sexual response. They had expected that intercourse would open them to their own erotic self. The experience did not provide this. But their sexual ignorance permitted them to accept the inadequate sexual exchange as sufficient. Evie is still preorgasmic and does not masturbate. But the rest of the women went on in their twenties to explore their own bodies with masturbation. When they finally experienced orgasm, they understood the poor quality of their first sexual exchanges.

Young women have a negative attitude about masturbation and are often inorgasmic. If women are inorgasmic and do not explore their sexual response with masturbation until their twenties, they will be unable to complete their sexual response with a partner. In addition, women need to acquire assertiveness, self-interest, and sexual initiative in order to direct the sexual exchange so that they are

satisfied. Young and immature men are less willing to accept this direction. It may well be that heterosexual women do not find women-focused sexuality until they are with male partners who are experienced, older, emotionally mature, and open to giving pleasure to women. From the experiences related by these women, most men younger than 25 do not carry this attitude.

Some women were able to describe their experience of transformation into a female or self-centered sexual experience.

Rudy

Rudy was spectatoring during her first experiences with sexual intercourse. As she continued to practice intercourse with this partner she found herself changing. "A few days later in the morning he invited me into his room. I never saw him naked the night we had sex. That morning he had an erection, and all I could think of was a turkey neck. And he said, 'Do you want to try it again?' And I said, 'No.' But he coaxed me, and we did it again. I still didn't feel much of anything. But I didn't feel nearly as empty. He said, 'Did you like it any better?' And I said, 'No.'

"A few months later, I moved in with him and a roommate of his. We had a mattress in the kitchen on the floor. His roommate had the bedroom. By then I decided sex was something I could do. It wasn't great. It didn't hurt. It was akin to going to a movie you don't want to see with someone who wants to see it a lot. That was my attitude about sex. I didn't feel I had to do it. I did it to make him happy. Then I started to love it. It was miraculous. I don't know what the turning point was. I couldn't get enough of it. I wanted to try everything. I was vibrant, alive, funny, goofy. I had been pretty unaffectionate and suddenly I was hugging everybody. Something inside of me loosened up, and I had a great time. He was shocked but more than willing to play with me. I didn't know what orgasms were, so I didn't know what I was missing. I was very aroused. We would go on for hours and hours. Looking back on it now, I don't think he knew if I was having orgasms. I don't think he knew what to do to facilitate me having an orgasm. And I didn't know there was more to do. At that point, sex was play. It was play that made me feel good. I didn't have my first orgasm until six years later. I was 25."

Sanura eloquently describes the transformations she has experienced in the process of taking control of her sexuality. This process goes far beyond the physical awakening that Rudy began to enjoy. She says, "Looking back at it, in the beginning I knew very little about how to meet my own needs sexually. Most of what I was taught was that my sexual gratification was the result of the sexual gratification of my partner. I don't think I was ever taught growing up how to satisfy myself. It's been a slow evolutionary process.

"When I was in my late teens, sex was not satisfying. Something was missing for me. I saw a picture of a woman in *Cosmopolitan* and she was flushed in orgasm. That didn't happen to me. I talked to my girlfriends. They said they weren't having orgasms, but it was okay because sex was the process and the orgasm was the icing on the cake. I felt this was true, but not the whole picture. So I started taking a look at the process. I decided I wanted more. I wanted the thrashing orgasms. I wanted to be in the process." Sanura was informed through her self-selected reading that there was more to the sexual experience. Throughout her twenties she began to consciously examine her sexual interactions in order to learn how to improve them.

Annie, Claire, Barbara, Cheryl Jean, Devorah, and Mitzi had all masturbated to orgasm prior to their experience of intercourse. They looked forward to a deeper intensity of this experience with a partner. They were disappointed because their partner did not render it. They understood that something was missing, but they did not have the skills to initiate sexual activity that would lead to their completion of the erotic cycle.

Teenage women had to overcome their original feelings of disgust about sexual intercourse or the fear of the pain of sexual intercourse before they could think about planning to perform it. They had to find a comfortable and private setting. They also had to obtain adequate birth control in order to dispel fears of pregnancy. They discovered that teenage boys are less than the ideal partner, immersed as they are in their own sexuality. The process of moving to a womanly self-expressive sexuality has taken them years after these first steps.

LEARNING ABOUT LESBIANISM

Today it is understood by social scientists that lesbianism and bisexuality are normal expressions of sexuality. It is simply that some women prefer other women as sexual partners, and some women are able to experience sexual fulfillment with both genders. Women are exposed to heterosexuality in infancy and they learn about sexual intercourse on the average by the age of 10. But the interviewees did not learn about lesbianism until the average age of 14. Women who developed into lesbians and bisexuals learned about sex between women at the same age that heterosexual women did. Until they reached adolescence, sex, even for most lesbians, meant heterosexuality. It is in adolescence and in the high school environment that most women learn about this form of sexual expression.

There are three important features to the acquisition of sexual information about lesbianism that set it apart from learning about heterosexuality. It comes at a later developmental stage when puberty is well in process and young women are considering the option of a sexual partner. And it usually occurs in a high school environment, where lesbianism is presented by peers and teachers alike as a negative perversion. Finally, girls' introduction to heterosexual partnered sex is some sort of presentation of physical contact, usually sexual intercourse. But lesbianism is introduced as a mysterious

kind of physical sexuality without a vivid description of what exactly lesbians do.

There is a negative valuation of lesbianism that is different than the valuation of heterosexuality. Most people do not view lesbianism as the normal sexual variation that it is. Instead it is seen to be outside the boundaries of good sexual expression. This ethos is so strong in the culture that few young women are able to be nonjudgmental about partnered sex between women. Those teenage women who are interested in other women as sexual partners soon discover that this is another deep, sexual secret that they must keep. Teenage lesbians and bisexuals who live amidst homophobia (hatred and fear of gay people) are more at risk for suicide than heterosexual teenagers. Their steps into partnered sexuality begin in an entirely different context than the heterosexual teenager. Like heterosexual teenagers, they must overcome the negative judgment that women should control their sexuality within marriage. But many of them also need to overcome the erroneous belief that there is something wrong with sexual expression between women.

Most heterosexual young women learn about lesbianism through gossip at school. Others are informed about it by their family socializing with gay people. The reactions of the young women to learning about this form of sexual expression are varied.

Peer acceptance is one of the prime concerns of the high school woman. Fitting in, being part of the social crowd, and social approval are the processes that absorb adolescents. As teenage women are taking their faltering first sexual steps with a male partner, they learn from other teens and from pornography that women can have sex with each other. The common reaction of the women to learning about lesbianism was that it was "gross," "weird," "disgusting," "abnormal," "socially unacceptable," and "perverted and sick." Some women said they simply could not understand it. When they were younger, these same women first thought of sexual intercourse as gross and disgusting, but never considered it abnormal or sick. The homophobic high school environment ensures that women who are thinking of themselves as heterosexual will not give serious thought to lesbianism as a realistic option. Shelley is 34, and she emphasizes the negativity about lesbianism: "I thought it was awful. In junior high I heard about it from kids. It wasn't normal. Dad was homophobic." Shelley points out that she simply accepted the negative attitude that was reinforced by her father.

The negative judgment about lesbianism creates an unhealthy atmosphere for young lesbians and marks the first separation among girls around issues of sexuality. In a way, all the girls were the same when they shared their secrets of looking at each others' bodies and traded misinformation about sexual intercourse. But when some girls are labelled "lesbian," they become a separate entity. Angela, 24, states: "I had a friend whose sister was a lesbian. When we saw her, we would be nice. Later, behind her back, we laughed probably for tension release, because it was different. In a group, I felt it was abnormal. But it didn't bother me personally." Angela went along with the crowd though it did not reflect her own feelings.

The negative judgmental attitude about lesbianism that pervades high schools affected lesbians and bisexual women. Many of them reacted just like heterosexual girls. Polly is a 34-year-old lesbian: "I was appalled in a way because it touched close to home. I thought it was wrong, horrible, totally deviant, perverted, gross. It was less than human." This echoes the responses of heterosexual women. Not until years later could Polly confront her interest in lesbianism.

The high school negativity is not limited to other students. Teachers can be the victims. Margot remembers being 13: "We thought our physical education teachers were doing it. I remember becoming aware of the possibility. I talked to my friends. We fantasized about what they were doing. I thought they were gross." Fran, 42, who remembers the open secret when she was 15: "In high school, my sophomore year, it was openly discussed about the high school gym teacher. She was masculine and had a female roommate who travelled with her. I felt repelled."

Girls who learned about lesbianism in preteen years also heard of it in a context of negativity, though they often did not understand what lesbianism was. Fatima, now 23, asked her mother when she was 7: " 'Why can't women marry?' My mom said, 'That's nasty, you don't do that.' So I assumed the attitude that it was wrong." Susie, 33, asked her mother about lesbianism when she was 11. "Mom told me women have sex together, and it wasn't okay with her. It seemed daring, exciting, and a short-cut to having to wait to grow up for boys." Susie is heterosexual, but she found the idea of sex between women inviting. She knew enough about keeping sexual secrets not to reveal her thoughts to her mother. Susie reflects the attitude seen in the discussion of children's secret sex play: Keep your sexual secrets from your parents. They will not understand, and they will condemn you.

Lynette is 21 and first heard of lesbianism when she was 8 years old. "On the playground some girls started calling me 'lezzie lizzie,' and I asked someone what it meant. I asked a girl. She said, 'It's when women love each other.' Someone dared my sister and a friend to touch tongues together, and they did. I thought it was gross. The 'lezzie' name was negative to me. They were teasing me. It was a play on my name." Lynette learned two unfortunate lessons from this event. One is that there is something wrong with women loving each other. The second, that she personally will suffer if she is one of these women.

The negativity, while predominating, was not universal. Some women report initial positive reactions to the concept of lesbianism when their families were accepting of sexual variations. Julie was 15, and "there was a lesbian lady in our town. The whole town talked about it. I overheard adults talk about it. I got a job in the phone company and listened to the two lovers talk on the phone. My reaction was matter-of-fact. My mother had affairs with married men, so I think I learned not

to be judgmental." Consuela, 42, was 18 and remembers: "Our uncle had a gay friend. He was part of our family. It was there. We grew up with it. I heard about it from my grandmother. 'Oh, they like each other, ha, ha.' I knew they had sex, but I didn't know how they did it." These families accepted their homosexual members. They were different, but normal.

Some women were in a college subculture that advocated openness to sexual forms. Kamiko recalls when she was 17. "I remember having a conversations with some of my male and female friends in the middle of the night. We were talking about sexual relationships at the time. I would say we were all of one mindset and we tried to come to a general decision. It was okay as long as it was between consenting people. I felt at that time it wasn't something I was personally comfortable with." Within her friendship group, Kamiko perceived herself to be heterosexual. She had not yet explored the concept of lesbianism for herself. Concepcion is 37 and recalls: "Friends of my mother's were lesbians. I didn't think of them having sex. Then at 15, I read *The Fox*. I felt quite fine about it. It was a provocative idea. I saw the film, and it had more than I imagined. It was fine." Knowing real lesbians while a child permitted Concepcion to be more open-minded about their sexuality.

Pornography was an introduction to lesbianism for some women. Robin, heterosexual and 29, never heard of lesbianism until "I saw lesbians in a porn film. I thought it was unusual because it wasn't the traditional way of having sex. I didn't feel it was bad, but I had a sense of curiosity about it. I understood how it might be preferable because there is a different sense of intimacy between women. Women could intuitively know what a woman would like and enjoy." Robin saw lesbian sexuality in a positive way. Violet, recalls being 13, and "I was babysitting at a house where there was a book on a table that was about lesbians. I read it, and it seemed natural, and I got turned on." These women saw depictions of lesbianism in pornography before they were exposed to it in the disparaging high school environment. Pornography is written to excite the reader and to present sexuality in a raw form. These young readers easily fell under the spell.

Lesbians and bisexuals also discovered lesbianism in pornography and were positively stimulated. Skye says, "I thought it was weird. When I was 14, a schoolmate pointed at lesbians and said, 'They have sex with each other.' It was emotionally and intellectually stimulating. I found X. Hollander's book, *Call Me Madam*. She has sex with women. I thought it was okay." Maybelle is 50 and learned of lesbianism when she was 17. "I read it in a dirty book. It was intriguing and very, very stimulating. I was interested. I made no value judgment because it was such a forbidden turn-on." When Sandy was 12, "I thought it was hot. I read it in a dirty book my brother had hidden in his room." Rachel was 13 when she looked at pornography. "It really excited me. Scenes of two women in *Hustler* really excited me. So did cunnilingus. In junior high everyone

said one girl was a lesbian. I thought she was weird. She was sleazy and an outcast." So while lesbian sexuality was something Rachel was interested in, she developed the same negative judgment against the one lesbian she knew.

Some heterosexual women had had secret play with girlfriends. Experiencing the fun of sex with other girls normalized it. Laura is 35 and heterosexual. "I thought, 'Oh, well, that's interesting. It made more sense than sex between men. I used to cuddle with a friend in seventh grade, and we'd suck on one another's breasts." Claudia, 40 and heterosexual, says, "I probably heard of queers and that it was wrong. But I had wonderful sexual experiences with girls as a kid. And that didn't feel wrong." As adults these women have no interest in female sexual partners. Yet, their positive childhood explorations, fondly remembered, create an open-minded attitude toward lesbianism.

Bisexuals and lesbians who were accepting of lesbianism were also interested in experimenting with it. Georgia is 31. When she learned about lesbianism, she felt "interest, curiosity. It was a pleasing thought. I thought about it before I heard about it." Daphne is 29. When she was 12, "some kids in school told me about it. I don't remember exactly the circumstances. I was interested but I knew other people wouldn't approve of it. It was a positive reaction, curiosity." Audrey is 42 and learned about it when she was 18. "I thought it was a great idea. I heard the word 'homosexual.' I thought it was only men. When I came out at age 18, it was perfectly normal and natural and always what it was supposed to be." Marion is 57. When she was 18 and learned about lesbians she became "very excited. I wanted to pursue it because this is what I wanted. I realized that I wasn't the only one who felt this way. Women in college brought me out to gay people and gay bars. It opened my eyes to walk into a gay bar in San Francisco in the 1950s. I went bananas!"

Guadalupe

"My best friend made a snide remark about two women. Her friend had shown an interest in me. So she said something about the two of us. To me, women were more bonded friends than what we had with guys. We knew and understood each other, worked and supported each other. I didn't leave that bond in the locker room; it was part of the relationships as a whole. It made me almost sweat. It was like someone turned up the heat under my skin. I didn't think about myself that way yet. It was exciting. It was scary, but I liked the idea. But I didn't want anyone to know that yet. I wanted to find it in me first."

A common response to learning about lesbianism is to wonder what women do with each other. Kenya, who is 25, remembers: "In high school there were rumors about different people. With women I kind of understood. With men I couldn't understand. I was grosssed out. Sex itself was gross. What would two women do together? With no penis, what could they do?" Kenya carried the confusion that teenage women feel about this subject. She heard some vague information about male sexuality and the concept that homosexual men perform anal intercourse. Sex, after all, is intercourse. Women with no penis cannot perform intercourse, so what is it that they do?

This lack of imagination about lesbian sexuality is a reflection of the concept that sexuality *is* intercourse. Melanie, 34, recalls: "I was shocked, and I didn't believe it. Two girls in my high school were gay, and kids talked about them. I didn't see how they could do it." Trudy, 49, was "disgusted. I couldn't figure out what they did. And I thought, 'There's so many men around, why take a woman?' " Leslie, 33, reflects on the misconception she carried: "I heard of two men first. I never thought women would do it as a lifestyle but as an unusual, occasional event."

Though lesbians and bisexuals grew up to eventually do sexual play with other women, many of them, on learning of it, wondered what women could do together. Star is 48 and bisexual. When she was 14, "a woman friend and I talked about how women were more interesting than boys. But we couldn't find information about lesbians. We wondered if we knew any lesbians. We couldn't figure out what they did. We were curious. I don't recall how we invented the idea. We were attracted to women but not each other. We knew the word *lesbian*."

Maggie is a 35-year-old lesbian, and at age 16 she wondered: "'How can that be?' I was curious what two women could do with each other. Was there satisfaction beyond cuddling? I read *Everything You Wanted to Know About Sex*. It was negative about lesbianism. I was ambivalent about it. Lesbianism was not an option for me." Maggie had both the curiosity about lesbianism and the guilt imposed by social condemnation. She stifled her secret desires. It was many years later that lesbianism became her choice.

Roselle is 32 and lesbian. She remembers: "As a teenager I wondered what they'd do together. I read *Everything You Wanted to Know About Sex* and remember its negative comment that one vagina plus one vagina equals zero. I was with girls at a young age. We manually stimulated genitals and rubbed bodies. We didn't want to get caught, but it was fun. I knew society would see it as wrong." Roselle discovered lesbian activity with her childhood friends, yet she thought adult women would do something different. She did not label her youthful play as lesbianism.

The title *Everything You Wanted to Know About Sex* would seem to have offered these searchers the information they wanted about lesbianism. But the author denigrated lesbian sexuality and failed to offer a description of lesbian sexuality and relationships. These readers were left to explore the mystery of lesbianism at a later age.

If some part of the woman's personality acknowledged that she was interested in lesbian sexuality, she often felt many different emotions. A bisexual, Bianca, now 20, states: "When I was 11, I saw a porno movie with two women. They were alone and then a man steps in. I didn't consider it lesbianism. The whole movie threw me. I was in shock and astonished. I'd heard about lesbianism but never contemplated it. My best friend's sister was becoming a lesbian. She was thinking about being sexual with her girlfriend. I thought it was weird, but I wasn't grossed out. It was strange." Toni is 50 and lesbian. She states: "It was one more taboo, so it gave it more attraction. There was a certain creepiness about it." Weird, creepy, yet attractive, a volatile mix that Toni stored in the recesses of her mind. Only in her adulthood was it a taboo she was free to violate.

Bisexual, Rebecca is 25. "I grew up in San Francisco. I knew what a lesbian was—someone who was with women, not men. But I didn't think of it as sex. Which is typical. Not thinking about women as sexual. I didn't think about sexual things until college. Part of it had to do with getting in touch with my own attractions. I've always had a woman or girl who I was totally in love with. I didn't see it as sexual. I didn't think of myself as a sexual being. I feared lesbians in high school. I saw them kiss, but I didn't think of it as sex. My mother had lesbian friends. I told my friend, 'That's gross.' I think I was threatened because I had those feelings, too. I grew up sexually liberated, but I didn't think about lesbianism as sex." Rebecca expresses her love for women, fear of sexuality, disgust at lesbians, and a sense of an internal, but undefined threat. If she had acknowledged that she was one of those women whom she feared, she would have had to restructure her self-image. Now that she identifies herself as bisexual, she has processed this reorganization of self and is comfortable and outspoken about it.

Ellen is 57 and bisexual. She states, "I learned about lesbianism as a teenager in a teasing, embarrassing way. l knew it was connected to me. I thought maybe women just cuddled. I read *The Well of Loneliness* at age 16 and got a clearer picture. I was curious, but not ready to explore it. It was scary. I wasn't ready to explore sex with men either. But sex with men was culturally okay. With women, it seemed like it would be loving and gentle." Like Rebecca, Ellen could not absorb the sexual component of lesbianism. She was fearful, curious, and attracted to the idea.

When Phoebe, a bisexual, was 15, she felt "a little coerced. I had been pursued by a female. I had a sexual experience at that age. I felt guilty, felt really bad. Later, through contact with other women, talking to other lesbians, reading, engaging in sex with lesbians as an adult, and having a positive experience, I became aware that the guilt arose from my former misinformation about homosexuality. The turmoil involved an unhappy high school period in my life. I was rebellious, and I felt guilty about the one lesbian contact. Up to that point all my sexuality involved guilt." Phoebe was cast into a sexual situation with a woman before she was mentally prepared for it. It appears that she is now conceptualizing this experience as sexual molestation. However, due to her passivity and sexual naiveté, she experienced the emotions at the time as confusion and self-

blame. She came to terms with all this much later in her mature adulthood after a heterosexual marriage.

Some young women knew immediately that they were lesbians. Their interior sense of sexual attraction to women was strong so that on learning the word, they found the name for their identity. Claire is 58 and recalls when she was 12, "The girls were talking about queers. They had a lot of misinformation. It wasn't surprising to me. There was a lack of information. I had a friend, and we would lay on top of each other and kiss. I didn't find out much information in the library. I felt it couldn't possibly be wrong, but I couldn't figure out why some of what I read was negative. I got the idea there were only a few women like this. I wondered where I would meet a woman like this. It made me nervous around girls because I knew I was looking at girls like I wanted to kiss them."

Cath is 45. "I had a crush on someone older than me. She was in eighth grade. I was in sixth grade. I heard the words 'homosexual' and 'queer.' So I started reading my dad's abnormal psychology books about homosexuality. I found out they were deviants, sick. My reaction was fear that I might be one and that I was sick." These women discovered homophobia and the fear of being found out by the wrong people who would punish them for being themselves. They also experienced their isolation in a heterosexual world. They wondered where the other lesbians were.

Some lesbians easily acknowledged their attraction to women and their feelings that it was right and normal. When they understood the cultural proscription against lesbianism, they took a critical stance against society. They did not respond by finding fault with themselves. Alana is 44. "I knew I was interested in women, but I never heard anybody talk about it. I read the part about lesbianism in my parents' book on sexuality, and it made me very angry to read the part on homosexuality. Angry because it said it was deviant behavior. I knew I had those feelings. It didn't feel deviant to me. I felt I had the same way of looking at the world as other people, so I was angry at that judgment." Jolene is 40. "In high school I wanted to go further than back rubs with girlfriends, but I didn't know what it would be. I was aware of wanting to cuddle and be with girlfriends. I didn't have a label for it. I just felt in love with different women friends. I would get possessive with their time. I never talked about it then, but I can see it now. Then I couldn't identify it. I remember being aroused by reading D.H. Lawrence's *The Fox*, wondering about it. Mom would tell me gayness was repulsive. Knowing my mom felt that way, I wouldn't get into it." Jolene's mother's supervision was sufficient to prevent her from exploring her desires as a teenager. But when she left home, she began her lifestyle as a lesbian.

SEXUAL TRANSFORMATIONS

Heterosexual women face the possibility of a transformation to an open-minded acceptance of lesbianism and, later, an understanding of the complexities of women-identified-women relationships.

Since the culture is so pervasively homophobic, many of them never make this transformation. The women interviewed for this book are a politically liberal and college-educated sample. Very few of them stated that they still thought of lesbianism as gross or sick. Women's negative views about heterosexual sexual intercourse became more positive after experiencing it. But they became more accepting of lesbianism without the experience of being sexual with a woman. This transformation was an intellectual exercise, not a physical one. For most heterosexual women, the transformation to a more open-minded attitude came from exposure to lesbianism through literature, from college courses, or from meeting and knowing lesbians. The experience of interacting with lesbians made this aspect of sexual expression less threatening.

Justine, 24, considers the value of her own experience and perceptions over what she was taught as a child. "As I got older, I changed from what adults had taught me. I started thinking for myself. I accept anybody's lifestyle as long as they don't force it on me. As long as they accept me. Some of my comfort about homosexuality came from my friendship with a transvestite in one of my classes. He was one of the most caring people I ever met." Justine found that meeting a member of a sexual minority in college normalized the person. But she is not sophisticated enough to be aware that the lesbian lifestyle is not at all similar to that of a male cross-dresser. Like her, Kristie, 23, found the college campus opened her mind. "I feel pretty open about lesbianism. As I grew older I became more open to life and different lifestyles. I was a peer counselor in sexuality at the university."

Yvette, 25, illustrates someone in transition. She is open-minded, but ambivalent. On one hand she has dropped religious moralizing, but on the other she compares lesbianism to drug usage, a negative behavior. "Entering college helped me become more tolerant. I met gay men in classes. I kept spiritual belief, and cast aside religious belief. I compare lesbianism to drugs being pushed. I wouldn't mind a gay person as long as they don't push it." Yvette has not reached the point of seeing lesbianism as just another sexual alternative.

Several women found friends transformative. Camille, 40: "At college I was curious about learning about it. I accepted it, but it wouldn't work for me. I had lesbian friends. About one half of the women I knew were bisexual." Donna, 46, recounts her changes: "I don't think it's nasty now. I was playing tackle football. I didn't realize most of the gals were gay. Now we're friends and respect each other's rights." Fran, 42, finds that she can accept her friends, but her children might be another story: "The first time I had close gay friends (males), I began to change my attitude. Today I feel accepting. But there's a little Archie Bunker in me who would have a hard time if my children choose a gay lifestyle."

Silena, age 30, also expresses a deeper transformation: "I no longer wonder what women do together. I let go of a rigid approach to sex. My best friend got into group sex and homosexuality. I have gay and bisexual friends. Knowing them made me wonder if I would ever get involved with a woman. Now I see sex as a whole that encompasses a lot of different behaviors." Silena is seeing lesbianism as another sexual option. She wonders if she would be sexual with a woman, but for now it remains a fantasy.

Susie, 33, expresses a broader acceptance of lesbianism: "I think it's daring and individualistic. Lesbians don't have to slow down for men. Men can't handle liberated women." Susie still prefers men as sexual partners, but she sees that in some ways lesbianism might be a better option. And Melanie, 34, also considers that lesbianism can be fulfilling: "About ten years ago, I found out a good friend was gay. She told me a lot about her relationship and also about the fear of oppression she had when she was young, and even sometimes now. I was surprised, but I got over it. Sometimes her life seems better than mine." Robin, 33, takes a holistic approach: "I think it's great. I like to see people in love. I always root for passionate involvement."

Sanura

Sanura, 32, vividly describes the process of her transformation in understanding lesbianism. "I was in the fourth grade. I was walking down the street with my girlfriend with our arms around each other. Some guys in a truck yelled out, 'lesbos' or 'lezzies.' We didn't know what it meant, but from the look on their faces it wasn't good. I remember the boys produced a negative reaction in us. They were teasing us. It is too bad it took something fun and innocent and made it have completely different connotations. For somebody to yell out the car on the street had a high impact. That was the cue for me that I was doing something socially unacceptable."

This event, men denigrating an innocent girlhood friendship, was Sanura's introduction to the context that lesbianism is unacceptable. It was effective because Sanura and her friend stopped their public affection. She was not sexually involved with her friend, so the sexual connotation of the word 'lezzie' was not salient. When Sanura was older, the issue arose again.

"From early on I knew that heterosexuality was my designation. I was to be attracted to boys. But when I was in junior high and high school, my older sister used to tease me for not having a boyfriend. She used to say it was because I was gay. I used to tell her 'that isn't true.' But I had an element of doubt. All my friends had boyfriends, and I thought, 'What's the matter with me? Why aren't I attracted to boys who are giving noogies to my friends' heads and punching them in the arm?' I thought that maybe there was something wrong with me. I don't know if she placed a fear of being gay in me. In high school there was a suggestion that a p.e. teacher was lesbian. My reaction was that it was deviant behavior."

Sanura felt herself to be heterosexual, but the accusations from her sister caused self-doubt. She had little information about lesbianism, and she had no partnered sexual experience. Sexuality was still a mystery. She was left to wonder about her own sexual inclinations. Like most girls in high school,

Sanura saw that lesbians were singled out as the "other." Being different is a problem that no teenager wants to bring on herself. In addition, she learned that lesbianism was considered abnormal. She had no desire to go in the direction of the lesbian social outcast.

Sanura continues, "At 16 I started professional modeling, and I met a lot of gay men. I remember thinking I could picture two men together but not two women together. But I had not met any lesbians until I was 18. One of my good friend's cousins stopped by with her girlfriend. They were in their early twenties. It's funny, I was afraid to look at them. I was afraid they would think I was staring. I was constantly averting my eyes because they touched and sat closer than most women I'd seen before. Then, while in my early twenties, I got to know women who were lesbians and who enlightened me about my misconceptions."

Sanura found that meeting lesbians who were often likable and not too different from herself altered her perception about them. She saw the lesbian terrain through their eyes. It was not frightening, but fascinating.

Bisexual and lesbian women also went through transformations about the concept and practice of sex between women. Some initially reacted to the idea of lesbianism as abnormal and wrong. These women began their transformation when they adopted more liberal and tolerant attitudes about sexuality. It progressed when they met women who were lesbian or bisexual. It then further evolved when they experimented with sexual exchanges with women.

Bisexuals who found themselves thinking about sexuality with women personalized the accepting attitude that they were adopting. Leanne, 41, says, "I got away from religion. I started looking at people and my own feelings in a different way. No labels. No judgment." Hoshi is 37. "Through self-growth I have come to feel it is natural. It could be a very beautiful experience. If it happened, I could go with it." Hoshi is taking a bisexual identity label even though she has not yet experienced sexuality with a woman. Amy is 25 and found her ideas changed when she was 18. "I had dreams of being with women. I read about it, and it made more sense and became acceptable." Jody is 25 and understands that "lesbian is a very strong, positive word. Lesbianism is a positive thing. It's a powerful statement a woman makes about herself and her autonomy." Like Jody, Skye is 25 and says, "Now lesbianism has an honorable place in my life. It's also commonplace and daily, whether I'm sexual or not. I daily talk about it with lesbians, and I daily think of women being with each other." Each of these women has gone beyond acceptance into claiming a lesbian identity for herself.

Discovering that they felt love and romance toward women, with all the accompanying warmth, brought many lesbians to recognize the goodness of their desires. Audrey is 42 and recalls: "I didn't have a label for feelings and fantasies about women as a teenager. I still dated boys. When I was 17, we moved, and I had to start all over. I would find the right man, and these feelings would go away. I had a crush on a woman. We ended up necking, and I knew this was a real thing. Women did this. I found a gay bar and thought I'd gone to heaven. Nobody ever brought me out. I knew exactly what to do." Tina is 36: "I changed by having a woman kiss me on the mouth and being glad. I smiled, and walked into her lesbian household. The feeling is serenity, absence of fear, courage, and acceptance."

Most lesbians and bisexuals experimented with sex with women once they met women who were interested. Bianca is a bisexual who is 20. She recalls, "I lived in Africa until I was 14. When I was 15, there were rumors about so-and-so being gay. I thought it was gross and terrible. Heterosexuality was normal. But when I was 18, I became more liberal about sex. Just a year ago, a good friend told me she was gay. I had no idea. My friend being gay did not bother me at all. Just recently I decided it was okay for me, too." Bianca changed her attitude about sexuality toward a more accepting one. When her friend announced she was a lesbian, she was prepared to accept it. Soon thereafter she too was able to acknowledge her own interest in sex with women.

Alexa is 33 and bisexual. She was 16 when she transformed her attitude about lesbianism in a simple experiment: "A friend and I talked about how we masturbated. We decided to experiment with each other. It was pleasurable and heightened our sense of closeness with each other." Polly is a 34-year-old lesbian who when she first learned about lesbianism was "appalled, probably because it touched close to home. I thought it was wrong, horrible, totally deviant, perverse, gross, less than human. But after I had relationships with women it began to change. With the first relationship it didn't feel wrong. If you love someone, what difference does it make?" Maggie is a 35-year-old lesbian. "I changed my attitude about lesbianism after I was married. I was with my husband's friends. We went skinny dipping. Later a woman and I went into the bedroom. We were drunk and began kissing. This was the turning point. I kissed a woman, and it was nice." Rene is also a lesbian. "I have more understanding now. In college, I was drunk and got kissed by a woman. I wasn't sure it was right, but I liked the hugging and kissing. I had a panic over the sex part. The panic disappeared with more experience."

When Lakeisha was 19 she "had sex with a woman. It was wonderful, fulfilling. It felt right, and I was immediately in love. I met her through a religious organization. She was with me and my family in a cabin in Lake Tahoe. We shared a room and had sex. The next day I felt it was all over my face, like everyone would know. Actually, I just opened my eyes to lesbianism. I think it chose me. Once I started having sex with a woman, I knew I was a lesbian. It felt like I was home to the core of my being." Polly, Maggie, Rene, and Lakeisha, after they acted on their desires, found that the mutually pleasurable exchange was enough to cast aside early negativity. They embraced their experience and were at the beginning of a new identity as lesbians.

Rebecca's transformation began in college when she was 19. She was away from parental constraints and found new and different people. "In college I found a label, a community, and a context. I had friends who were bisexual and who explained, 'This is what it means.' I came out when I was 19. I knew I was in love with Lisa. My feelings were more than friendship. I had previously had a sexual relationship with a man, and I recognized the feelings. I was a sexual being, and I realized I could be a sexual person with Lisa. I realized I lusted and had sexual fantasies about a woman. But I didn't identify as a lesbian because I didn't want to give up men. I became an active part of the women's community." Rebecca was thrown into a new subculture, and she found her place in it as a bisexual. She was able to acknowledge the feelings that she felt toward women and to create a sexual identity label that allowed her to maintain the possibility of sexual activity with men.

Ellen, 57, recalls that when she was 24 she "had lusting sex with a woman. We did deep kissing, penetration, cunnilingus. It was a positive experience. I wanted to fit in the lesbian culture, but I felt desire for men and couldn't talk about it with lesbians." Bisexuality was more hidden when Ellen was in her twenties. She lacked the community that Rebecca found to validate her sexual feelings for both men and women.

Guadalupe is 29 and sees her acceptance of herself as a lesbian as an ongoing process. "I'm constantly evolving. I left home one week after I turned 18 and went into the conservation corps. The women there were nonfeminine. I could identity with them just by how they dressed, walked, and talked to each other. The older ones took me under their wing, 'You don't understand yet.' I was naive and introverted. It's been a very long period of evolution of who I am—a lesbian. It's more than just being with another woman. When I was 18, I was a pebble rolling on the ground. As I've grown older, and picked up more experiences, I've continued to roll and become a bigger stone. I haven't yet come to a stop. This is an ongoing lifetime experience. You never stop growing up." Guadalupe eloquently describes the transformation that lesbian women are making about their sexuality. It is a continuous process, full of challenges in a culture that disparages women's sexual fulfillment, especially if her object is another woman.

A SEXUAL REVOLUTION

If there had been a sexual revolution, young women would begin their sexual lives supplied with the sexual information, self-awareness, and communication skills necessary to create a fulfilling sexual exchange. Instead, the teenage years are the time for experimentation with partnered sex. They hope to learn about good sex by trying it out with a partner. For most women, the first partner is male. After sexual intercourse with a young man, heterosexual women transform their childhood negative attitudes about intercourse into a more interested and positive viewpoint. It is the mere fact of experiencing sexual intercourse that marks this transformation, even if the woman was not orgasmic. She may not be having a completely erotic exchange, but the new territory of sexuality with a partner becomes a valued, even necessary aspect of the young woman's sexuality. Sex with a partner may be awkward, but for them it marks the beginning of sexual maturity.

For most teenage girls, sexual intercourse is not satisfying because they do not know how to manage the sexual exchange so that it includes their orgasm. In addition, boys who are only interested in the physicality of the sexual experience do not meet their emotional needs for intimacy and trust in the exchange. Not until later, in their twenties, with the benefit of a number of sexual experiences behind them, do women develop the ability to transform their sexuality into an interchange that is more erotically and emotionally fulfilling.

After a sexual revolution girls would learn about lesbiansism in a nonjudgmental manner and at the same age when they are told about sexual intercourse between men and women. But now it is in high school that most women learn about lesbianism. The majority of them assume a judgmental and homophobic attitude toward it. Yet some are more liberated and are accepting and interested. Teenage women who will grow up to be lesbian and bisexual women learn and adopt similar homophobic attitudes, only to discard them as adults. Only a few teenagers are aware enough of their sexual desires to identify themselves as lesbians or bisexuals and wonder about how they will be able to explore their sexuality. After the revolution teenagers who recognize in themselves a sexual interest in other women will easily accept it and will not be traumatized by homophobia.

Today lesbianism is mysterious because most young women cannot envision what constitutes lesbian sex. Sexuality is defined as intercourse, and so it would seem to be impossible for two women to do. After a sexual revolution, information about lesbian sexual acts would be common knowledge.

In this prerevolutionary period, a transformation to acceptance of the lesbian lifestyle does not occur for all heterosexual women. But some take on a more tolerant attitude. This tolerance is a result of an intellectual valuation of individual sexual rights. This shift is a different process than the shift toward more acceptance of the act of sexual intercourse. Most heterosexual girls were initially nonaccepting of heterosexual intercourse, but their attitude changed after experiencing it. Heterosexual women drop their initial negativity toward lesbianism without experiencing the act of sex with a woman. Many of them discover friendships with gay people and so are enabled to free themselves of negative judgments.

Bisexual and lesbian women become less judgmental about these sexual orientations as they begin to identify with them. They create an ongoing personal sexual revolution as they begin to explore the possibilities of these lifestyles. Acting on their sexual desires results in a satisfied state that reinforces their new choices.

In childhood and adolescence, women share the same sexual context and experiences. This changes when women sort themselves out and align themselves along sexual orientation. They begin markedly different sexual travels. Lifestyles becomes dissimilar when women identify themselves as heterosexual, lesbian, or bisexual. The next chapter will illustrate the range of directions that women take, the kinds of choices they permit themselves, and the transformations that each lifestyle brings.

chapter three

ADULTHOOD: WHO WE BECOME

HETEROSEXUALITY

The road to heterosexuality is mapped out for women before birth. Their parents are heterosexual, and they are surrounded by heterosexual relationships. Sometime in childhood, they begin to imitate heterosexual relationships by adopting the role of girlfriend to a boy or, for the more aggressive girls, by seizing a boyfriend. Children play at being married, and their parents approve. The high school environment entrenches heterosexual relationships when girls explore their first sexual experiences with young men. Lesbianism is looked down upon in the homophobic atmosphere of high school, so it is never an option except for the few young women who experience an attraction to women in their youth and who are assertive enough to risk sexually

approaching their girlfriends. Many women marry soon after high school graduation. Others continue their quest for a mate in the dating arena. They have accepted the definition of their future as a life within monogamous marriage. Their sexual travels involve erotic adventures, going from one partner to another after significant conflicts arise, but always moving toward the desired outcome of the perfect, compatible husband.

When teenage heterosexual women move toward seeking male partners, they give little or no thought to the fact that they are involving themselves in a particular sexual orientation. While sexologists view all sexual orientations as valid or normal, many heterosexual women see only heterosexuality as normal. Most of them never consider lesbianism or bisexuality. Those lifestyles are considered foreign, unfamiliar, and scary, whereas heterosexuality is predictable, understandable, and highly valued. Heterosexual encounters are what most women experience in their carnal travels. Indeed, for most women there is never any thought that there is anywhere else to go. While they may be aware of lesbianism and bisexuality, these are not real options in their minds. There is more than enough to challenge a woman in the land of heterosexuality. She is planning her future by charting her course to find the "perfect man," by trying to understand the male mind, by learning the communication patterns of a "relationship," and by considering how children or career or economic security fit into the picture. All this demands her energy.

Heterosexual woman see themselves as naturally flowing into sexual relationships with men. It is at puberty or in adolescence that this process begins. They are attracted to boys, and they want to date them and to explore the world of heterosexual relationships. They are supposed to take on the trappings of femininity and become the opposite to the male gender.

Choosing Heterosexuality

Of the women who stated that they were heterosexual, 82 percent stated that they were exclusively heterosexual, and 18 percent stated that they were not. Some of the women who saw themselves as heterosexual admitted that at some time of their lives they had explored sexuality with other women. These were side trips for the sexually curious. Curiosity satisfied, they continued down the path of heterosexuality.

I asked women if they chose to be heterosexual. Most of them had never pondered this question. To them, sexuality with a partner meant sexuality with a man. Their heterosexual lifestyle was just the average progression of any woman into adulthood. What is there to choose? Fifty-seven percent stated that they did not choose to be heterosexual.

Forty-three percent of heterosexual women stated that they did choose. How balanced this choice was for them remains another question. In a culture in which lesbianism and bisexuality are denigrated and kept secret, can heterosexuality freely be chosen? When they were children, heterosexual women learned about heterosexuality and their future in it as married women. Little girls grow up, get married, and have children. Every woman does it. In high school they learned about lesbians, but lesbians were usually perceived as the object of scorn. Who would want to be one?

These were the issues for women when they considered why they were heterosexual. Most women felt they were steered directly into heterosexuality. Rosie, 38, says, "I'm heterosexual by persuasion. Everything around me persuaded me to be heterosexual." Leza, 24, "I always took my heterosexuality for granted. Until recently, I never considered anything else. I don't think people can choose a thing when they don't know the options. I was socialized to be heterosexual, so no other options existed for me." Chloe, 22: "I always thought I was heterosexual. It was the way I was brought up. Being a lesbian was not something that was an option. I was raised to be heterosexual, and that's the way my friends were around me."

Kate, 31, examined this question more deeply: "I began to think of myself as heterosexual at age 15. I probably didn't think that much about other options. I had the idea that other options were not right from my parents. My parents wanted me that way, but I made the final choice. I have not had any thoughts or desires to explore the homosexual part of me. But I believe that I was born to be either. My parents trained me so that the heterosexual lifestyle would be the most likely. Socially, it is the easier choice."

Other heterosexual women who felt that their heterosexuality was a choice they made attributed their choice of sexual orientation because of their sexual attraction to men. Lynette, 21: "I grew up understanding that heterosexuality was the norm and understanding that I was one. But as I grew older and knew there were other options, I chose heterosexuality because I liked men. I wouldn't feel comfortable being bisexual or lesbian. Still I think it's learned. I learned it."

Other women emphasized that they are not attracted to women. Piper, 22: "It never crossed my mind that people had a choice until I was 13. But then I never thought that I wanted to be gay. It's never been a conflict in my mind that I'd have to

choose." Cheryl Jean, 42: "My heterosexuality is just what I feel. I could have chosen to do other things, but I'm just not interested. If I fantasize about a female, it's more about my sexuality than about being with a woman."

Innate Heterosexuality

Most heterosexual women were unconcerned that lesbianism was never an option for them. Sixty-one percent of these heterosexual women stated that they thought they were innately heterosexual. These women believe that their heterosexuality is something they were born to be. It is part of their nature or part of their biological make-up.

Vanessa, 21, explains her progression, which she sees as "natural": "When I was 9 years old, I got interested in boys. Heterosexual is what I am, I did not make a decision. I've only had romantic feelings about males. I think sex preference is biological. I don't think it can be changed depending on what you would prefer to be."

Shaniqua, 24: "Heterosexuality was all I saw growing up. It wasn't because of those images that I considered myself heterosexual. I was born this way. Inherently my nature is that I'm attracted to the opposite sex."

Whether or not they had a choice, whether or not it is socialized or innate, these women do not seem to care. They are comfortable with men and are not interested in women sexually. Their heterosexuality is socially approved, and they are happy relating sexually to men.

Curiosity and Choice

But being heterosexual is not so simple for everyone. Some heterosexual women are curious about sexuality between women. They imagine that women are better lovers than men because they think women would understand a woman's body. Most heterosexual women keep these ruminations in the realm of fantasy. Forty-four percent of heterosexual women stated that their sexual fantasies involve both men and women.

Fifty-one percent of the heterosexual women experienced sexual attraction to a female. The average age for feeling this sexual attraction was 21 years. But being attracted to women and fantasizing sex about them does not necessarily challenge the heterosexual woman's sense of herself as a heterosexual.

Blythe, 34, makes a distinction between emotional and sexual attraction to women. "You can love someone of the same sex, but not want to have sex with them. I became convinced that I was heterosexual when I was 31 years old. I had a bisexual girlfriend, and we had a close bond. We did have group sex once, and she and I just felt each other's breasts. That made me wonder. Maybe because society is geared toward heterosexuality I can be more free with a man. I never considered being with a woman when younger, except in fantasies."

Ten percent of the heterosexual women had experienced a sexual encounter with a woman. The average age for this experience was 19 years old. These women feel that they tested out their bisexuality, and they came to the conclusion that the heterosexual lifestyle was for them. Karen, 28, speaks for many heterosexual women. "I never thought of myself as anything but heterosexual. In the fifth grade I was attracted to a boy, and that might have been the point when I became heterosexual." But Karen created situations where she was sexual with women. "I have had three experiences with women, and it wasn't what I wanted. It seems to be a different experience for my lesbian friends than what I had when I experienced women. I had sex with a woman when I was 18. I felt there was something missing. Yes, I had an orgasm. It wasn't at all a negative experience. I've had sex with three women. All were with experimenting straight women.

"If I compared the women to all the men except my husband, they were more positive, caring, and concerned with what I felt than the men were. There was more verbal communication during the sexual experience. I didn't have a relationship with any of these women. My husband offers more qualities, because it is a relationship. Women weren't exactly right for me. It wasn't my thing."

Laura, 35, went further in her explorations by forming a relationship. "I lived as a bisexual for six months. The sex was great—I was orgasmic 100 percent of the time and was completely satisfied. We did clitoral stimulation with our hands or mouths. We were able to communicate, in spite of problems that arose. There was a willingness to communicate feelings and thoughts. Because of this relationship with a woman, I would know by now if I wasn't heterosexual. Or I would have pursued more relationships with women."

Sanura

For Sanura, becoming a heterosexual involved testing out the sexual experience with women as well as with men. When she was a young adolescent, others accused her of being lesbian. This created in her self-doubts about her sexual orientation.

"I always thought of myself as heterosexual, but there was always an element of doubt. I knew lesbianism wasn't socially acceptable, so it wasn't something that I wanted to be. So, instead of exploring any feelings, I disengaged myself from them. But I didn't realize that this was happening until much later. When I was 21, I explored other people's and my own fear of looking at other people's bodies. But it wasn't until I had the experience of being with a woman intimately that I really understood what homo- and heterosexuality were.

"I don't think that I can control the level of attraction that I feel toward someone. When I was growing up, I was heterosexual because that was the way it was supposed to be. So I didn't have a choice. It was compulsory rather than based on a gut feeling. I really think that no one fully understands who they are if they haven't allowed themselves to explore the feelings they have toward the same sex. If you don't explore all these feelings, you've cut off part of who you are.

"I was 26 when I had sex with a woman and man together. I knew them, and they invited me to have sex with them together. We talked about it, and it happened at a later time. I found it distracting and difficult to focus on both of them.

"I made love with the same woman alone a year later. We were on a camping trip together. We started talking about the other incident. She was heterosexual at that time. We both had the same reaction afterwards. I said that she seemed soft and feminine and I felt very masculine. She said the same thing when we were driving home in the car.

"It was nice. But what I learned was that it was just a different kind of experience: soft, sensuous, and warm and comforting at the same time. It didn't have the zing, the extra step of being really stimulating. It was nice and much mellower than the experiences I have had with men. I did wonder whether if I had been with a more experienced woman, my perspective would be different."

Barbara

Barbara, 52, also gave herself permission to experiment with a woman. "I think I probably did consciously choose to be heterosexual. In graduate school in the 1970s there was a time of intense adventure. One evaluated all aspects of one's life—sexuality; spirituality; the meaning of life, truth, and beauty. It was a time of no rules and no prescribed scripts to follow.

"I was going to bed with everybody—with strange men, with my best friends, and with one woman. She was a roommate and a friend. She was exploring, too. She was having sex with other women, and so we just tried it. I remember it as being pleasant, but I wasn't turned on. I went to bed with her again maybe a year later. By then she was a committed lesbian. It was more friendly than anything, not a turning point. It wasn't a huge turn-on, but it was comfortable. She was my friend like before and afterwards. We were still friends.

"I think after that i chose to be heterosexual. I don't think I've questioned that since. I could be innately bisexual, but I haven't really been motivated to explore lesbian sex more than I did. I think I'm probably heterosexual. I think if it were more of a part of my sexuality it would be more of a conflict with me. Women are not in my fantasies, but I know I've been attracted to some women. That is why I think I'm somewhat bisexual."

Twenty-six percent of the heterosexual women believe that they are not innately heterosexual, but innately bisexual. Most of them have not acted on these feelings. They realize that they carry a potential to be sexual with women, but they don't do it, for a variety of reasons.

Most heterosexual women are aware of homophobia, the fear of and persecution of lesbians and gay men. As long as being with men is sexually rewarding, why put oneself in the position to be a victim by becoming sexual with women? Janelle, 30, sees that she has made sexual choices "because of sexual experiences and the choice of whether or not they would benefit me. I don't think I'm locked into anything. I was pushed into a mold as a girl. Those who were different were persecuted." Beverly, 47: "Like everyone else, being heterosexual was part of my programming. I didn't know much about gay people. I didn't know what a lesbian was. I would like the option of deciding to be homosexual, but I feel that society today is homophobic. I have told women they could have me. But right now I'm not really interested in sex." Beverly is stopped from pursuing her bisexual self by fear of social criticism. She is sexually passive, telling women they can have her, but not actively pursuing them. She also has a low sex drive, so she is happy enough not to put energy into seeking a sex partner, either female or male.

Wendy, 37, also has found that her sexual passivity and her contentment with men has contained her bisexuality. "I was attracted to women in the past, and I might have explored it if they had liked me. I never considered being with a woman until I started smoking pot or, rather, when the hippie days started. In the current phase I'm in, I've chosen monogamy. I would not follow an inclination now as long as I'm married. I don't remember making a choice. Heterosexuality was just the thing to do. My main choice as a sex partner has been a man. Nothing ever happened with the couple of women I was attracted to."

Noting that she is in a phase, Wendy is holding different options for the future. She does not view her sexual identity as immutable. Instead, her sexuality is part of her personality, which is open to change and the acceptance of new experiences.

Nicole, 42, has mixed thoughts about her own sexual orientation. "The first time I experienced an orgasm was with a man. I was 19. Prior to that, I knew that a heterosexual relationship was expected of me, but I never saw myself in a married role. I chose to be heterosexual because it's pleasurable and it's more socially acceptable. Those are my reasons for choosing it. I also chose the relationship itself and what I get out of it. I experience an orgasm most of the time with men, too. It's what I'm the most comfortable with. When I think back on my homosexual explorations, it was a period of time to explore the body with my close friends and become comfortable with it. Today, if a man or a woman relationship came along, I'd explore." Nicole has been comfortable with a heterosexual lifestyle, but she knows she could be intimate with a woman. Like other heterosexual women, she is also taking a passive attitude, waiting for someone to come along rather than actively seeking out a female partner.

Confusion about Sexual Orientation

Thirteen percent of the heterosexual women stated that they were confused or did not know whether they were innately bisexual or heterosexual. Some did not have a ready answer for this question, because it was a topic they had never considered. Did sexual fantasies about women mean they were bisexual? They had no experience with women. How could they know? Fatima, 23, is a virgin from a very sexually controlling family. She has never dated, and she doesn't masturbate. She has not developed sexual fantasies, so she questions herself. "All my life I've thought of beautiful women to admire, but I don't want to have sex with them. Am I normal or not? Would I be labelled as queer if I admire my own sex?" Without the benefit of any sexual experience with either men or women, and with a lifetime of sexual repression, Fatima has not developed the self-knowledge needed to guide her exploration of who she is as a sexual being.

Yvette, 25, found that she could not give a clear response to the question of her sexual orientation. "When I was 16, I felt sexually turned on to boys, and I chose to have relationships with men. I chose sex, which plunged me into heterosexuality. This question confuses me. I haven't made a decision to be heterosexual. If I watch two women in a porno film, I'm turned on because it's sex. A sexual act of women to me is stimulating because it is a sexual act." Although she is aroused by the fantasy of two women being sexual, Yvette does not acknowledge that it might be tapping into her bisexuality. This is an ambiguous and confusing area for her, and so she retreats to her comfortable familiarity with heterosexuality.

Leslie

For some women, this issue is more problematic and painful. Leslie, 23, wonders how she will find happiness. "I never saw there was another option. It wasn't something to think about. Heterosexuality was supposed to be natural. It wasn't until I understood there were other options that I could see heterosexuality as a label. I didn't make a conscious decision to be heterosexual because I did not see it as a decision. When I realized it was, I didn't want to choose it, and that's when I chose to be a lesbian. I wanted to be a lesbian after a bad relationship with a man when I was 19.

"I met a lot of bisexuals, and I felt comfortable with them. But it was a handful of people, so how do I know if that's bisexuality? At the time, I was angry with men, and I went to the gay pride march in D.C. I thought of it as support for human rights. But straight people went out of their way to show they were straight. I didn't, and people thought I was a lesbian. But I didn't feel comfortable in the gay culture. I didn't feel accepted, although I wanted so badly to fit into it. I came away and realized that it won't just take a weekend to know that this is where I belong.

"It's been a personal journey for me. Bisexuality is not something I feel pressured to become. No one is telling me this is the way I should go. It's in my mind where I would like to be and where I would see myself."

Leslie is unique on a number of levels. She is a young woman coming into her sexuality at a historical moment when it is easy to find lesbian and bisexual associations. She has found out that there is an option to heterosexuality. Her open-mindedness about human rights and her genuine friendships with bisexuals and lesbians mean that she has been able to start out on her sexual trek with a wider view of the entire sexual landscape. Her strategy has been intellectual and practical. But she has been unable to use her experiences to come to a solid, definitive sense of her own sexuality. She is tentative and unsure of who she is as a sexual being.

Leslie has fostered her sexuality differently from the women I interviewed. Women who came to identify as lesbians or bisexuals uniformly state: "Then I fell in love with a woman." They were not, like Leslie, angry with men when they found themselves in a romantic encounter with a woman. Leslie has placed herself in settings where she could be available to both men and women. But so far no beautiful romance has transpired. At the time of the interview, Leslie had decided to be celibate. She knows that a sexual relationship for her carried so much meaning and risk that she did not want to plunge herself into an experience for its own sake. With a commitment to celibacy Leslie is free to develop deeper friendships, without playing out from her desperation. She is hoping that the future will draw to her the lover she deserves.

Leslie is at a crossroads. Is she becoming bisexual? Or will she experiment with women as Barbara and Sanura did and discover that she is heterosexual? Leslie's life illustrates that sexual orientation is not a simple path that is set from childhood. Knowledge of the sexual territory and experiences with men and women all shape the lifestyles that heterosexual women create for themselves.

If we add the 26 percent of heterosexual women who feel that they are innately bisexual to those who are confused about their sexual orientation (suggesting that they have unexamined feelings of bisexuality), 39 percent of the heterosexual women feel that they are innately bisexual or that they might possibly be bisexual. However, only 10 percent of heterosexual women have ventured into the sexual experience with a woman. They have found it to be rewarding, but not as fulfilling as their interludes with men. For them, bisexuality was not interesting enough to pursue as a lifestyle.

What prevents most heterosexual women from testing out their bisexual proclivities? First, they are socially conditioned from childhood to see men as the objects of relationships and as sexual partners. It is a daring risk to hazard sexuality with a woman. Second, homophobia, the social condemnation of lesbians, is very apparent to heterosexual women. They do not want to be so victimized. They do not want to give their associates the opportunity to condemn them on the basis of their sexuality. So sex with other women is kept in fantasy. Third, women are trained to be sexually passive. Men initiate dates, and women make themselves available. Some women who want to venture into sex with a woman take the same passive stance. "If a woman came onto me, I'd go for it." If the woman she would like to approach

her is equally passive, neither will know that the opportunity is there. Heterosexual women do not take the initiative with other women. Fourth, heterosexual women are sexually satisfied with men. Their sexual and relationship needs are met by men. If they are not in a sexual relationship, they have the skills to socialize with and date men. They expect that a future relationship with a man will be sexually rewarding. Finally, heterosexual women are comfortable in a heterosexual lifestyle. Their friends and acquaintances are primarily heterosexual. The shared activities, attitudes, and expectations of heterosexuality are enjoyable. There is no dissatisfaction that would send them to another realm.

LESBIANISM

Beginning as a Heterosexual

Like all girls, lesbians are born into a world of heterosexuality. Their parents are heterosexual and have the same expectation for their daughters. The lesbian girl approaches life from the stance that heterosexuality is her future. It is the only way to be. In childhood she is just like the other girls. She learns a female way of being. Lesbian girls see before them the same heterosexual freeway that stretches out in front of all women. Eighty percent of the lesbians I interviewed started out thinking of themselves as heterosexual. Thirty-nine percent of these women had been married to men. When I asked lesbians if they chose to be heterosexual, 21 percent said they chose it, and 73 percent said that they did not choose it. Their reason is similar to the responses of heterosexual women: There was no option. Lesbianism did not exist.

LaQuita, 29, "I started to think of myself as heterosexual when I was 12, and I started being interested in boys and falling in and out of love. Heterosexuality was the only thing I knew. I had no other options presented to me as a Jehovah's Witness. I was directed to become heterosexual. So I did it all, got married and had children." Now 48, Rita experienced the same absence of lesbians. "When I was 15 years old, I had sex with my fiancé. I chose sex, and that was what was available. I had a fantasy about women. But in the 50s in the South you didn't have an option of choice."

Rudy

Rudy was not sexually interested in boys, but she took refuge in the concept that she was heterosexual. "When I was a teenager, about 16, I had no desire to have sex. I didn't like males very much. There was a rumor about my best girlfriend and me. People thought we were lesbians, but we weren't. Laurie and I were best friends and did everything together. People would talk. She suggested we go out on dates with boys. I considered it fortunate that I was not a lesbian at that time because I would have been really traumatized had I been trying to keep it a secret. As it was, I thought it was funny. As a teenager I had four dates: the two proms and the one ball. I only

had one regular date and that was a disaster.

"I had sexual feelings but I didn't understand them at the time. They were always fantasies. I had erotic fantasies about Elizabeth Taylor. I was in love with her. But it wasn't realistic. I had dreams and pictures of her. I attributed it to admiration. Later I realized it was a crush.

"I considered myself heterosexual. I don't see that I had a lot of options. I didn't know any lesbians that I knew were lesbians. I hung out in a heterosexual world. I didn't think of other options until I was 21."

Nancy, 34, believes her life could have been different. "I was heterosexual from birth. I grew up thinking that heterosexuality was all there was. I assumed it because I did not see anything else. Once I became aware of other options, in my late twenties, I realized I had had desires for sexual intimacy with women prior to that. But those desires were unconscious. I did not let those desires surface in me. If I'd had any role models to give me an idea of options, I would never have been heterosexual."

The heterosexual lifestyle pervades every aspect of life. Women are raised to think that heterosexuality is all there is. Ryfka, 47, lived her adolescence and twenties as a heterosexual. "I think you don't think about it [lesbianism]. You only think about it when you challenge it. When you think about sex with a woman, that's when you think, 'No, no, I'm heterosexual. I don't do this.'

"There's a presumption of heterosexuality. It's like the white skin privilege. It's not something you notice unless someone raises it as an issue. In general, unless one recognizes at an early age that one is different, heterosexuality is the presumed norm, and you don't think about it. You only make an assumption when you think, 'Oh, maybe I'm different.' You don't recognize sameness until you challenge it."

Some young lesbians did wonder if they were different. As teenagers they felt an unnamed attraction for other girls, but they could not face this in themselves. If all girls want to date boys and to be sexual with them, what were they to make of these strange yens they felt for other girls? These feelings were nameless and outside the category of heterosexuality. There was no indication from anyone around them that other women had these feelings. These attractions must be a personal quirk. Delphine, 35, as a teenager was aware of peer pressure. "I tried to be like everyone else when I was 14. There was no choice. I had to be accepted, so I was a heterosexual. I was aware of queers, but I wasn't one. I have always been attracted to women, even when I was trying to be heterosexual. I hated the fact that I wanted to be close to women. It was a feeling that warned me that I was different no matter how I acted."

Her fear of her own lesbian tendencies caused Rosalie, 46, to react powerfully to the possibility of attraction to women. "I was exclusively heterosexual and began dating boys at 14. When I was

17 I was approached by a lesbian teacher. I reacted negatively. I chose heterosexuality because I didn't recognize my own lesbian tendencies. It wasn't a big deal. I chose it because it's what was there. If I'd known of lesbianism then, I wouldn't have chosen heterosexuality." Rosalie was not at ease with her teacher's advances. If she did think about it at all, it was that she was establishing that she was not like the teacher, a hated queer. It was in her adult years that Rosalie established mature relationships with women and experienced lesbianism as an entirely different entity.

Cath, 45, was vaguely confused about her sexuality when she was young. "At one point in my life I didn't know there was anything else to be. I never really was heterosexual, I just considered myself one. That's what everyone was. Unless you were crazy. Those were your options: heterosexual and normal, or not heterosexual and crazy, queer. Those years trying to be heterosexual were a lot of wasted years."

Like Cath, Lakeisha, 32, had no way to assimilate her own internal experience of attraction toward other women. "I think that until I was aware I was a lesbian I assumed I was heterosexual. I was sleeping with men. I was attracted to men until I started having sex with them. Then any sort of physical attraction was gone. My first fantasies were about women. When I masturbated, I thought about women. During puberty I felt comfortable with women, and I didn't like men. I had homosexual feelings that I know now in retrospect. Before, I thought I was weird and confused." In a world where lesbianism doesn't exist, young women like Cath and Lakeisha had no way to understand their own attraction to women. They had no context for the emotions and could only assume that it was their own peculiar idiosyncrasy.

Some young lesbians chose to be heterosexual in order to pass as one and to play the game. They knew they were different, but they also knew of homophobia. It made life easier, so it seemed, by pretending to be heterosexual. For Concepcion, 28, adolescence was confusing and dismal. If she pretended to be heterosexual, would she become one? What was she to make of the forbidden desires that haunted her?

Concepcion

"I thought I was heterosexual from when I was 13 to 17 years old. My mother was into the Seventh Day Adventist church. So I was involved in the philosophy of that church, which is structured in family—men's and women's—roles. I adopted the philosophy and got a boyfriend. We were not sexual. I was afraid of sex with men. I was attracted to females, even as a child. I realized I had to be normal, so I chose heterosexuality, as it was the normal thing. So I tried to be straight. It was a real struggle. I had no one to talk to about it. I got religious, I prayed to be straight. At the age of 17, I overdosed to escape this situation. I wanted to die. My mom found me unconscious. In my culture, parents would rather see their child dead than gay. So this experience was terrifying.

"I had a close relationship with a woman in college, but it was not sexual.

She was a friend and was having sex with her boyfriend. I had a boyfriend but no sex. I couldn't deal with being homosexual. I was reading, and I learned about bisexuality. I thought the label bisexual would explain my feelings. I still suffer sexual anxiety from childhood conditioning. I chose bisexuality the same way I chose heterosexuality. The realization of being a lesbian was too hard. It was easier to think of myself as bisexual. When I was 23, I was finally sexual with a woman. It was comfortable. I had done reading on lesbianism. I was feeling sexual, and I was surrounded by women. At age 23, I finally had the nerve to be what I was since I was 9 years old. The other labels were attempts to avoid its realization."

Concepcion's tale reveals the psychological pain she endured because she could not accept her own lesbianism while living in a culture that made it invisible. She had no context for her love for women. She had no word to describe herself. She knew that she was different and that she would be condemned by her parents. The isolation and loneliness she suffered was only relieved when as a young adult she left home and found other women like herself.

Claire

Claire's account is different. She had more social advantages than Concepcion, and she knew and accepted that she was a lesbian. "I felt my first sexual attraction to another girl when I was 12. And I labelled myself a lesbian when I was 20. I don't know if I have a choice to be lesbian. If I was attracted to women, did I have a choice? When I made a conscious decision to get married to a man, I wasn't changing my sexuality. I never claimed the heterosexual label for myself. Even when I married, I did it for my family. I was fearful that I would have a difficult time being active sexually with women in college. I knew I would have to be very discreet. I consciously saw marriage as a cover. Then after I got married, I realized I wouldn't have the freedom to pursue women. I didn't enjoy sex with my husband. I didn't anticipate that. I found that I didn't want to have sex with him. If I had had orgasms and wasn't sexually frustrated, it would have worked out. We didn't have sex before marriage. He didn't want to; he didn't believe in premarital sex. I left the marriage after one month. I don't think I thought it through. It wasn't fair to him. I thought, 'Either I get out of it now or drag it out and make us both unhappy.' "

Discovering Lesbianism

There is a wide range of ages for when women first unearth their sexual attraction to other women. Twenty percent of these women believed they were innately lesbian because they were aware of being attracted to women from an early age—some as young as 6 years old. At the other extreme are women who were not sexually attracted to females until the age of 39. The average age for being aware of the first sexual attraction to a woman was 17 years old. Ten percent of the lesbians were first aware of their sexual attraction to women after the age of 30.

The average age for the first sexual experience with a female is 20 years old. Twenty percent of the women had some form of sexual experience with another girl in childhood or prepuberty. Thirty percent explored another teenager. Fifty percent of the lesbians were older than 20 when they first became sexually involved with a woman, and 10 percent were older than 30. Most of the women had already been sexual with men before they acknowledged to themselves their attraction to women and acted on these feelings.

Being sexual with another female does not necessarily mean that a woman will label herself a lesbian. It takes some time for women to come to terms with lesbianism as a sexual identity. Twenty-four percent of the lesbians discovered this part of themselves after they were 30 years old. They spent their adolescence and their twenties as heterosexuals, pursuing relationships with men.

Lesbians universally describe their discovery of the lesbian territory as a wonderful experience of coming home. Suddenly, their sexuality, emotional life, and attraction to women all neatly form into a harmonious reality. They find a peaceful and sexual resting place. This is always a turning point in the lesbian woman's life. She is changed and will never again be the same. She is in transformation when she actively turns away from intimacy with men and embraces a complete affiliation to women.

Stephanie

Stephanie, 25, was raised in ignorance of lesbian life. "I always thought I was heterosexual. Heterosexuality was expected of me. I was told that one day I would find a man and get married. I never thought I had a choice, though I knew that the lesbian lifestyle was there. Mom was involved with bisexual men, and lots of gay men came over to the house. But I never saw it in terms of women. I lived with a man as housewife. I always felt inadequate. I'd cook, and he didn't eat it. I felt a lot of pressure to be involved with men: from myself, friends, and family.

"When I was 11, I made love with a girl, but I did not see this as preventing me from being heterosexual. I did not think of this as lesbian. It was just a nice thing that we shared. Then when I was 21, I took my first women's studies course in college and learned more about lesbianism. I fell in love with a woman in dance class. I went to a gay pride workshop. It felt so right, like I'd gone home. That marked the end of my marriage."

Jolene, 40, found that her transformation to a lesbian was a gradual process. "When I was 12, I was fighting with my tomboy image. I was trying to turn into a girl, not liking it, but doing it. Mom and society were pressuring me to be more femme and get interested in boys. It was expected of me to be a heterosexual, so I just assumed the role until I chose to change it when I was 24. I'm basically gay.

I was born gay, but late in learning about it. My stomach topsy-turvied for girls, never for a man. In the phase of my life before being lesbian, I got into a three-way, live-in situation with a man and a woman. I thought I was bisexual. Then I wanted the man out of the picture, while she wanted me out of the picture! It was a step to being 100 percent lesbian. It was the way I phased myself into it. I decided I didn't want to be with men ever again. It felt normal. I put men behind me. I was tired of men. I liked the softness of women, emotionally and physically. The love experience with women seems more real. I fought it all my life. My attractions were always for women."

Cath, 45, was initially heterosexual because the alternative was to be "crazy or queer." As a young teen she secretly tried to find out about herself. "I had a crush on someone older than me. She was in eighth grade, I was in sixth grade. I heard the words *homosexual* and *queer* together, so I started reading my dad's abnormal psychology books about homosexuality. I found out they were deviants, sick. My reaction was fear that I might be one and that I was sick. When I was 20, I fell in love with a woman, and I decided that loving couldn't be sick. I was still afraid about being socially condemned, but I decided that it wasn't sick. It was actually the first time I felt good in eight years."

Rudy

Rudy was heterosexual because she saw nothing else in her environment. "I was not walking around an angst-ridden lesbian. I was walking around a heterosexual person with this part of me that wasn't awakened. I led a heterosexualized life. The options were either to be alone or be with men. It never occurred to me that women could be other than friends or sisters. After I met some lesbians, I thought these unnamed feelings could be lesbian feelings. Then I tried it and it was a reality. If I were 16 now, I might have been much more aware that a close relationship with a woman could be more than a friendship. A male friend of mine came out in the 1950s. He had feelings but didn't know what it was. He discovered it in French philosophers, and he thought he had to go to France for it. Now there is more openness in movies and media. For me there was no place like this."

After Rudy became friends with a homosexual man, she found the concept of the gay lifestyle to be fascinating. "I didn't think of other options until I was 21. I became friends with a gay man, and I was curious about his life. I began an intellectual process about the significance of women in my life. The passionate relationships that I had as a kid were with women. Crushes on teachers and movie stars. My best friend in high school was a girl. I wasn't interested in boys at all. I had no interest in men until I met Jeff. He was the first man I had sexual or emotional feelings about in my life.

"So Charles was a gay man who was open about what that meant to him. He was involved in gay liberation and was open publicly about himself. He wasn't apologetic about his relationships at all. He answered any questions I might have. (Later he told me he thought I was a

lesbian, and he was waiting to see if I'd figure it out.)

"I asked Charles if he'd introduce me to a lesbian so I'd have one to talk to. He introduced me to his friend, Susie, who was 26. Later, we met again at a night class at college. We sat and talked in her car for two hours. I asked her how she knew she was a lesbian and how to meet them. So she took me to a lesbian bar for a beer. It was Wednesday night. There was hardly anyone there. She had been out for a long time, since she was a teenager. I was nervous that I would offend somebody and act like a dolt. We were at the bar talking, and what was difficult for me, making me nervous, was the gender bending that was going on. Some women looked like men, and a man came in and he looked like a woman.

"When Susie went to the bathroom, a heterosexual man came up to me, hitting on me with, 'Baby, I got the cock that'll make you straight.' I didn't know the etiquette. I didn't expect this, and I didn't know how to behave. I told Susie when she came back. She told him, 'She's with me.' Finally she planted a kiss on me to back him off. So we started making out. She asked me if I wanted to go home. I said, 'Yes.' At her house there were no expectations; it was up to me. But I thought I was up for it.

"She was living by herself, and we went back to her house. I had no awkwardness, and it felt natural. We sat on the couch in the living room for a while. She was not pushy at all. She asked me if I wanted to go to bed with her. I said, 'Yes.' I think she asked me a couple of times if I was nervous. I wasn't. I remember thinking

I would never go home with a man from a bar, but I felt safe with her. We went into the bedroom. I didn't have an orgasm. I took the lead from her. It was mostly fondling, touching, kissing on the mouth. I don't remember if we had oral sex. She was into penetration so we finger fucked each other. She did it to me first, and I was taking mental notes about what we were doing. I had only been with four men. I was not sexually experienced. I knew more about men's bodies than my own. I had never had an orgasm, and I didn't with her. She did. She loved sex. She was open about it. It felt good to her. She was a sexual person, and she had orgasms really easily. Then we just curled up and went to sleep.

"My change into becoming a lesbian took three months. I saw Susie and spent some time at the bar. I didn't see myself as bisexual, but just as a sexually free person. This was 1970 or '71. I was thinking about sex with men, 'I don't want to do this anymore. This doesn't feel as good as the lesbian world does.' At that point I hadn't been in love with a woman. I had five to ten sexual partners, a few one night stands and some for a few months.

"In six or eight months, I fell in love with a woman, and that confirmed it for me. It was difficult at first to be in love with this woman. She didn't think she was a lesbian. We were friends from school, and we were doing everything together. I told her I was falling in love with her, and she said, 'You can't do that. I'm not a lesbian.' She kept saying that she just happened to fall in love with a woman, me. She was closeted, and we hung with a heterosexual group. We didn't have lesbian friends. After a year, I found out that she'd had two previous lesbian lovers! And she's been with women ever since.

"By the time I realized I was in love with her, I had not been with a man for 11 months. I didn't miss men. I liked the sameness of us rather than the difference. I liked being with someone who knew what I meant when I said, 'Remember when you started your period?' I liked the experiential commonality. I liked women's bodies. I had never found men's bodies particularly appealing. I was never with a man again."

Rudy discovered the culture of lesbians and slowly made her move into the lesbian world and away from the heterosexual mainstream. Each step led her deeper into a territory that felt familiar and safe. She found that she could express more of her personality in this arena. She felt more understood, and she experienced deeper love than she had with a man. The sensuality and physicality with women was infinitely more appealing than what she knew with men. Her moves into lesbian space were forthright and conscious. She never looked back to men.

Anita had a 20-year marriage with an alcoholic and abusive husband. She worked blue-collar jobs and raised her seven children with little help from him. She was trying to keep her marriage and family together. As her children became teenagers, they tried to protect her from her husband, and they urged her to leave him. Her self-esteem was raised from being successful at her jobs, and she ended the marriage. Once on her own, she fell in love. She was surprised that the person she loved was a woman. "I just assumed I was heterosexual. There were no options to consider—if you were female, you got married and had children. So I did. After my divorce I had my first experience falling in love with a woman. I was 47. Then I explored what it meant to be a lesbian in society, and I realized it was the only sane choice. The more I learned about myself, the more I became a woman-loving woman. The more I found out about patriarchy, the more I got in touch with anger, and that influenced my decision. It is almost impossible to have equality within heterosexuality. I never had strong female role models. Mom was always with a man. I decided to be a different role model for my children and grandchildren. They see my partner and I, two women sharing a life in a loving, respectful way." Anita went from struggling for her survival as a battered spouse, to a loving and supportive long-term relationship with a woman. It was a transformation she could never have imagined while she was married, but when it happened, she won joy in her life.

Redefining oneself as a lesbian is usually a process that happens over months or years. When women begin this process as adults, they generally have a full heterosexual life established, and it must be altered or dismantled.

Ryfka

Ryfka, 47, was in an unhappy marriage, and she had two children. She was working and going to school. She could not make any instant changes. "My children's father and I lived next to an apartment with a lesbian couple. He got sexually involved with one of them. Because he was shtuping one, the other and I decided to hop in the sack. One day we realized that the only reason we were in bed was because our respective partners were in bed together. I was not sexually attracted to that neighbor. We ended the affair. A few months later I was separated from my husband. I realized I was attracted to a friend, so I propositioned her. She was straight. She said, 'Ooo, I love you, but not that way.'

"Not until I was 34 was I with a woman where it was reciprocal. I was teaching a college class, and a student in the class started to come to talk to me in my office hours. She walked me back from class, then she met me to walk before class. I didn't think it was a big deal. Then she sent me a note, 'I enjoyed our conversations. Want to have a beer sometime?' I said, 'Sure.' Suddenly I realized, 'She's hitting on me!' She started meeting me; brought me balloons for my birthday. We started talking about getting involved. She was living with another woman. She said something about coming to visit me at home. When she came to my house I realized there was more to this. I told her, 'I have no intention of doing anything with you as long as you are in a class of mine.'

I was in a custody fight, and I had a good case to get full custody of my kids. I didn't want to take any risks. Then there was a graduation party. She graduated and we kissed on the dance floor and went to bed that night. We had a great time.

"Until then I thought of myself as heterosexual. I learned about lesbianism in terms of women's liberation literature. And I had lesbian friends so it was not such a big deal to become one. My reaction to that night was, 'Ooo, this is good, fun. I like this.' It felt like, I've come home. I immediately knew I was a lesbian. I didn't think of labelling myself. Except for my concern about child custody, it was no big deal. My friends didn't give a shit, and I had a close lesbian friend.

"I was going through this terrible introspective period, and I was in therapy dealing with the loss of custody of my stepson. I talked about sex with a woman. My therapist said, 'Does this bother you?' And I said, 'No.' So she said, 'Enjoy it.' So I changed the label. Lesbian just seemed to fit. Being a lesbian wasn't a major epiphany. I never went to a debate about 'What does it mean about me, my life?' I had no turmoil. It felt natural. I didn't agonize over it. I like women's bodies better than men's. I dropped my interest in men. I was no longer interested in dating men. Women are more interesting.

"I hung out with the former student for a couple of months. She wanted to move near me, and I refused. I was worried about custody. Then she moved to the other side of the country. I had other more important things going on in my life. I didn't put a lot of investment into her.

"It took me a while to be with a woman because I had just not met a particular woman I was drawn to or was drawn to me. I don't think I was in a setting for it to happen. When you hang out with straight people, you don't get ideas about queer people. Coming out was organic and natural and not a problem. The only problem was keeping it secret due to the custody battle. It wasn't that I found sex with men bad. It just felt great to be with women and that is my primary sexuality."

Ryfka's story illustrates that once the opportunity to be in a sexual relationship with a woman began to surface in her consciousness, over time a process gradually moved her into a lesbian identity. Her relationship with the world as a mother, and therefore a presumed heterosexual, precluded full involvement in a lesbian subculture. The acts of living her daily life with the new sexual openness to women gradually led her to meet women who reciprocated. The slow pace of this transformation made it feel to her like a comfortable evolution.

There is no simple standard or format for a lesbian lifestyle. There is no simple progression into marriage and children, as there is for heterosexuals (although some lesbians form long-term domestic partnerships, often living with their children). Challenges from homophobic people at work or in social settings force lesbians to redefine themselves. Despite these problems, lesbians find that loving women is amazingly rewarding.

Lesbians and Bisexuality

Forty-nine percent of the lesbians say that they had a period of time during which they identified as bisexual. The range of time was 1 month to 12 years, and the average time was $3^1/_2$ years. The average age at which lesbians labelled themselves bisexual was 28 years old. All lesbians saw this as a transition phase. They could not immediately acknowledge that they were lesbians. They did not want to sever all intimate sexual and emotional connections to men. They were gradually moving into lesbian territory, keeping their options open to return to the world of men. Seventy-six percent of these lesbians believe that they chose to be bisexual. They chose to express and explore their sexual interest in women, and they were still somewhat interested in men at the time.

Thirty percent of lesbians see themselves as innately bisexual. They have the capacity to be sexual with both men and women. But they are making a choice to limit their emotional, sexual, and intimate bonding to women only.

Kameko

Kameko, 21, once identified as heterosexual, but she makes a distinction. "I've come to believe I'm innately bisexual, because although I'm mainly attracted to women now, I have been and sometimes still am attracted to males. I called myself bisexual from the age of 19 to 21. At 21, I labelled myself a lesbian. I am innately bisexual, but I also chose bisexuality. I think of being bisexual as just being attracted to other people. I believe that it can't always be a male/female attraction. Gender is not that important. What matters is that you like them.

"This year I chose to be a lesbian by resolving to myself that I really wasn't attracted to men. (I don't like penises.) That was bolstered by the realization that relationships with women were more emotionally satisfying. I found myself what I hope will be a permanent relationship with a woman. And a part of it is trying to convince myself I'm not attracted to anyone else, particularly men. I get a lot of support from peers to not be interested in men. Becoming a lesbian was part of my development. Choosing female partners was something I had to do to take care of myself."

Kameko is at a decision place in her life. She perceives herself to be bisexual by nature and capable of a sexual relationship with either a man or a woman. Today she sees that her healthiest sexual choice is to stay in her monogamous relationship with a woman. Will this be a lifelong sexual lifestyle? She is young and at the beginning of her sexual trek. Kameko may find that her sexual choice leads her back to bisexuality and sex with men. Or, she may, like so many lesbians, find that the intimacy she experiences with women becomes more and more rewarding than what is available from men. Her choice today may be a lifelong commitment to lesbianism.

Bisexuality can be a comfortable place of transition for lesbians who acknowledge the worth of their relationships with men. With a reasonably good marital relationship and two children from the marriage, Willa, 37, travelled from her marriage to bisexuality. "I didn't consciously think of myself as anything but heterosexual. This is a heterosexual culture, so kids grow up assuming that is normal, natural." But she moved on to identify as lesbian as a political statement and a philosophical belief. "I think bisexuality is the healthiest sexual orientation. Normally, I would label myself so now. But it's politically better to be a lesbian to stand up for women's rights. I believe people should be able to love who they choose. Sexuality should be based on who is attractive. I went through a stage of not really being a lesbian. Part of me doesn't believe I may never fuck a man again. I used bisexuality as a transition to feel good about loving women. To be a lesbian you have to choose because it's so condemned, ostracized, and hidden away."

Virginia

For Virginia, 35, the concept of being a lesbian is much more than a sexual choice. Her movement into lesbian territory involves opening to a new way of being within herself and to a new culture, lesbian women's culture. "I am a lesbian because I love women; but sexually, I'm bisexual. To be lesbian is a political choice. I love women socially, spiritually, politically, psychically, and sexually. Bisexuality is a sexual choice and a result of a desire not to be labelled as queer.

"Once I got involved in a relationship with a woman, I had an awareness that a man couldn't give me what I was looking for. The kind of relationship I wanted I had a much better chance of finding with a woman. The kinds of qualities that a lesbian appreciated, a powerful woman, vital, strong, into her body, assertive, older, were not appreciated by men. These were qualities I aspired to. Lesbianism is the most comfortable choice. I couldn't be anything else. I can't imagine being with a man in a relationship. I love women and women's culture."

LaQuita

LaQuita also moved from her marriage to lesbianism with a bisexual phase in between. "I was bisexual. I liked both men and women and had no problem being intimate with either. I stumbled across it. I was married and had sex with a woman. It was a new experience, and the world was filled with so many pleasures—love of men and love of women. At first, it was just this one woman. I did not immediately label myself bisexual. Bisexuality was another safe place for me. I felt people could deal with it better than the word *lesbian*. It was easier to break the news to straight people of color. I was concerned that my family would reject me.

"I didn't like heterosexuality as a power play, ownership, dominance and submission, no equality with men. Marriage I hate. I hate to be told who I can or can't love. I was looking for an alternative. My definition of lesbian is a woman who loves women as friend, intimate, who fights for the rights of women, who refuses to live within the norm. Lesbianism questions the role of women in society. It's a whole concept of life—no power play in a relationship, equality with a partner. A whole different way of life; putting women foremost in my life."

———

This theme of involvement in the culture of women marks the "no turning back" point away from bisexuality or any close affiliations with men for many lesbians.

Nancy

Nancy, 34, made the typical progression. She was heterosexual, then bisexual. "I was attracted to both sexes and had relationships with both sexes and had no clear preference for one year. Then I came out for one year as a lesbian. Then the following year I had a relationship with a man, so I called myself bisexual. This is an issue now. Until recently, I would've labelled myself bisexual, but now I choose to be with women both sexually and politically. It's becoming more and more difficult to relate to men the way I once was able to. I'm more identified with women. Sexually, I prefer women. The interest I have in men is habit rather than conscious choice. Men are easy—roles, pattern, and way of being. There's a lot of support from job, family, and peers for being with a man. I am looking for a lesbian support system. Lesbianism encompasses a culture for me—women's music, values, socially, too. Politically, lesbianism encompasses those shared values and way of being: nonsexist attitude, nurturing, equality, being nurtured, environmental concerns, listening, talking about feelings."

———

As lesbians like Nancy, Virginia, and LaQuita become more involved with the subculture of a society of women, lesbian women's values and interests take hold. The creative energy of women-only groups becomes more and more fascinating. Lesbians have formed spirituality groups, political action groups, environmental action groups, and many other interest-based organizations. There is lesbian theater, visual arts, music, and literature. When lesbians begin their walk into this domain, they find a multifaceted universe that can nourish any aspect of their creativity. As they investigate this diverse world, the company of men falls into second place and finally disappears from the ground of interest. Lesbians find that women offer personality liaisons that are different from men. For lesbians these differences are essential. Female values, the personality characteristics of being nurturing and emotionally sensitive create a special woman-to-woman bond.

Innate Lesbianism

Sixty-eight percent of the lesbians see themselves as innately lesbian. They believe that being lesbian is part of their personality and perhaps a biological tendency with which they were born. If they were heterosexual once, or if they had a period as a bisexual, they see this as a result of social conditioning. As women they were programmed into heterosexuality. It took them time to discover the lesbian hidden within, shrouded under the veil of heterosexuality.

Some lesbians knew and accepted this part of themselves from childhood. But they are a minority, only 20 percent of the lesbians interviewed. All of these women are matter-of-fact about being lesbian. Alana, 44: "I'm not sexually attracted to men, only women. I wouldn't have a sexual relationship to someone I'm not attracted to sexually. Being a lesbian is just something I intuitively know—that I came into the world this time loving women. Period." For Lindsay, 22, it is as simple. "I never thought of myself as heterosexual or bi. I have no interest in men sexually. I labelled myself lesbian when I was 15. I felt more comfortable with myself being a lesbian, and I didn't have to be what others expected me to be. I think I am an innate lesbian because I always had feelings for women that I didn't have for men." It was the same for Reed, 27: "I was never with a man. When I was 22, I chose to find other women like me who were experiencing some of the same problems. I was under undue stress, feeling I had unnatural feelings. When I found there were other women like me, it resolved these feelings and problems. I am an innate lesbian. I remember dreaming about women at the age of 2. I was always more attracted to girls. Girls were special. I had crushes on girls but never on a boy. I had no interest in boys at any age." Polly, 34, adds that the interest in women is beyond a sexual one. "I was attracted to girls and women from as long as I can remember. Emotionally I always wanted to be with women. I found support, connection, emotional everything with women." Danielle, 42, is unabashed in her praise of women. "Nobody made me a lesbian. Women are so much more wonderful than men. I'm very biased about it. Men are creatures I tolerate under certain circumstances. This is based on the chemistry stuff. Men taste and smell bad. Men do not appeal!"

Rudy, 44, does not think of her lesbianism as innate. "I choose to live as a lesbian. I don't think my feelings and impulses are inherent or genetic. They are a culmination of experiences and growth. I know heterosexual women who wish they were lesbian, but couldn't get it together. A woman can choose to live in denial; to be celibate; to hide. To be lesbian and not to do it is to create a fabric of dishonesty woven into the center of your life. I have never chosen to live my life dishonestly. I value the process of awareness a lot. To be so aware, you have to be aware of yourself, and you can't accomplish that if you don't live openly to yourself. I think this is no news to anybody. One's identity clearly is certainly at least more than what you do sexually. I've been celibate ten years and I don't lose my lesbian identity because I stopped sleeping with women. Part of it is where I see the potential of relationship. I don't look at a man and see the potential for an intimate sexual relationship. I see potential for companions and comrades but never as a potential lover."

Most lesbians think of themselves as born with a lesbian orientation. Some think of themselves as bisexuals who have chosen to be in relationships exclusively with women. Others prefer to think of their sexual identity as a fluid process that involved the influences of culture, personality, opportunity, and desire. These women feel that they have been on a sexual trek that led them to the lesbian territory. For all lesbians, there is no interest in returning to the heterosexual world or the arena of relationships with men.

BISEXUALITY

If lesbians are invisible, bisexuals simply do not exist. Many people believe that bisexuality is a phase of the transition to becoming a lesbian. They think it is not a permanent sexual orientation. Bisexuality challenges the social order of dividing people into bipolar extremes: heterosexuals and lesbians. A woman who is bisexual can disappear into either community. When she is with a man, she is presumed to be heterosexual, and when she is with a woman, she is identified as lesbian. Many bisexuals melt into the culture and the

friends of their current lifestyle. Since sexuality is such a private issue, a bisexual is not going to address her relationships with women of the past when she is socializing with heterosexuals. And if she is with a lesbian, she knows that lesbians are not very interested in men as a topic of discussion. If she does refer to a past with men, it is assumed that men would never be in her future.

Is there such a thing as a bisexual lifestyle? Is there a subculture for women who are openly bisexual? In the late 1980s, bisexual activists appeared on the public scene to demand recognition in the gay community. The San Francisco Bay Area has a large bisexual network of women who refuse to pass as either lesbian or heterosexual. These women are actively exploring their psychological state as bisexuals. These women feel that their bisexual identity and lifestyle challenges contemporary myths about sexuality. They feel that they are living on a daring cutting edge with special risks and rewards.

Some women who say they are innately bisexual are not included here. These are the heterosexual women who said they were bisexual though they had never explored a sexual experience with a woman. Some lesbians who were formerly heterosexual stated that they were innately bisexual. However, they have found women more desirable than men, or they have made a political decision to devote themselves to women and to stay in solidarity with women. For them, future sexual relationships with men are out of the question. These lesbians are lesbian by choice and are renouncing their bisexuality. I call these actively heterosexual or lesbian women "theoretical bisexuals" because they are bisexual only in their own psychological theory about themselves and not in practice.

Beginning as a Heterosexual

Sixty-five percent of the 44 bisexual women interviewed once thought of themselves as exclusively heterosexual. These women grew up in the same heterosexual world that all girls experience. They were trained to be the female counterpart to the male. Brandy, 24, echoes the familiar refrain of both lesbians and heterosexuals. "I was heterosexual. I never thought of anything else. I assumed it. It's just what everybody was. It was what I was before I gave anything else a thought." Leah, 45, was in the closed heterosexual field: "I was always heterosexual. It was an assumption. It just was what everybody was as far as I knew. I didn't know anybody who was any different than heterosexual."

Alizon

Alizon, 31, touches on the difference between heterosexuals and all other orientations. "I started out as heterosexual. I just thought that that was what you were. I didn't think of my sexuality because normal people don't. They just are. It's when you're out of the norm that you question and think about things. I didn't know there was a choice. I just did what

everyone else did." Alizon is right. Those women on the freeway to heterosexuality who find it compatible just move right along with the path created for them. It is only those who eye the lonelier outlying trails of sexuality with women who begin to analyze their sexuality.

May

May, 30, remembers that in high school sexuality was not on her mind. She had not had a sexual awakening, but her girlfriends were already preoccupied with it. "It never occurred to think of myself any way at all. One day my roommate said she and friends had been talking about who was gay and who was straight. And they decided I was straight. And I kind of went, 'Oh, thanks.' I thought maybe it was a good thing that they decided that I was straight. It was presented to me to give me the sense that it was the norm to be straight. Figuring who was gay was trying to figure out who was weird or something—status-quo high school.

"The high school I went to was a very upper middle class, Episcopalian church school, and if you weren't normal you got in a lot of trouble. I was eccentric by the school's standards, and I had a hard time because of that. I was too quiet and too bookish, and I hung out with the nerds and the techy weirdo types who knew how to fix the Xerox machine. My best friend was someone the others didn't like much. When we were roommates, someone wrote 'lesbian' on our door, and I got very upset about it. It felt like an attack. I had a male classmate who everyone thought was gay, and I saw how he was picked on. And I saw how difficult it could be if people thought you weren't straight."

As a teenager, May was not in her sexual awakening. Who she was as a sexual being was not yet part of her process. But she was a careful observer of what was going on around her. Being gay was not acceptable. She felt herself an outsider in other areas. She did not need to add another. Fortunately, she had no inkling of a sexual interest in women, so she thought she could be heterosexual, since that was "normal."

The culture of heterosexuality pushed women onto the predictable track of dating, marriage, and children. Forty-six percent of the bisexuals had been married. Their marriage was the fulfillment of their passage into adult heterosexuality. Like all women who marry, this was to be their permanent lifelong relationship. The unexpected arises when the yearning for sexual experiences with a woman begins to flower as a powerful desire in their psyches. But it does not necessitate an immediate change. Giselle, 44, says, "Heterosexuality was expected of me: that I would have children in the context of marriage. It never occurred to me to be anything else. To be a woman in love with a woman would be out of our religious norm, so I never considered it." Giselle went on to get married three times and to have four children. It was not until she

was 37, divorced, and meeting lesbians that she looked into herself, and "I finally accepted my sexuality. I finally relaxed and let it be. I stopped fighting it. I made a choice to stop pretending to be heterosexual. I did not know the word *bisexual*, so I called myself eclectic."

Unless there is a possibility of a complete affiliation with a woman, a bisexual woman can keep her bisexuality in a dormant state. Rachel, 35, is one of these women. She is happily married and wants to keep her monogamous marriage as her primary focus. But her experiences opened up another side of her personality.

Rachel

"My preference right now is heterosexuality because I'm in love with a man. I feel attraction to both men and women after I get to know them. I am heterosexual in behavior because I want monogamy. Anyway, a woman is not usually my first choice for a sexual partner, men are. When I was 20, I had my first sexual experience with a woman. I was swimming naked with two women in someone's home pool. We were drunk. They made love to me at the pool with four people watching. Then we went to their room for privacy, and people followed us, so we stopped. My next experience with a woman was an experience of group sex with my husband and my best friend. Now my friend is gay. I was also influenced by the novel *Brave New World*. It explained that social conditioning makes one heterosexual, and I began to think about bisexuality. My fantasies involved women, too. When given the chance, I wanted to try sex with a woman."

Rachel came to terms with her bisexuality through an intellectual approach, reading and thinking philosophically about it. Her sexual experiences with women were not in the context of relationships and the deep emotional milieu that women create. These purely sexual adventures do not challenge the stability of her marriage. She has chosen to keep the woman-centered aspect of her sexuality nascent.

Moving into a Lesbian Identity

The average age that a bisexual woman first experienced sexual attraction to a woman was 18. I asked bisexual women when they think they were first attracted to women but did not recognize it as such. Their answers are that they were sexually attracted to females at an earlier age than when they consciously began thinking that they were lesbian or bisexual. When women have these early attractions, the memory of them slips from consciousness quickly. There is no context or understanding for the sensations and emotions. Women may notice them in a way that Peggy, 48, did.

Peggy

"When I was 16 I had a best girlfriend in high school, Maria. We did everything together. I thought she was gorgeous, that she looked liked Elizabeth Taylor. One day there was a violent blizzard, and school was let out early, but none of the buses were running. I had a two-hour bus ride, and it looked like I would not get home. It was 60 degrees below zero with the wind chill factor, so I did an extraordinary thing. I went home with Maria because she lived near the school. Her mother was worried that we were frozen from the walk to her house, so she gave us shots of anisette. I had never had liquor before, and I was surprised that a parent would give me some. But I was polite and drank it. Then her mother told us to go to Maria's room to crawl into bed and warm up under the thick featherbed. So we did. I used to sleep with my sisters because we didn't have room for separate beds, so being in bed together was not too odd. We were lying next to each other, and I was in a sisterly space, thinking about each of us having enough room and not crowding out the other. Suddenly I felt a compulsion to lie on my side facing her and to rest my hand on her breast and maybe kiss it. I didn't move, but I examined this feeling inside myself. I clearly remember thinking, 'What a strange impulse I'm having right now! I am such an odd person! Whatever could this be about?' I thought it would absolutely freak her out if I expressed the impulse, so I didn't move. And I guess we just laid there and talked about school or whatever until dinnertime.

"I never talked to anyone about this compulsion to touch her. I didn't know a thing about sex, only that it was what married people did to make babies. And that women put up with it for love of men.

I had no way to say to myself, 'This is a sexual feeling.' And if I had been able to label it sexual, I probably would have thought it was another eccentric thing about myself. I already felt I was an oddball, the 'brain' at school, and I didn't need another weird thing about myself. I think that not talking about it kind of erased it from my consciousness. It wasn't until I was almost 30 and experienced those same feelings again with a woman, after I had had my sexual awakening with men, that I remembered this incident with Maria and finally had a name for it, *lesbianism.*"

Peggy's experience is one that is common to her generation, but this delayed acknowledgment of bisexuality may be an element of the past. Young women today are exposed to more sexual material. Gay activists, the publicizing of gay freedom marches, the identification of celebrities as lesbians—all these give young women information about the range of sexuality and a context for their own feelings. Today young women are more likely to label themselves lesbian or bisexual, unlike the generations before them.

Amy, 25, was one woman who began to think about sex with women in her young teens. "When I was 13, I was called a lesbian, and I learned that there was more than heterosexuality. I could avoid it and still call myself heterosexual, not bisexual. But I recognized the feelings and chose to realize that this is what it was. I was born this way. It was part of my personality that was showing up."

Bianca, 20, has identified as a bisexual for two weeks. She is in the beginning of her creation of her bisexual identity. She points out an experience similar to Amy's. She never saw lesbianism around her. And she had internal feelings of sexual attraction only to men. When she became interested in dating at the age of 16, she thought of herself as heterosexual. "Heterosexuality is out there. It's just what you're told to do. If I was given the choice a year ago I would have said, 'men.' I never would have considered women at all. Now I'm attracted to both sexes. I was never attracted to women before. I like it. There's more of a choice. I am more attracted to women now. I can't explain how I am now more attracted to women. But I am around lesbians now. I have an attraction for both males and females sexually. Right now I have a girlfriend, and I'm happy with her. We do more things than friends. I like women as women. I don't want them to pretend to be a man. A lot of it was influenced by my environment. Prior to meeting lesbians and falling in love, I never even thought of it. I never imagined myself with the same sex."

Bianca has found herself on the new mysterious ground of an intimate union with a woman. Suddenly she is in a new world, and she is shifting within her personality to create an expanded concept of herself and the possibilities of her future life. The predictability of dating and marriage to a man has just disappeared as the secure probable expectation. Her thrilling happiness in her new liaison has pushed aside for the moment any trepidation she might have.

Fourteen of the 44 bisexuals considered themselves lesbian at one time. The average age at which they labelled themselves lesbian is 25. The average length of time that bisexuals labelled themselves lesbian was six years.

Lesbians often say that bisexuality is a phase on the way to developing a lesbian identity, and for lesbians this is true. But when bisexuals identify as lesbian, it is lesbianism that is a phase. This happens most commonly when a bisexual woman falls in love with a lesbian and develops a relationship with her. The bisexual woman enters the lesbian community and considers herself a full-fledged member. If her thoughts of men are overshadowed by the depth of involvement in this subculture, she assumes a full identity as a lesbian. This was Jody's experience. "I was attracted to men and women since I was a child. I was about 14 when I had my first boyfriend, and I felt committed. I identified as heterosexual. Before then I didn't really think about sexual orientation. I decided after I became a feminist and involved in the lesbian community, I didn't feel different with women sexually as opposed to men. It was fine with men and fine with women. I changed from bisexual to lesbian when I had my first serious relationship with a woman. Then I turned back to bisexual after one and a half years of considering myself a lesbian because I fell in love with a man. I identified as a lesbian, because I was attracted to many women and politically active and producing a lesbian newspaper, receiving love and support from lesbians almost exclusively. It seemed the way I wanted to live my life, very healthy and powerful."

Jody is not unique in this experience of a mutable sexual identity. When some women throw themselves into a relationship, it reflects on their whole identity. Daphne found that she swung around with her sexual identity. "There have been periods in my life when I've been attracted to men and women. I have been sexual with men and women, so now I don't like to label myself. It's too complicated. It feels like a choice to be bisexual because originally I felt I was heterosexual. Since I feel attraction to men, it would be easy to ignore my feelings for women and be involved with men, in terms of society. At age 19, I became involved with a woman for the first time. Then I fell in love with her, and I didn't feel any attraction to men anymore. It was hard to believe it was gone. It was so intense with her. So I said, 'I'm a lesbian.' When I was 26, I found myself attracted to a man again. So then I scrapped labels."

Alexa, 33, believes she is innately bisexual. She began to think of herself as bisexual from the age of 16. But from the ages of 22 to 24, she was a lesbian. She explains, "For a couple of years I was involved in the lesbian community and lived with a woman as lovers. The woman I was living with thought I would leave. She felt more comfortable if I called myself a lesbian. At the time, I was disillusioned by my first marriage. I was trying to cut men out. I wasn't sure what I was doing. The reason I stopped being a lesbian is because I still felt attracted to a couple of men I knew, not just intellectual, but sexual attraction."

Thirty-five years ago, there was not the public face of lesbianism and bisexuality that there is today. For Ellen, 57, there was no context, no one she knew who was like herself. "I knew I loved men and women. I was different, but I had no label for it. I was secretly a bisexual. I stuffed it and tried to be a lesbian in the lesbian community. I had a coming out process as a lesbian, but I felt I was a half-breed. I could not be public about it." After living as a lesbian for years, Ellen fell in love with a man. This forced her to reexamine her sexuality. It took more years for her to weave her identity into bisexuality.

Star

Star, 48, is of the same generation as Ellen. She passed through all the sexual orientations. "Since the world is heterosexist, I just fell into heterosexuality. The rare heterosexual who opens herself up to sexually explore the same sex may choose heterosexuality after her adventures, but heterosexuals are not forced to deal with it or to challenge heterosexuality. I am from a very Catholic family. There were no other choices given. That is just beginning to change due to gay and lesbian liberation."

When she was 32, after living as a heterosexual, Star came out as a lesbian. She was in a relationship with a woman. She chose to be lesbian "because it was the only label available to me at the time. There were no bisexual role models for me.

All my friends were lesbians. I love women, and of course I wanted to be in the club. So that added up to me being a lesbian." After four and a half years as a lesbian, Star "fell in love with a man. He identified himself as a bisexual and said, 'Girl, you can't call yourself a lesbian. It doesn't work that way.' It was the best relationship in my whole life. It was the first time I fell in love as an adult. That made it more valuable. I knew more and I understood who I was more than when I was 16 and fell in love with my husband." Since that time 12 years ago, Star has identified as bisexual. "I live with the potential to be romantically and sexually involved with human beings depending upon the chemistry. I've lived my whole life in a way where I've related to people, and their gender has not been important. I just didn't know there was a name for this attitude, bisexuality."

Jody, Daphne, Alexa, Ellen, and Star discovered lesbianism after a sexual first step as a heterosexual. For them, lesbianism was the second step on the way to integrating all the aspects of their sexual beings into the identity that includes their range of sexual interest: bisexual.

But life as a heterosexual is not always the starting point for bisexuals. Some bisexuals always recognized in themselves their attraction toward women, even as children, though they may have had no name for it. When they became interested in sexuality as adolescents, they pictured themselves with women.

Molly

Molly, 35, was aware of sexual interest in women when she was young. She called herself bisexual when she began her sexual life, but sex with men was not very rewarding, and her first clear sexual identity was as a lesbian. "As a kid, I enjoyed both boys and girls. I never desired to call myself heterosexual. It doesn't describe my behavior or my feelings. In college I defined myself as bisexual, though I hadn't been with a woman sexually. I thought about it a long time. I was dissatisfied with men as sexual partners. I went to a gay rights demonstration in Washington, D.C. We had a hotel room with four women and two beds. I was sleeping with a lesbian who put her arm around me. I felt a potent mixture of fear and lust. I had limited sexual experience at that point. I moved to San Francisco and came out as a lesbian immediately. When I came out as a lesbian, I pulled out the qualifier that I could be with the right guy.

Molly was surprised to find a novel sexual interest in a man surfacing when she was 30. "I spent two years not sleeping with anybody, and I started thinking about what I really wanted in a lover, and I realized my fantasies were different from what I had chosen. I had been a ghettoized lesbian. I had no heterosexual friends. The issue of dating a man was to lose the lesbian community. As a lover, Roy was the person I thought of. It took me months to acknowledge this attraction and act on it. I feared being ghettoized in a heterosexual suburb. A friend told me, 'Each one of these things is a separate decision.' That gave me the reassurance to go ahead. I wanted a relationship with Roy. I realized if I didn't do it, it would be because I was afraid.

"So I had to overcome my fear of bisexuality and its stigma. It was a choice but a reluctant choice. It was Roy and not men in general that I wanted to bring into my life. I don't like heterosexual practices, and I don't have heterosexual friends. To a certain extent, that is a point of contention with him."

Unlike the more common scenario of beginning as a heterosexual and moving into lesbianism, Molly moved through her territory of sexual passion first as a lesbian. When she was attracted to a man, she felt pushed to realign her sexual identity to coincide with her actions. Her bisexuality took shape after a love affair with a man.

Creating a Bisexual Identity

Becoming a bisexual is a process. This process takes time. Women do not begin with a full-grown, strong identity as a bisexual. Their growth as a bisexual takes place on a number of planes. One plane is the internal coming to terms with the fact that one is sexually attracted to both genders. It also involves experiencing sexual intimacy with both genders. And, for most bisexuals, in time they form close relationships with both men and women. Bisexual women believe that every intimate relationship further informs their identity.

For most bisexual women (70 percent), it is the recognition of their sexual attraction to women and their subsequent sexual experiences with women that move them into thinking about themselves as bisexual. However, just because they discovered this new attraction, their sexual interest in men did not end. If they began to live with a woman, they identified themselves as living a lesbian lifestyle, but not as *being* a lesbian. Brandy, 24, has discovered that her new life is truly rewarding. "I'm living a lesbian lifestyle, but that's too exclusive to me. I like sex with men. I wouldn't rule out sex with men, but I'm happy with whom I'm with. I found being with a woman opened up a new world, a new area of feelings I hadn't felt before. Everything was more intense. I feel more. With men it was paler, not as strong."

Bisexual women examine their personalities as they consider whether a lesbian lifestyle and identity is meant for them. Mandy, 29, began her sexual life as a heterosexual. "For a long time I didn't know I had an option. Once I did know, for a long time I chose to be heterosexual. But I became aware that I have had so many limitations placed on me I don't want to put any more on myself. I had been heterosexual, and I did a year's research on being a lesbian. I decided the best choice for me was to be bi. What pushed me in that direction was I fell in love with a woman, and I made a choice to pursue a woman."

Not all bisexuals can come to their identity with the permanency that Mandy seems to. Whether they are in transition or are unable to project their future possibilities, not all bisexuals are committed to the identity. But it is not with the expectation that they will return to familiar heterosexuality. Georgia, 31, is in the midst of her excursion away from heterosexuality. "I was heterosexual. It chose me. I hung around with my brother and boys, and I liked boys. But I would dream sexually about women. I consider myself a soul more than a body. So it means I can experience my life in many ways. I wasn't comfortable being heterosexual. But I'm not to the point in my mind that I would be strictly gay. I may get there, but I haven't yet." Georgia has been influenced by the theory that bisexuality is a phase on the path to being a lesbian. When she looks at herself at this moment, she experiences herself as bisexual. But she does not project a static future. Today she cannot predict whether bisexuality is a permanent aspect of her nature or whether she will move into a lesbian identity.

Thirty-five percent of bisexual women never had a phase as a heterosexual. They always knew they were bisexual. Most thought of themselves as bisexual from an early age, though they might not have had the word. They knew that they were sexually attracted to men and women. Amity is 18 and has thought of herself as bisexual for three years. "I never considered myself heterosexual. I always knew in the back of my mind I'd be with a woman at some point. I had talked of it with my best friend, but we started being sexual with boys at school. I'm more attracted to people than people of a certain sex. So I think I can have a fulfilling and working relationship with a man and a woman, and I have had satisfying relationships with both. I believe we're all born bisexual." Amity can be so clear about her sexual identity at such a young age because she is becoming aware of herself in a cultural moment in which lesbians and bisexuals are a visible presence. When she felt attracted to women, she had a name and a context for it, unlike the bisexual women who are now in their thirties and forties. Amity easily accepted this aspect of herself without fear. She is standing apart from her society like an anthropologist and can see that although heterosexuality is reinforced, she can live outside of the mainstream.

Claire

When Claire, 37, retrospectively examines her formation of a bisexual identity, she decides that she really did not begin as a heterosexual. While she behaved as a heterosexual, her innermost feelings were bisexual. But she could not allow herself to fully accept this. "I feel I was highly encouraged and rewarded to be heterosexual. I was given the message strongly that not relating to men and relating to women was horrible and wrong. And I fought my feelings of sexual attraction to women."

Even though she was directed into heterosexuality, Claire recalls persons and events that meant to her that she was always interested in the gay lifestyle. Her bisexual identity is a process that started in her youth. As a girl, it was vague and unformed. "In high school it was a faraway thing. In tenth grade, I did a report on homosexuality, so it must have been on my mind. In high school I had a gay male friend from church. An older woman in my church thought he was wonderful, and that made it feel okay. I initially had some closeness with gay men, but I still kept a distance from the idea of lesbianism. I was fearful of lesbians. It was different than male homosexuality. It was more threatening. I felt that lesbianism was gross. I was squeamish about it. Gay males had nothing to do with me sexually, so they were safer. Women can enjoy some safety with gay men that's similar to what straight women can enjoy with each other. They are not after us for something.

"I came to accept lesbianism in other women and had lesbian friends in my twenties but there was still something inside of me that stopped me. When I was 19, I had a game with a roommate. We pretended that we were girlfriends, and we were silly. I was terrified to go further." Eventually Claire lost her fear of becoming sexually involved with a woman. An available and nonintimidating woman was her turning point. "When I first experienced a woman sexually, it confirmed my attraction to women, and it didn't take away any of my feelings for men. I didn't feel straight or lesbian. I was 25 in 1982. I was unaware of a bisexual community or if it was a valid identity. But it seemed accurate as a description, so I used it. My impression of them was that bisexuals were nonpolitical, but now I know that isn't right. So I politically identified with the lesbian feminists. I felt I was an odd one. I knew that it was fine to be bisexual, but it was unpopular in the lesbian community. I didn't feel there was a basis for the criticism about bisexuals. But I was still honest and told them I was bisexual."

The experience of falling in love with a woman and being sexual with her is usually the one that sets a woman into the direction of thinking about herself as bisexual or lesbian. But some women are more intellectual and look into their future sexual travels as something to plan and prepare for. Devorah, 25, is one of these women. She was over 100 pounds overweight as a teenager and consequently felt that she would be rejected by any possible sexual partner. She maintained an asexual status as she considered her possible future sexual paths. "I was willing to identify as bi from the beginning. I was aware of the potential. It felt weird to come out as bi before I had any sexual experiences. When I was 20, I read *Woman on the Edge of Time* by Marge Piercy. And I thought, 'If I had a utopia, this is what it would be like in terms of race, feminism, and sexuality.' And I thought, 'In an ideal world I'd be bisexual.' So I thought, 'I should think about how I have a choice. About how I want to be as a sexual person.' It wasn't choosing an orientation as much as a way to live in an honest way and allowing myself to recognize 'This is how it would be in an

ideal world. This who I am now. Yes, I am bisexual.' It was not the first time I thought about same-sex relationships, since my mother was a lesbian and my father was straight."

May

May, 30, is also very self-reflective and takes an intellectual approach to her life. She was late in coming into her sexual awareness. Even though May had sexual experiences with girls, she did not label their games as sex. Sex happened between males and females. "Some information about bisexuality must have dribbled in there into my mind over the years. By the end of high school I heard 'bisexual,' and I knew these two girls who fooled around, but they also had boyfriends. Bisexuality wasn't taken seriously. When I was thinking about college, one school was Sarah Lawrence. There was an article about a lesbian community there, and it made my mother discourage me from going there.

"I ran into lesbians when I went to college and got better information about it. There were a few 'out' gay men and lesbians at college. It was intriguing and alarming. The rumor was a lot of the feminists who went to the women's center were lesbians, so I didn't want to go there. I was worried that they might come on to me, and that would be weird. But I hadn't thought it out. It was knee-jerk reaction."

May's fear of lesbianism is not unusual. She knew lesbians were outsiders, and she already felt she was labelled as on the fringe, due to her intel-lectualism. She did not want to be tossed into another group as an outsider. But things began to change for May when her attraction to women began to surface in her awareness. She discovered that she could not deny her sexual interest in women.

"I was 19 and enjoying a great sexual relationship with a man. In a dance class there was a woman who was really sexy and flirty with me. I think she admired me and always wanted to hang around me in class. And I thought she was cute, and I decided it didn't mean anything. It was just a crush, not sexual. So I wasn't going to worry about it. Then I got a vivid image of going down on her. I was seeing a psychologist trying to sort things out—who I was, where I was going. This was a bolt out of the blue, a new thing I had to integrate. My shrink said it was rebellion against my parents. But he was wrong, it had nothing to do with my parents.

"But I accepted it, my attraction to women. Once I got there, it was easy. It was a few months before I told anyone. It was easier to tell men. I was afraid women would be alienated from me. I felt men would understand because they were attracted to women, too. And they did seem to accept it. I was at a very politically left college. And if you hung out with the left crowd, many people assumed you were bi. In three years all my friends knew.

"It fit for me at the time. I was into being politically liberal and trying to find value in all things and all people. It was satisfying to think I could love women emotionally and sexually, as well as men.

It helped that I was sent to a liberal community where it felt safe and a fine thing to be bisexual. I had no moral dilemma. I also decided I was an atheist at age 16, so I didn't have to contend with dogma. I've had support for being bisexual all along, except with the occasional lover."

May's evolution into a bisexual woman included an intellectual process. But there was also her clear interest in sex with particular women that fired her awakening of this desire in herself. May did not "think" herself into bisexuality. She experienced sexual attraction to both men and women. Her reflections on her experiences as well as her development of her personal ethics together created her evaluation of her sexual identity.

Bisexuality as a Political Statement

Bisexuals can melt into the heterosexual culture if they are partnered with a man, and many do. Given the homophobia in American culture, if a bisexual woman falls into a relationship with a man, the apparent return to heterosexuality offers a respite from the persecution of being a lesbian "outsider." But bisexual activists believe that there is a kind of dishonesty to this action. For some women, claiming the bisexual label is an important way to take pride in themselves. Carolyn, 29, first describes herself, "I'm equally attracted to both sexes. I am not willing to give up one for the other. I believe that choosing a label is a way of confirming, validating, and identifying myself."

Rebecca, 25, expands the thought that the bisexual label is validating. "I took the label because it's the best available option politically. And socially it's important to have a label, to come out publicly and combat homophobia. It's being honest with myself and embracing my connections to men and women. It's who I am. But I could have chosen to suppress either half. In this society you have to make bisexuality a choice."

May has reflected on the meaning of being a bisexual woman. "I feel bisexuality is a valuable thing in a larger social context. I feel people who are straight or gay are limited. They grow up with and are given a mold that they are supposed to fit into: They should marry someone of the opposite sex and have children. And gays go to the opposite end of the mold. As a bi, I don't have that easy framework. There is a lack of role models, and the bi movement isn't visible. We have to create what our lives are going to look like. It would be good if others had to make such conscious choices about what they do with their lives. People who aren't bisexual could learn a lot from our discussions. It's healthy not to be living in a conventional mold. I have had to think about what I really want and act on that and to integrate it into my life in a positive way. What I find unhealthy is when people just do whatever is easiest. When my stepmother found I was interested in women, she said, 'Wouldn't it be easier to stay with men?' That is appalling. She was basically telling me that she thought a better way to live was to deny my feelings

and stay in the status quo to get acceptance. And I know I would try very hard not to get myself into that kind of situation."

As Devorah thought about bisexuality, she developed her political analysis of its place in the social structure. "If I were in a world that wasn't so compulsory heterosexual, I don't think gender would make a difference. In a heterosexually dominated society and gay-hating culture, it made it difficult to come out as a bisexual." As she examined the lifestyles of people around her, Devorah became contemptuous of some. "I don't think I chose to be bisexual. It is my nature. But if I had a choice, I would chose bisexuality. I find heterosexuality dull and uninspiring, not an exciting, interesting place to be. Coming out as not straight forces so much looking at the world in a different way, to examine gender roles and life. Without that questioning, heterosexuals plod along in very uninteresting lives. I don't like going to family gatherings on my dad's side. Their lives are so boring. Both of my sisters are straight. One is married, has kids, manages a store, lives in the suburbs, and has the most boring life I can imagine. I don't think that she questioned who she was. 'Who am I? What do I want? How will I live my life?' These are essential questions one asks when one comes out."

Rebecca

Rebecca's political analysis of her own life places the bisexual lifestyle as a fulcrum for deep changes in how men and women relate. "It's hard to be in a relationship with a man. We are on the horizon. We've been with women and know what it's like. I have had my sexuality forever changed by that. My sexuality was changed radically by having sex with a woman. I learned how to relate to a woman's body, to explore someone else's body who has the same body parts as I do. I also experienced my own homophobia. Once you experience homophobia in your bed, it changes you. Sex with women is so natural. It isn't so different from sex with men.

"Once you open the possibility of same-sex sexuality, the concept of compulsory heterosexuality is seen in a different light. You see the contradiction between what your parents tell you and what you experience. When you've had good sex with women, it's hard to put up with shit with men. Those men who go to sleep right away and don't prolong sex play. For me, there isn't an automatic gender power imbalance with women. So the next time I have that kind of sex with men, it drives me crazy and would be intolerable.

"To be with a man as a woman with a woman-identified consciousness is a challenge to traditional heterosexual relationships. It challenges men's sexism and gender roles. In some ways, it is a feminist act to be bisexual and to be sexual with a man. We bisexuals challenge those patterns. Lesbians sometimes work in a vacuum. It's easier for a lesbian woman to be a separatist from men. Feminism is not just a thinking issue for us, it's a feeling issue. We're confronting sexism in our bedrooms, in our relationships.

"Bisexuality is a challenge to heteropatriarchy. It's shaped my relationships with men. It's not why I have relationships with men, but when I happen to be attracted to a man, these issues come up for me. There is often an element of sexual coercion with men. By sexual coercion, I mean that a man does not understand I mean 'no.' I think that attitude is pervasive, even with men who consider themselves progressive. They do not care about learning what gives a woman sexual pleasure when they don't know.

"My relationships with women changed my expectations about communication with men. Men wanted me to be less emotional. They wanted me to stop crying. I wanted to be comforted while crying. Or, they didn't tell me what they wanted. Then there's the way men deal with the world as men; the way they deal with their roles and their sexism. This can get in the way even if they define themselves as feminist. Sometimes men just don't get it. That's a fundamental difference. I don't know what to do to overcome that. They'll never understand what sexism really feels like to us. Straight men can be threatened by my connections to women because they think I'll leave them for a woman. 'Would you love me more if I were a woman?' Or they think they are unable to meet my emotional needs or they can't live up to my standards on being nonsexist. It could be their whole dick trip: A woman might satisfy me more sexually."

These activist bisexual women see that their bisexuality adds a strength and power to their feminist consciousness. When they relate to men, they bring this awareness with them in the form of a demand for a truly egalitarian relationship. They insist on full sexual exchanges that fulfill their sexual needs. They want open and complete communication similar to that which they have experienced with women. They want all the affection, attention, and loyalty of a total ally. They expect an understanding of feminism and the personal social struggles that they face as women in a sexist world. They believe that placing these demands on men will educate them toward the experience of true equality in a relationship.

Innate Bisexuality

Eighty-two percent of bisexuals say that they are innately bisexual. One of these is June, 28: "I believe we're all born bi, but I chose to acknowledge it. That's the difference between me and a heterosexual." June represents the majority of bisexuals who theorize that everyone is bisexual, but that most people never face this possibility in themselves. Alizon, 31, responds using herself as a personal reference: "I am attracted to and enjoy relationships with both men and women. It's just the way I am. I don't think you get to choose your sexual orientation any more than you get to choose your parents." For Alizon, regardless of one's particular sexual orientation, it is a reflection of an inborn characteristic.

Ten percent of bisexuals say that their bisexuality is part of their development as a sexual being, an evolution of the self. Leah, 45, feels that being bisexual is a result of her development of her sexuality and of her growth as a self-evolving woman: "There wasn't a choice for me to be bisexual when I was a heterosexual girl. If I grew up knowing about choices and possibilities, I might have decided to be bisexual at an early age. And it might have been clear to me. When I was 17, I babysat for a woman and I saw the movie *The Children's Hour*. And I thought, 'What if I'm a lesbian because I like when so-and-so hugs me?' I had no understanding about sexuality, not even my own. Today I'm a bisexual because I've experienced sexual pleasure with men and women, and I have sexual attractions to men and women."

Sixty-seven percent of bisexual women say that they chose to be bisexual because the alternative would have been to consciously suppress their sexual feelings for either women or men. They chose to acknowledge and act upon all these feelings. Bianca, 20, says, "You could call it a choice. Heterosexual is the way you're supposed to be. Your parents don't say as you grow up, 'Oh, you can be with men or women or just women.' You have to find it for yourself." Patricia, 37, sees her choice to live a bisexual lifestyle as partially based as a statement of resistance to society. "I feel I chose this because it's not an accepted lifestyle. So being bisexual goes against a lot of people's beliefs, both gay and straight. I made a conscious choice. I'd been fighting labelling myself. When I accepted myself, I made a choice to be what I am."

Coping with Biphobia

Universally, bisexual women are very aware that homophobia creates a milieu of negativity against lesbians and bisexual women. They have all heard antigay sentiment and are knowledgeable about gay oppression. The usual way of coping with homophobia is to be selective about to whom to reveal one's sexual orientation. Daphne, 29, has protected herself: "I'm not very out. Those who know me would not criticize me." Devorah has placed herself in an unusual environment of open-minded people. "Most people have been open and accepting. The last job I had in computers was with six gay men and a straight woman. Even though I was out as bi, the men referred to me as a lesbian. It was something they chose not to see at times. I was out with one of them recently, and I mentioned about being bi. He asked me what I would choose, and I said, 'Not to be straight, because I like to fuck girls.'

"Most of the straight people I'm out to try to understand. My older sister has been interesting. I take a perverse thrill out of shocking the hell out of her. She was very homophobic when my mother came out as a lesbian, and she is disrespectful of my mother's lover and relationships. She's made a point of not rejecting me, though. The people who matter to me are mostly gay and bi. So the straight people I'm out to are family and college friends. In general, I'm in a liberal environment, so that if people don't believe in gay rights, they know better than to say so. I test people's accep-

tance by telling them my mom's a lesbian. So I don't risk myself."

When Devorah, 25, told her lesbian mother that she was bisexual, she expected her mother to be happy for her and wholly understanding. That is not what occurred. "The worst anti-bi bigotry I came up against was when I came out to my mom. She didn't take me seriously until one of my friends asked me how hard it was to come out to my mom and my mother heard my response. Later she said, 'When you grow up, you'll be a lesbian. Bisexuality equals nonmonogamy, which equals promiscuity. And are you promiscuous?' This took a while to work out with her. It was extremely painful for me. We were very close. For her not to understand something like this was very hard. Her lover got it more than she did. Bisexuality does not mean that I sleep with just anyone or have three-ways."

Friends are considered to be safe confidants. But bisexuality can be very threatening to friends, especially when the woman is in the process of transforming to a bisexual lifestyle. Molly, 35, was a lesbian active in the lesbian community in San Francisco when she suddenly found herself sexually interested in a man. As she pursued this involvement, her lesbian friends shared their opinions of her new transformation. "I was living in a lesbian household when I was introduced to a heterosexual male and decided to have sex with him. One lesbian roommate became furious with me. In contrast, there was no conflict when I came out as a lesbian. I was afraid of losing all my friends if I took a man for a lover. It was a matter of honor. I wasn't going to let other women push me around. I used my friend, Trudy, as a chaperon on two dates. Why I thought I needed a chaperon, I don't know! Maybe I was afraid of sex with him. One night she came back to the apartment, and we were in bed. She gave me a ten-minute harangue that 'by sleeping with Roy, you are threatening my sexuality!' I lost a number of lesbian friends. Now most of my women friends are bisexual. Many lesbians have a problem with bisexuality. They cannot ignore it because I'm married to a man now. On the other hand, the heterosexuals I know through my husband are not critical. I don't know if they are approving. They may not be used to talking about sexuality. I don't want to pass as heterosexual. I identify as queer, so I won't change pronouns to cover up an experience or anecdote."

Claire

Claire, 37, is cautious about how she chooses to let people know about her sexual orientation. She perceives heterosexuals as potentially dangerous. "I'm more afraid to come out to straight people, especially if I hear negative things about queer people. Men have cared less if I'm bisexual. It's more of a problem with lesbians because of the feminist aspect. There's the viewpoint of 'You're either with us or against us. The bi's are with men and can't be trusted. They just take from women and don't give.' This is a blanket stereotype. If I called myself a lesbian it

would be different. There are women who behave sexually like I do and call themselves lesbian so they don't experience criticism. They have sex with men but keep it secret.

"I'm a feminist. This includes independence from men. And whether that's believed or not by lesbians, it's true. I've done political work for women. I transcend some of my personal worries about what people think because I'm doing the right thing. I'm being myself. Over the years, some lesbians have changed their minds about bisexuals after knowing me.

Bisexual women are especially vulnerable to criticism from lesbians. Lesbians and other bisexual women are their community of possible lovers and close friends. An arbitrary rejection based on their sexual orientation excludes bisexual women from a terrain of sexuality with women that they desire to enter. Like Claire, May has experienced this exclusion. "There's this large-scale political problem between bi women and lesbians in that a subset of the separatist lesbian community does not think well of women who are queer and are involved with men. We get called 'traitors to the women's community.' So, in general, I feel defensive around lesbians.

"There is also an element of this in the bi community, with women who are strongly woman-identified. I have a feeling that they would not think well of me for sleeping with men as much as I do.

That may be based on my own paranoia. These bi's are attracted to men, but more comfortable with women. But I haven't had much experience with women, and I'm afraid I'm not taken as seriously as I would like. I tend to worry about approval, and I'm hesitant to put myself out socially. I'm a bit of an introvert."

Rebecca, 25, places these personal experiences of censure from lesbians in a broader context. "Criticism from lesbians is more painful on a personal level. But that doesn't compare to the horrors of heterosexual oppression. I'm not afraid of assault from a lesbian. I expect more from lesbians. I assume that heterosexuals will be less accepting."

Molly, May, Claire, and Rebecca have been living close to the nexus of the lesbian world, so they experienced criticism from lesbians. Lynette, 33, was married, and she was castigated by heterosexuals. "My first husband criticized homosexuality by his derogatory comments to men. And he wouldn't allow my homosexual friends to come over. He was rude, threatening, and physically violent. Other heterosexuals said, 'Yuck, how could you do that?' when I told them I'd been sexual with women. Some heterosexuals wanted to get me into three-ways."

Bisexuals who are very open about their identity say that they have experienced criticism from both gay people and heterosexuals. Star, 48, concludes that "people are threatened by someone who is prideful of being bisexual. It forces people to question their own sexuality if they are monosexual." But the kind of threat experienced from gays and from heterosexuals is different. Ellen, 57, explains her perspective on why gay people respond negatively to bisexuals. "People don't understand you can love more than one person at a time and that one can love both sexes. I have an alliance with the gay/lesbian community. I have worked as an activist for rights for gays. As a civil libertarian I can understand oppression from gays more than I can from heterosexuals. It's like reverse racism. Gays have bad feelings due to people not coming to terms with lesbianism. They feel that being bisexual is a cop-out from being gay. But heterosexuals are much more hostile than gays. I consider myself part of the gay community, not the heterosexual one."

Bisexual women see themselves standing in a territory that is apart from heterosexuality. Heterosexuality is perceived as rigid and unyielding and allows no room for their existence. Heterosexual lifestyles do not offer them the freedom of self-expression that they desire.

Since they do not psychologically reside in a heterosexual land, bisexuals are a sexual minority like lesbians and gay men. Lesbians have, with difficulty, claimed their space and are reluctant to make room for bisexuals, who have the possibility of returning to the appearance of safe heterosexuality. Therefore, bisexuals are forming their own networks, fashioning a new country that uniquely can include bisexual men and women. They prefer to envision it as a new open space, not another sexual ghetto. Future decades and the next generation of bisexuals and lesbians will shape the outcome.

THE SEXUAL REVOLUTION

The sexual revolution around sexual orientation is not one that immediately affects the lives of heterosexual women. Heterosexuality is taken for granted and is socially approved. The sexual revolution around sexual orientation will be made when all sexual orientations are equally accepted and respected as an individual's preference for a love object. The revolution is in process as lesbians and bisexual women become more open about their sexual orientation and as they take part in political activities as members of a sexual minority. Most women say that when young they never heard of lesbianism or bisexuality as a realistic option. Today there are many falsehoods proclaimed about lesbians and bisexuals. They are not depicted as average women from every walk of life and in every ethnic minority. In addition, there remains widespread intolerance and hatred against these women. When all young women can consider lesbianism or bisexuality as an option without fear of reprisals and when there is no discrimination or violence perpetrated against these women, the sexual revolution will have been made.

chapter four

MASTURBATION:
THE COMFORT
OF HOME

Masturbation is like the comfort of staying home from the sexual trek. The territory of one's own body is the logically obvious starting place for women to explore their sexuality. A woman can choose the time and the place to explore her body in privacy, safety, and comfort. It is an opportunity to experience perfect physical gratification without the demands of the presence of another person.

Some women never explore their own body's potential for pleasure. Others are well travelled in their sexual journeys with partners before they return home to discover masturbation for the first time. Some are not so sure that it is okay to stop and explore the physical delights of their own body. Still, many women do relax and enjoy the innocent entertainment of masturbation.

EARLY CHILDHOOD

The infant discovers the existence of the body from the caring touch of her nurturers and from simple bodily functions. She touches herself to discover the boundaries between her own existence and the environment. It is natural that the infant will discover the delights of her labia and clitoris. But very few women told me that they remember masturbating as a very young child.

People think of masturbation as an activity that starts in childhood. It is the young person's first discovery of the body's erotic sense. This may adequately describe the male experience, but it is not true of most women's sexual exploration. Only three women remember masturbating at a very young age. Gloria is married and at the age of 44 is going to college after her two children left home. She says, "I can't remember not masturbating. At third grade I learned from a priest that I was committing a mortal sin, but I continued anyway." Anita, a 50-year-old lesbian, athletic with graying hair in a long braid: "I must've started masturbating when I was very young. By the time I was three it was an established fact." Guadalupe is a 29-year-old lesbian. "I remember being in my crib. Because we were poor, I slept in a large old crib until I was in kindergarten. I had this fuzzy toy rabbit. I put it between my legs, and it felt stimulating. I lacked physical touch and emotion as a child, so it was a kind of touch. It felt good to my vagina. I did not have orgasms, but it was a warm pleasure, and I can't dismiss it as nonsexual."

None of these women recall this early experience as orgasmic. Instead they describe a feeling of nestling and comfort within themselves. It was natural and easy for them to place their hand between their legs. Touching their genitals was a retreat into themselves. It was a withdrawal into an innocent pleasure and an emotional center of the child-self. It was a quiet place in which to rest.

CHILDHOOD

Women who discovered masturbation when they were children had no name for what they were doing. They received no sexual information from their parents. They experienced physically pleasurable sensations, but they would not have labelled these as sexual feelings.

It was a special warm feeling that did not usually include orgasm. Their discovery of masturbation was purely accidental. Only 40 percent of the women with whom I talked discovered masturbation before the age of ten.

Girls are instructed to keep their genitals clean. Hygiene is the only reason to touch themselves "down there." But some girls discovered that soap and water on the labia is a very pleasant feeling and their place for masturbation was when bathing in the tub or playing with the water as it came from the tub's faucet. All these women talk of homes where modesty was the rule. When they were old enough to bathe alone, it became a very private activity. Without ever being told, the girls learned that the place to pleasurably explore the genitals was in the privacy of the bathroom or, if they had their own room, the bedroom.

Without a conscious plan, little girls learn that their first explorations of their bodily home are a secret adventure. Cath, 45, remembers, "When I was a kid, I rubbed on a pillow. Sometimes I put my hand on top of the pillow, and I'd hump it for more firmness at night in bed. It was really a trick when my sister was sleeping next to me in her own bed next to mine. I was trying to do it quietly so I didn't wake her up." Ryfka, 47, remembers a similar bedroom activity. But sometimes her sister heard her. "I would masturbate by riding a pillow. My sister would ask, 'What are you doing?' and I would say, 'Practicing horseback riding.' She accepted that. I had orgasms. I never talked to anyone about it. It seemed like a real private thing to do. I don't know if I knew it was sex. I don't remember being told not to touch myself." By keeping their little secrets, Cath and Ryfka were able to enjoy themselves without being shamed or punished.

Girls need reassurance from their parents that their bodies are their own possession. In the context of a conversation about how wonderful it is to have a body, girls can be informed by their parents that the good feelings that can be produced by touching their genitals are for their own private time to enjoy. They need to be told that it is their right to refuse to let others, especially grown-ups, touch their bodies in their special place.

Most children are not given this information from their parents. No one talks about the pleasures of self-touch. Their discovery of it is a special secret. They think there is something special and unique about themselves. Or they acquire shame for it if the secrecy is interpreted as hiding a bad activity.

Without parental instruction and support, children are liable to be victimized by adults who sexually abuse them by taking advantage of their sexual ignorance and their compliance with adults. A girl who is sexually abused experiences her body as someone else's object and can be traumatized by this humiliation. If she perceives an awakening of sexuality, it is embedded in guilt and shame. If she experiences any pleasurable sensations in her body, she carries the confusion that good feelings are at once pleasant, shameful, humiliating, evil, and debasing. She has no

understanding that she should be protected from sexual touch or that she has a right to refuse it. She will need to take steps to shed the negative emotions that become intimately associated with her sexuality.

Now 28 years old, Guadalupe was the youngest of 11 children. Both parents worked and still the family was impoverished. Guadalupe was often under the care of her siblings. Guadalupe's innocent play with her toy rabbit changed when she entered childhood. In a molestation experience where she was threatened to keep silent, she learned more about what masturbation could be. "I masturbated to orgasms when I was 11. I was exposed to the seedier side of my brother. He was a career criminal. I was 10 and he was in his twenties. He molested me. There was no penetration. He masturbated in front of me. So I started it myself after that. I never discussed this with my mother. That molestation influenced me. But it was part of a chain of experiences. I saw my brother's pornography, and that gave me ideas. I didn't feel good about how I came to the knowledge. But masturbating felt good, so I enjoyed it. Of course, I had mixed feelings. It physically felt good, but I felt it was dirty or seedy because of how I learned about it. I could never tell my mother this. I felt I was a liar, not worthy of being her child."

It is clear that the secrecy and silence about masturbation coupled with the sexually abusive and degrading manner in which she learned more about it created conflicts for Guadalupe. But later, in a relationship with her lesbian lover, she learned to reclaim this part of her sexuality and to separate it from the context in which she was first exposed to it. She says, "Now I think masturbation is important. I had a girlfriend who masturbated in front of me as part of our lovemaking. It was exciting and good. She taught me a lot. She was healthy, both sexually and spiritually, and she helped me to start moving out of denial and shame to wonder and excitement. Because of her, I feel better about myself. I would be tormented to this day by my brother without her influence. The molestation is a secret. I never described what occurred." As an adult, when masturbation was part of a healing and self-affirming love relationship, Guadalupe found the route to reclaiming good feelings about her body. In a new and caring context, she could venture into self-pleasuring for pure joy, leaving behind the prurient sensibilities of her brother.

PUNISHMENT BY PARENTS

Some girls received a severe message to avoid self-exploration. They were taught to think of their labia as dirty. Physically located near the orifices of elimination, they supposed that their genitals were contaminated. Consequently, many girls did not explore the pleasant sensations of stroking their genitals. They learned that bathing is a practical chore to be carried out efficiently and quickly. The girls were told, "Don't touch yourself there!" Melanie is 34 years old and heterosexual. She recounts a vivid memory: "I can

remember as a young child (about 6 years old) my mother seeing me playing with myself in the bathtub. She yelled at me, slapped my hands, and told me never to touch myself or anybody else. I was really scared." Despite this terrorizing tactic, Melanie continued to masturbate. She learned to be extremely secretive about it. In addition, she acquired a belief that she was a bad girl for pursuing the good feelings in her body.

Melanie's misguided mother set in motion a faulty and shameful outset to Melanie's awareness of herself as a sexual being. A healthier response would have been for her mother to comment that it is nice that the body can feel so good and that Melanie should explore those nice feelings when she is alone. She could have allowed her privacy until she was tired of masturbation and ready to continue her bath. In a calm tone she could have added that she should not let anyone else touch her special place. This communication would have validated Melanie's good feelings and also prepared her to refuse to comply with adults who might abuse her.

Trina

Trina, 24, was also punished for masturbating. She was doing it in secret, but her father took his prerogative to enter her room. "My parents told me not to do it around anyone. When I was 9, they busted me for masturbating. One evening I was in bed, and my dad came in and saw me masturbating with the end of a brush. He told me to pull my pants up, and he took the brush. It was scary that he came in the room like that. I didn't think he'd pull down the covers. I didn't think he had any business pulling down the covers to see what I was doing. I felt intruded upon. I played with myself, but I wasn't orgasmic. They never said not to do it, just not to do it around anyone. It was a mixed message."

Trina was given permission to masturbate, but at the same time, she was punished for it. She was following the admonition to masturbate in private, but her parents did not explicitly state that it had to be in secret. This set up a conflict. Masturbation was okay, but, simultaneously, it was wrong. This experience set her up to be more secretive, especially from her parents. Trina's parents set her out on her sexual path with a sense of confusion. They taught her that touching herself was at once all right and also it was a dirty little secret that would embarrass them if anyone knew about it.

As well as enforcing secrecy, scolding produces a sense of shame and embarrassment in many girls. Janet remembers an experience of being physically abused for masturbating: "My aunt caught me masturbating and scrubbed my genitals with soap till they were raw. 'You're going to ruin your body!' she said. We were never to touch ourselves down there. It made me feel very dirty." Today, Janet knows that her aunt started some very negative attitudes about her own body. Her aunt taught her that good and pleas-

ant bodily sensations are wrong to experience. At 43, she still is not very comfortable with masturbation and only permits herself this pleasure about once a month. She is trying to replace these attitudes with a sense of love and enjoyment of her body.

Sometimes parents lie instead of directly shaming the child. Martha is 42, married, and mother of a teenage boy. She says, "When I was growing up, my mom said, 'Everything will fall out of you if you do that!'" Fortunately, when she was 14, Martha discovered that her body would stay intact, and she began enjoying herself. But she learned that parents are not a resource for good information about sexuality. If her mother could deliberately lie about an uncomplicated aspect of sexuality, her word could not be trusted for anything more complex. So sexual secrecy and silence between Martha and her mother was established.

Once this punishing attitude about masturbation has begun, parents are not the only ones who reinforce it. Lakeisha recounts a story of how her brother assumed the role of shamer to his own advantage: "My brother found me masturbating when I was 8 years old. I was alone in the bathroom using my favorite toy. I would rub the handle of the hairbrush against my clitoris. My brother walked in on me, saw what I was doing, and threw the brush out the bathroom window and over the back fence. He got me to do things like clean his room for him by threatening to tell our parents. He told my brother and sister. They'd sing: 'Lakeisha plays with the green scratcher!' Even now as an adult, they tease me with this phrase."

Sanura

Sanura, 32, recalls how her childhood innocence was punished. "Nobody said anything about masturbation. But when I was seven I was just exploring myself with my fingers in my bedroom that I shared with one of my older sisters. She came in, and I stopped. She asked me what I was doing. She urged me to show her, and I bent my head over and spread my labia apart. I was telling her, and I looked up and my sister was in belly rolls of laughter while my mother was watching me from the doorway. She had a strong, powerful look of disgust. I was ashamed."

When family members induce this kind of embarrassment in the child, they do not stop or prevent the girl from masturbating. Instead, the girl learns to protect her privacy more carefully. Sanura explained, "I continued to play with myself, but it became a much more private experience."

Lakeisha, too, always made sure her door was locked after the incident with her brother. Still, the purity of the pleasure in knowing and enjoying her own body was stolen from her: "I felt nasty and bad every time I masturbated. Sex was not discussed in my home, and I never heard my parents having sex. The silence might have contributed to this idea of it being nasty, or vulgar."

Sometimes the shaming is lost from memory, or it was so subtle that the woman does not remember the source of the information, but she does remember what she did and felt. Annie, a 43-year-old heterosexual, remembers being around five and "lying in my bed at night or early morning. My panties had come off, and I felt totally guilty. I felt like I was going to get caught. I felt like I had to do penance, so I was going to lie there for the rest of the night with my arms crossed across my chest. I don't remember touching myself, but I think I was."

Many girls learn that the simple pleasure of this first excursion into sexuality is tainted by the reaction of adults. The vivid and volatile emotions that adults display on discovering girls touching themselves imprint a message that it is wrong to experience sexual pleasure. At some age it will not be wrong, but how will the girl know when she has reached that age and can shed her guilt? Most girls secretly continue this sexual journey and continue to believe that they are very bad girls for doing so. The undoing of these negative messages becomes another sexual passage for the adult woman.

NONORGASMIC MASTURBATION

For the women who discovered masturbation before they were 12 or 13, it was an easy and comforting way to relax. Only a few experienced orgasm during childhood. Leanna is 20 and heterosexual: "I think I discovered masturbation in the shower. I was not orgasmic. It was just kind of a nice thing to get away and relax. It was a secret. I just really didn't know if it was okay, so I thought it might be bad. I had no direct messages about not touching myself." Today, Leanna is still inorgasmic with masturbation, and she does not do it.

Shaniqua

Shaniqua, 25, recollects her discovery of her clitoris: "I was in the bathtub playing with a little toy sailboat. Occasionally it would scratch up my skin, and one day it rubbed up the clitoral area. I identified that it was a pleasure zone. I did that for a good six months or so. Then after a while I stopped. I don't know why. It was a matter of exploration. It wasn't something I looked forward to doing as an isolated event. I was not orgasmic at that time.

"Later when I was 12, I started again. This time with my hands, and not with toys or objects. I think that it was the time I started developing pubic hair, and I ran my fingers through my hair. I remembered it was the same spot, a pleasure zone. At that point, I discovered orgasm. Probably I did it once every two weeks. In church at that time, all the lessons were about being a virgin and staying a virgin. I probably indirectly associated this with masturbation, although it was never mentioned. So I thought masturbation was something I shouldn't do. Also I shared a room with my sisters and I didn't want anyone to hear me in case I made a noise or made the mattress squeak. By the time I was 13, I was getting into boys and I thought, 'You don't do that when

you're trying to date boys.' Since then, it is still a rare event."

Shaniqua's story shares many elements that we see with other women. She innocently discovered masturbation as a child and knew somehow to keep it a secret. She lost interest in it, perhaps because she was not orgasic. With the arrival of sexual feelings in adolescence she rediscovered masturbation, and now she became orgasmic. Then when her sexuality became directed toward partnered sex, masturbation became less important.

Most little girls are compliant and docile. If they do not spontaneously discover masturbation and they are told not to touch their genitals except for bathing, they are obedient. For others, it never comes to mind to explore the sensations of self-massage. At 58, Julie has two children who are now in their thirties. She did not start to masturbate until she was 40. "I didn't masturbate as a child. I didn't even think about it. In my thirties, I knew boys had wet dreams from the sheets I took off my son's bed, but I had no knowledge of it for girls."

TEENAGERS

Fifty percent of the women did not discover masturbation until they were older than 13 years. With puberty and the first experiences of sexual arousal, teenagers know that masturbation is a sexual act. Teenage women know the feelings of sexual arousal, and 28 percent of women discovered masturbation during the teenage years.

Chloe is 22 and heterosexual. She discovered masturbation on her own. "I discovered it accidentally. I was taking a shower, and we were on vacation. I was lying on my back in the shower and the shower hit me in the right place. It was a great feeling. I did it for a couple more years after. I thought of it as my own private experience. I didn't talk about it." Roseann, age 22 and heterosexual, was surprised to discover masturbation: "I was 12 the first time. I was playing with the Jacuzzi jet. It was a spontaneous thing. It happened and I went, 'Ooh!' I was with another girl. She didn't say anything, but I told her the secret later. She went out and tried it out later. From ages 12 to 16, I used the shower head. But between 16 and 19, I stopped masturbating. I had a boyfriend, and I thought, 'Oh, it's gross to masturbate.' Some peers probably gave me that idea." Roseann returned to masturbation at age 19, using her hand.

May

May is bisexual and 30. When she was 12, "a friend told me what finger fucking was, so I tried it on myself. I didn't get anywhere with it at first. I first started doing it when I was in the bathtub and I felt like washing my bottom off. I slid down so the water from the spout fell on my genitals, and then it felt nice on my clitoris. And so later I added putting my fingers in my vagina at the same time. I became orgasmic with this.

"I did it in the tub whenever I could because I couldn't figure out how to do it effectively with just my hands. So it was a question of when I could use the tub. I masturbated less often in high school. I was at a boarding school, so I could not use the tub there, and I had no privacy to masturbate alone." Once May was given some information, in secret from a girlfriend, she began her search for this private pleasure. Her creative attempts had to be negotiated with complete solitude.

Annie

Annie is 43. She remembers how she learned to masturbate: "I figured out how to masturbate after a date. I made out with this guy real heavy. I was lying on top of him, humping him with clothes on, and I had an orgasm. I figured out that I could recreate it with a pillow at home." Once she found out the joy of masturbation, it became a major part of her life. "When I was 15 we—my parents and sisters—went to the beach after school. Lying in the sun in the beach put me in a sensual space. I'd go to my own room and say, 'I'm gonna take a little nap before supper.' I was horny all the time! I masturbated at least every other day. I remember my sister saying she liked water dripping on her. My sister told me she used the water coming out of the faucet in a steady stream. She lay under the stream with it flowing on her genitals, but it didn't work for me. I talked to my sisters about masturbation, but never my parents. I always kept boundaries between me and my parents."

While Annie discovered masturbation for herself, she found that she could later discuss it with her sisters, her confidants. Masturbation was not something to discuss with parents. They are not a resource about sexuality.

Trina's sexuality went through a change when she began experiencing partnered sexuality.

Trina

"At age 17 I discovered masturbation in bed. I finally got good at it and became orgasmic. I'm not sure how I knew I could have an orgasm. I think I heard women could have them, but I didn't know how. I was overwhelmed at how great it was to get to that level of excitement. Then I wanted to do it all the time. The older I became, the more I did it regularly. The first time I had sex I was 17. I didn't have an orgasm the first time I had intercourse. I think after I had sex, I realized I could masturbate with my hand. I've gotten better at it. I know what it takes to have an orgasm, and I can get there faster than when I was younger."

Trina had a childhood history of masturbating for the purpose of a cozy comfort. With sexual arousal as a teenager, masturbation took on the complex form of her complete sexual cycle.

Mitzi

Mitzi, 32, discovered masturbation as she entered adolescence. "I read a book by Judy Blume. She was the author everyone was reading. There was a book, *Are You There God? It's Me, Margaret*. In one scene she was talking about touching her special place. I didn't know what she was talking about. Later I touched myself and realized that it felt pretty good. There was something about reading the sex scene that made me feel different in that area. The second time I masturbated, I orgasmed. My body went through this really bizarre feeling that I had never experienced before. I didn't quite know what was happening to me. I guess the next night I read the same part of the book and did it again. There were a couple nights where I masturbated so much that I couldn't fall asleep. I couldn't get enough.

"I didn't talk about it for a couple years. Until ninth grade I didn't have a close friend. There was no way I'd tell my sister or mom. My best friend, Elaine, and I confided in each other that we masturbated. Every day we'd ask each other, 'Did you?' and no one knew what we meant. We took turns using her sister's vibrator. I had been masturbating using an electric toothbrush. I don't remember how I figured that out. It was under my parents' sink. Years later in my late teens, my sister and I talked about how we both used it. By then, everybody in my family had vibrators. My parents got divorced. Then there was a big change in how people got along. My mom became more of a friend than a mom. She and my sister and I talked about everything."

Mitzi's story has a unique transformation. Masturbation was a private secret at home. But she found she was not the only one who did this. Later, when her family changed, open conversation about sexuality freed her to be matter-of-fact about self-pleasuring.

Devorah, 25 and bisexual, had a mother like Mitzi's who was very open about sexuality and explained her body to her. Consequently, she says: "I don't remember not knowing about sexuality and about what was possible. I remember when I was young wanting to have an orgasm and trying to figure out how I could do that. When I was 14, my mother offered to get me *Playgirl* if I was interested in what the male body looked like. So I asked her for it. I looked through the ads and found the sex toy catalogs. I sent to one to find out what was possible. So since I was young, masturbation has always been a part of my life."

Sanura, 32, recalls: "I read an article in *Cosmo* about masturbation when I was 16, and I put it to practice and had my first orgasm. Prior to that, it felt good to touch the area lightly and softly. The article talked about focusing on the clitoris

for an extended period of time. The article gave all different ways to try it."

Barbara is 51, heterosexual, and Jewish. Her mother inadvertently set her on her course with masturbation. "I was 18, and my vagina was itchy. Mom said, 'Be sure you get the soap off.' So I made sure I get the soap off. I was in the bathtub and ran the water over me from the faucet with my legs on the sides of the faucet, and I had my first orgasm. And it was fabulous. I used to take long showers to see how long I could come and how many I could have in a row. I used to vary the temperature of the shower and the strength of the flow. I was very clean after that! [laughs] I remember it fondly. I suppose it was quite a while after that I realized you could do it with a finger, too."

Teenage girls' discovery of masturbation is a result of their own experimentation with their bodies. Self-exploration, women's magazines, and sexual explorations with boys are the teenage girls' resources for discovering masturbation. Some of the girls later shared their knowledge with close girlfriends. At all costs, parents are barred from learning that the daughter is pursuing self-pleasure. The girl is allowed no recognition from them that she is a sexual being and that masturbation is a perfectly appropriate and safe way to experience her sexual self.

ADULTHOOD

The admonition "Don't touch yourself down there" is a strong one, and 20 percent of the women I talked with did not discover masturbation until after the age of 20. Claire is a 37-year-old bisexual. "I didn't touch myself until I was 20. My family was very religious, and very modest. When I was 20, I asked my 18-year-old sister if she masturbated, and she said, 'Sure I've been doing it forever. Don't you?' I felt cheated, like, 'Why didn't I get told this was okay?' She said she had done it as long as she could remember. But my sister was sexually molested by my father. It was negative for her, but she was more free. It was bizarre." Even without being told, Claire received the message not to masturbate. Her sister, due to molestion experiences, had discovered masturbation. Secrecy in this family stifled Claire's sexuality and protected the perpetrator of her sibling's abuse. Claire is relieved to have escaped sexual abuse but distressed that her sexuality was repressed. In this false dichotomy, sexuality is either repressed or one is made a victim. There is no room here for sexuality as a lovely, pleasurable experience of one's own body. This understanding is one that Claire had to discover for herself as an adult, free from her dysfunctional family.

Rebecca, is 25, bisexual and a college student with a full-time job. She says, "I started playing with myself as a teenager. I was relaxing myself to fall asleep. I didn't start having orgasms until I was 20." Beth, 38 years old and married for six years, did not start masturbating until she was 25. "I just never knew about it. It never occurred to me until I read a sex manual." Carmen is 48, married, with two teenage children. She finished two years of college in South America before she emigrated to the United States. She says, "I started late; after I took a human sexuality class when I was 32. Now I masturbate every day, making up for the years I missed!" Kim is 37 years old, single, and owns her own business. "I've had sex with 18 men, and I never had an orgasm with any of them. When my last relationship ended, I decided, 'This is it. I'm going to do whatever it takes to have an orgasm!' I started masturbating using my hand, and nothing happened. So I bought a vibrator and wow! I had my first orgasm this year. I've tried my hand again, but the vibrator is the only way I can come. Now I wonder if a new man will accept a vibrator into our sexual activity."

Leah

Leah is a married bisexual, aged 45. She came into her sexuality late. While she had performed intercourse at age 18, she had never experienced orgasm. She was determined to do so. It was the 1970s, when for a brief moment, sexuality was discussed more openly during the (failed) sexual revolution. "I was 23. I got started late, but I made up for it after a while. I was reading about women's sexuality and began to be concerned that I didn't have orgasms. I was going to sex, love, and intimacy workshops. I went to a Betty Dodson slide show. She said, 'If you have trouble having orgasms, practice touching yourself.' So I had to find my clitoris and touch it. When I was 24 I did sex therapy. I had married, and in that relationship I was getting frustrated that I wasn't having orgasms. There wasn't a pre-orgasmic group, so instead we did Masters and Johnson therapy with a therapist. I never achieved orgasm with that. Later, in a pre-orgasmic group for women, we were supposed to masturbate every day. We were instructed to use our hands on the clitoris and a dildo. Then I thought I had a mild orgasm after a lot of work spending an hour with my hand. At the time, every sensation was a big deal. Soon after that I got into a vibrator. I learned to go slower and how to use it, so I could often have an orgasm with the vibrator.

"My major feeling was frustration that I wasn't orgasmic. It was something I really wanted to work on. I felt inadequate not to have orgasms. Since then, I've had them without the vibrator with another person. I felt physically frustrated while being sexual and trying and trying and building up tension and no release."

As adults, these women were ignorant about their bodies. They became aware that they were inorgasmic when they were informed that orgasm is not solely a male prerogative but a physical possibility for women. Once informed, they took on the quest to experience an orgasm. Vibrators became a primary resource for Kim and Leah, who are incapable of orgasm without them. Leah searched every avenue available in order to achieve this experience. For her, San Francisco in the 1970s offered more alternative sexual therapies than it does today.

MASTURBATION AFTER EXPERIENCING INTERCOURSE

Of the women I interviewed, 24 percent began to masturbate some time after their first experience of sexual intercourse. For some, it was between 16 and 22 years later. Each of these women clearly states that masturbation was an activity that followed their experiences of sexuality with a male partner. They moved outward to shared sexual experiences before they had explored the interior of their own physical home. Peggy, age 49 and bisexual, says, "I experienced my first orgasm the first time I had intercourse with a man I loved deeply. I was 24. I remembered being astonished and thinking, 'So this is why women do intercourse!' A few days later I wondered if I could do for myself what he did for me. That was my first try at masturbation and my second orgasm. It was a step toward sexual independence. I got on the phone and called my 18-year-old sister to share the great news. She said, "I've been doing that for three years already! I take Mom's vibrator into the bathroom.' I said, 'So, why didn't you tell me about this?' She replied, 'You dummy, you're older than me. I thought you knew!'"

FREQUENCY OF MASTURBATION

Some women say they never masturbate. Younger women are more likely than older women to say they never masturbate. Twenty-four percent of the 18 to 25-year-old age group said that they never masturbate. Fifteen percent of the group of women 26 to 35 years old said they never masturbate. Only 7 percent of the group of women aged 36 to 58 said they never masturbate.

None of the women stated a moral or religious reason for not masturbating. And there was no statistical difference between women of different religions (including those with no religion) on how they talked about masturbation.

Not only do more women masturbate as they grow older, but they also masturbate with more frequency. The average times of masturbation per month was 4 for the age group 18 to 25; 5 for ages 26 to 35; and 8 for the age group of 36 to 58.

A difference in attitudes about masturbation is what may account for the differences in the groups. Younger women have more confusion about the normalcy of masturbation and a more negative attitude toward self-fulfillment through masturbation. Younger women are still unclear about whether masturbation is acceptable behavior. The following responses from younger women highlight this confusion.

Leslie is 23 and heterosexual. As a child she remembers, "I explored at night in bed just touching myself and figuring out what was going on in my body. I was not orgasmic, but it was pleasurable. I thought it was okay to do because it was part of me. Later, I realized sexuality was repressed in my family, so I stopped. Until recently, it was still negative for me. About six months ago, I met an open group of people, and we discussed these topics, and I realized it was okay and not abnormal.

Now I'm in flux. Right now I don't want to be sexual, so it doesn't give me pleasure to touch myself. Still, I do want to know how I can achieve an orgasm. But that is how it's been."

Leslie is going through a period of sexual redefinition, and she finds it safer to avoid exploring herself. She has never masturbated to orgasm, and she does not appreciate or understand her sexual response cycle. At this time in her life she is putting all of her sexuality on hold. She is not choosing celibacy, but is consciously suppressing her sexuality.

Danita is 22 and heterosexual. She has had sex with men, and she has learned about masturbation in a college human sexuality class. She states that she has never masturbated. "It never occurred to me." She has no religious objections to it. Masturbation is simply not part of her life.

Gayle is 25 years old, tall with dark hair. She masturbates once a month and almost seemed to ask for reassurance that it was okay when she said, "No one said it *wasn't* okay." Sondra is 24 and stated that she never masturbates now, though she started masturbating when she was 12 years old. She raised the subject of guilt: "I had no feelings one way or the other about guilt and masturbating. It wasn't discussed." Sondra is expressing some confusion. She's not sure if she does feel guilty about masturbating. In order to be guilt-free she plays it safe and doesn't masturbate.

Kenya is 25 years old and working two jobs while she's going to school part-time. She says, "I started to masturbate when I was 3 years old. I don't know how

I had orgasms when I was a kid. I only have vague memories. But I never masturbate now. Never!" She is implying that masturbation is for children. In her quest for sexual maturity, she is denying herself this simple amusement. Cindy is 21 years old and lives with her parents: "I've never masturbated. It was never something I desired to do. Of course, I do have sex with my boyfriend." Cindy is saying that she skipped the childhood activity and started with the "real thing"—intercourse. But Cindy learned a lesson about masturbation from a very specific silence from her mother. "When I was 9, my mother went through some sex books with me. She skipped the part on masturbation, so I was curious about that. She said that most people didn't do that." Cindy learned that masturbation is abnormal, and, of course, she wants to be normal. Therefore she never masturbates.

In her thirties and raised in a family where masturbation was openly discussed, Mitzi expresses very different views about masturbation and when and why she does it. "I use masturbation as an all-around cure-all. For example, feeling bloated, feeling frustrated, cramps from my period, feeling horny, feeling fat. It's like a homeopathic remedy. And if I'm feeling uptight I masturbate to relax. After I use the vibrator I'm a much nicer person. It peps me up or it can relax me, depending on the situation. I like to get off in the morning and start my day, and I like to do it at night and relax and go to sleep. I really think that sex with a partner and masturbation are entirely different things. Masturbation is quick, more of a physical release, and I can get off more times. Whereas with sex it's emotional as well as physical. It takes longer, and usually I can get off only once, though usually it's a stronger orgasm."

Ryfka

Ryfka, 47 and lesbian, thinks about masturbation in ways similar to Mitzi. "My masturbation activity changed from when I rubbed against a pillow in my childhood. In high school I started using my hands. I've always masturbated, even when I had partners. When I was married, my husband hated the fact that I masturbated. He thought I should just tell him, and he'd take care of it. I told him, 'I don't want you to take care of it. It's something I do for me.' I enjoy it. It helps me relax and fall asleep. I always masturbate if I have insomnia. And when I'm sick, masturbating makes me feel better. Today I like having my girlfriend watch me masturbate. I never did it with my husband because he didn't like the fact that I did it. It became an issue between us, and we would fight about it. He didn't want me to do it. It threatened his notion of his sexual power and authority."

Like Mitzi and Ryfka, Guadalupe, 28, also finds masturbation is a personal therapy: "I go through changes in masturbation frequency. It's usually four or five times a week. What makes a difference is my menstrual cycle. I do it to alleviate my cramps. Stress does not affect how often I masturbate. It is either desire and having the time to do it, or being too tired to do it."

Masturbation as personal therapy does not work for everyone. Cheryl Jean, 43, finds that her frequency of masturbation diminishes under stress: "When I was younger my pattern of masturbation was mostly consistent, but now there are interruptions. When I'm busy or distracted by other things. It's not related to when I have a partner. When I'm distracted by a crisis in my life, it stops me."

Rudy

Rudy, 44 and lesbian, did not begin to masturbate until she was 25. She describes her early thinking about masturbation: "It didn't occur to me in high school to masturbate because masturbation was sex and sex was bad. After I became sexually active at age 18, I had nothing against masturbation. It was like anything else. Why go to a movie by yourself? Why eat dinner alone? Sex was a two or more person sport and there was always someone I could go to bed with if I wanted to. Masturbation was something you did if you didn't have a partner, and I never experienced that.

"The underlying message about sex is that it's something women do for someone else. It's about giving what you can give. And we're discouraged from getting something for ourselves. Women are not to receive sexual pleasure without the exchange they offer men. Now I think masturbation is something to do with or without a partner."

In marked contrast to the younger women, most older women, like Rudy, express a positive attitude about masturbation. After almost two decades of sexual experiences, the older women have a stronger sense of their erotic selves. They are aware that they are sexual beings and that they have a right to express their sexuality without a partner.

NONORGASMIC MASTURBATION

Some women do not masturbate because they are not orgasmic. Twenty-two years old and living with her mother, Piper masturbates once a month. She says, "I masturbate, but I never have orgasms. It doesn't work! He [her lover] can do it and it'll work!" Similar to Piper, Leanna, who is 20, was never orgasmic with masturbation. So she never masturbates. She says, "I have a regular sex life, and that is what satisfies me now." Maureen at 38 is recently divorced and living with her teenage daughter. She says, "I don't achieve orgasm by myself. And that's probably why I do it infrequently, maybe only once a month. It's frustrating." These women are orgasmic with partners, but they do not know how to produce their own orgasms. Unlike Leah, who went to therapists and workshops and who read books to discover the key to her own orgasm, these women seem content to give the control of their orgasms to their partners.

Some pre-orgasmic women who do masturbate use it for relaxing in the same way that girls do. Bianca is a 20-year-old bisexual who says "I never have had an orgasm while masturbating. To be honest with you, I don't know how." Crystal, at 20, is heterosexual. She states, "I touch my body, but I don't have orgasms. I've never had one." Bianca and Crystal do not masturbate because they have never had an orgasm. For them, masturbation has no purpose.

In spite of the fact that older women tend to masturbate more often, this age group also has women who are negative about masturbation. Bonnie is a 52-year-old homemaker with a 30-year marriage. She says, "I never masturbate. I tried it once when I was 22 years old and it frightened me." She declined to elaborate about this terror. At 49 years old, Trudy is married and raising three teenage sons. Of masturbation she says, "I never did, I'm not even curious."

MASTURBATION AND PARTNERED SEXUALITY

Some heterosexual women relate all aspects of their sexuality with men, including masturbation. Evie is 21 and does not masturbate. "I first did something like masturbation when I had my first boyfriend. We did stuff together. I figured it out or he told me or we came across it. We probably figured it out before intercourse. I don't ever have an orgasm. I haven't masturbated alone. I've only done it with my boyfriends. I only think about it when I'm with a partner. I don't think of it as an individual thing." It is clear that Evie is being sexual with a partner, but she has not yet experienced her sexual awakening. She has never experienced orgasm so she has no sense of her sexual cycle. She does not know the physical sensations of sexual satiation and completion. Evie's sexuality is inextricably linked to her male lover's sex drive and his needs and definition of sexuality.

Also 21, Vanessa expresses the attitude most common to younger women. When she first experienced sexual feelings she linked them to a boy in school. "I liked a boy in eighth grade. So as I fell asleep I thought of him being there and where he'd be touching me. So I touched myself in those places. And I said what he'd say. We danced once. But other than that, this was fantasy. I'm not orgasmic with masturbation. And I'm a virgin. Actually I've never had an orgasm." Vanessa does not masturbate because she in not in touch with her own sexual self. She is waiting for the appropriate male sex object to appear so that she can begin exploring sexuality. She bears no guilt or shame about masturbation. It simply seems irrelevant to her.

Some women masturbate less often when they are in a sexual relationship. Their explanations of the decrease in masturbatory activity are various. Lily is 20 years old: "I am in a relationship with a man, and so I never masturbate. Masturbation doesn't make me feel as good as I do when I have sex with him."

Chloe, 22, has found that her pattern of masturbation is intimately connected to the kind of sexual relationship she has. "I've gone through phases. I stopped through high school. I first had sex my sophomore year. It was painful. It took me a year to recuperate from this. A year later, I had a permanent boyfriend, so I didn't masturbate. I rarely did while in college. I always had a boyfriend, so I had sex with him if I had a need. Without a boyfriend, I would masturbate once a week. I currently started masturbating again because of my boyfriend. He bought me a vibrator to help me get started again." Chloe had the idea that she matured into partnered sex and so could stop masturbating. It was her lover's encouragement and sexual openness that reintroduced masturbation in her life, not a surfacing of her own desire. While Chloe is almost a generation younger than Rudy, she expresses some of the same ideas about masturbation that Rudy held when she was 20. Sexuality has more to do with men than with one's own body. It is something to share and not to be enjoyed alone.

May, 30 and bisexual, began to masturbate when she was 12, but her pattern of masturbation changed. She went through a stage like Chloe and Rudy in which sexual satisfaction with a partner upstaged masturbation. "In college, I was almost always sleeping with someone, so I had an active partnered sex life. I was satisfied with a partner and had sex most nights of the week. In one relationship, we masturbated together. I felt vulnerable letting someone else watch me do that.

During a couple of years of being single or when I've been in a long-distance relationship where I didn't see the other person much, I masturbate more. Now I'm home alone a lot, and so I masturbate quite a lot. If I'm turned on or bored, I give myself an orgasm. Before I see my lover, I don't masturbate for a couple of days because it makes it easier to come." May reclaimed her self-love in masturbation, and she discovered something about her sexual response cycle. Once she felt that she had a limited number of orgasms available to her in a time period, she made a decision to allot some to herself and some to her partnered sexual experiences.

Shelley is 34 and single. She says, "How often I masturbate depends on whether or not my boyfriend is around." Paula is 41 and in a steady relationship: "I never masturbate. I have no need for it because I have sex with him pretty often, three times a week." Annie, like Paula, masturbates less now that she is married: "I masturbate about once every two months. I get so much sex now, I don't need to. I used to masturbate all the time until my present sexual relationship. Now I'm satisfied. I never was satisfied before. Even when I was dating other guys, I masturbated every other day. None of them satisfied me the way my husband does."

Leah, 45, found that her pattern of masturbation fluctuates with her ability to experience partnered sex. "When I wasn't in a relationship, it was more likely that I'd masturbate. If I was in a relationship with regular sex, I'd rarely masturbate. Sometimes if I had sex with someone once a week, I might still masturbate five times a week to relax and sleep, not from being horny." Despite the fact that partnered sexuality satisfies her sexual needs, Leah still claims masturbation for herself as a private way to relax.

Sanura says, "When I first discovered masturbation, it was several times a day for months. And later when I wasn't in a relationship it was similar. Because of the frequency of sex in my current relationship, I don't masturbate. I masturbate more when I am in a relationship where I have difficulty climaxing."

Mitzi found that her pattern of masturbation has changed within her own marriage: "From age 14 to 29, a daily orgasm was a must. My body physically needed it. Now that I'm married, it's changed. In the beginning, we had sex every day and I stopped masturbating. Then he thought that I was using his body. (So what if I was?) And so he started pulling back and became less interested in sex. In the last three or four years I masturbate much more than we have sex. Sometimes we masturbate together. But mostly because it's my thing not his, I ask him to leave the room when I masturbate." Marriage did not create a situation for Mitzi where she had a continually available sex partner. So masturbation remains for her a way to manage her strong sex drive.

Barbara

Barbara, 51, notes that her pattern of masturbation has gone through many changes. Some of these relate to her sexual partners, but in complex ways. "I have experienced substantial changes in the pattern of masturbation. Until probably I was in my early 40s, I masturbated an average of six times a week. Then with Ted, whom I lived with from age 42 to 50, we had sexual problems. One of the ways I tried to solve them was to repress my sexuality. For the first time masturbation struck me as a reminder that I was frustrated within our relationship, so I stopped masturbating.

"Recently I got back into my sexuality, and I began to masturbate again. I became sexual again because I met somebody with whom I had a very passionate and sexual affair. I think I am a sexual person, so I returned to where I had been. Having an available sex partner did not change my masturbation. It was more than being sexual and satisfied. It was a way to communicate with myself; to nurture myself and to be alone. Masturbation and partnered sex are two different kinds of relationships. One was with myself and one with my partner. Some of it was pure habit, a way to go to sleep and almost meditative. It became a habit, part of my waking hours."

Some women who don't masturbate reject it as an inferior form of sexuality. Pam, who is 31, shuns masturbation as inferior to partnered sexuality when she says, "If I can't have sex with a man, I do without!" Denise, a 39-year-old bisexual, says, "It takes a lot of energy. I'd much rather have someone else do it for me." But Camille, 40 and heterosexual, expresses the opposite sentiments: "It's much harder for me to come by myself than with a partner." These women express a range of attitudes about the relationship between masturbation and sex with a partner. Some find frequent partnered activity lessens their drive for solitary sex; others place a lower value on masturbation than on partnered sex; and others see masturbation as a wrongful act.

Single women enjoy masturbation as a completely fulfilling form of sexual expression. Masturbation is private time and valuable in itself. Shannon is 32 and a medical student, single by choice. "I just have so many things I'm doing, I don't want a sexual relationship right now. It would take up too much of my time. I have great sex with myself." Star says, "After my divorce, masturbation helped me through some lonely days. I knew that though I lost that relationship and sometimes I missed him, I didn't have to give up sex, too."

ANATOMY OF THE CLITORIS

Women discover masturbation by touching their genitals to discover what feels good. So women can learn to masturbate without knowing the anatomy of their genitals. However, it is important for women to know the sexual parts of their own bodies. The heights of sexual pleasure can only happen when a woman

FIGURE 4.1

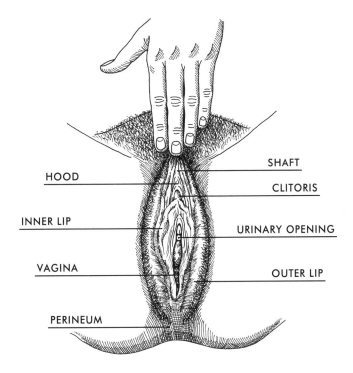

HOOD

SHAFT

CLITORIS

INNER LIP

URINARY OPENING

VAGINA

OUTER LIP

PERINEUM

FIGURE 4.2

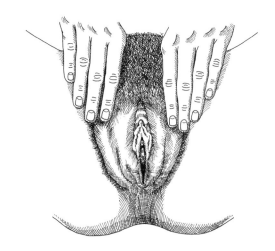

FIGURE 4.3

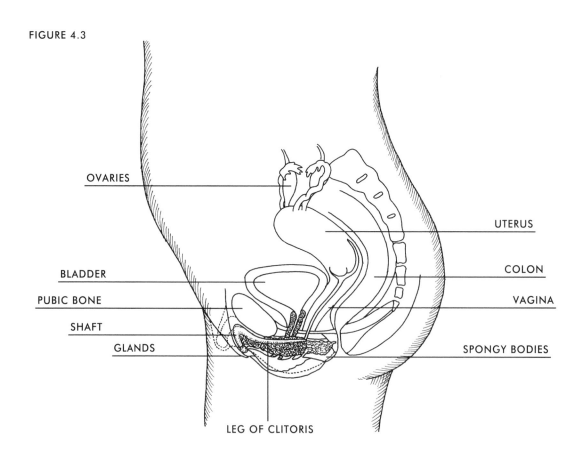

OVARIES

UTERUS

COLON

BLADDER

PUBIC BONE

VAGINA

SHAFT

GLANDS

SPONGY BODIES

LEG OF CLITORIS

understands her anatomy and the parts of her body that are the most sexually exciting. It is important for a woman to look at her body, to appreciate the beauty in her genitals, and to unlearn any negative thoughts or judgments relayed by others. By looking at her genitals, a woman will be able to better appreciate the complex physical aspect of her sexuality. Figure 4-1 can be used as a map of the vulva. The vulva's outer lips protect and conceal the openings to the body. The inner lips are folds of tissue that sometimes drape over the openings. There can be great variability in women's lips. Sometimes the inner lips are larger than the outer lips and protrude past them. Other women have very small inner lips, some so small that they cannot be identified as more than small ridges (see Figure 4-2).

The most sensitive part of the vulva is the glans of the clitoris, which is covered by the hood. There is variation in the size of the hood. Some women have a hood that completely covers the glans, and others have a glans that protrudes. If the hood is pulled up and back, the shaft of the clitoris can be seen as a ridge under the flesh. Below the glans is a tiny urethral opening. Below that is the vagina. The space between the vagina and the anus is the perineum.

Figure 4-3 shows the internal structure of the clitoris. The clitoris is composed of the sensitive glans, the shaft, and the legs. The clitoris has the same number of nerve endings that are in the penis (the male counterpart to the clitoris). The clitoris is also composed of a spongy concentration of blood vessels that expand and fill with blood when a woman is sexually aroused. These spongy bodies are completely internal and are the counterpart to the spongy bodies in the penis that fill with blood and create an erection. When a woman is sexually aroused, the shaft of her clitoris becomes erect. This is shown by the dotted line in Figure 4-3. The dotted line along the labia indicates that the tissues will swell when engorged with blood during arousal.

Figure 4-3 shows that the urethral sponge wraps around the urethra. It is anterior, or in front of, the lower one-third of the vagina. Some woman say that this part of the vagina, known as the g-spot, is especially sexually arousing. Stimulating the g-spot in the vagina is stimulating the urethral sponge on the other side of the vaginal wall. The perineal sponge extends from the labia toward the anus. This part of the clitoris is stimulated during anal intercourse.

Figures 4-4 and 4-5 show a view of the vulva when the woman is lying on her back. Figure 4-5 shows the legs of the clitoris and the internal spongy bodies. Women who masturbate by "humping" a pillow or contracting their thighs are stimulating the legs of the clitoris.

GENITAL SELF-EXAMINATION

After studying Figures 4-1 and 4-2, take the time to examine your genitals. This inspection of your own body will help you reclaim from your childhood the early innocent sense of your sexual self. Looking at yourself is a new starting point of love and appreciation of your sexual

FIGURE 4.4

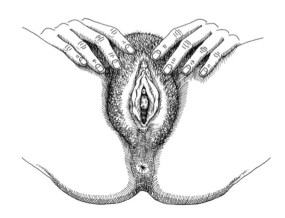

FIGURE 4.5

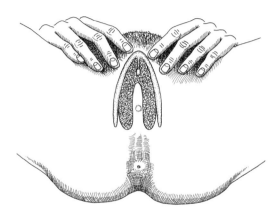

form. If you already have an appreciative lover, you will understand the attractiveness that he or she acknowledges. If you are without a partner, you can bring to your next liaison the expectation that (s)he will cherish your form.

Take some private time to relax in a comfortable position. A flashlight, or lamp appropriately positioned and a hand mirror will aid in this self-examination. Explore the pattern, thickness, and texture of your pubic hair. Admire the shape of the labia as they form a curtain protecting the inner structures. Gently separate the lips. Look at their tint. There

may be changes in the colorations from pinks to dusky dark browns. Your lips may be asymmetrical, one side larger or more pronounced than the other. Your inner lips may be larger than the outer lips. Or they may be small and indistinct.

Examine the clitoris itself. It is the powerhouse of your sexual energy. Find the hood that drapes over the top of the glans of the clitoris, very often like the hood of a cape. Pull upward and back on the sides of the hood to reveal more of the shaft of the clitoris. For some women this organ is clearly visible. For others it is very small and recedes into the inner recesses of the body. Separate the folds of the labia so that you can see the opening to the vagina and the small aperture of the urethra above it.

Examining the genitals is a way for a woman to truly own her body. She brings reverence and joy to the appreciation of her hidden jewel. No matter what her particular form, she can honor her unique vulva. Love and acceptance of all the parts of the body are essential for celebrating sexuality.

THE FEMALE SEXUAL RESPONSE CYCLE

When a woman is sexually aroused, the tissues of the genitals become engorged with blood, and the clitoris becomes erect. The walls of the vagina produce a fluid that lubricates them and the labia. The pelvic platform (the muscles that support the inner organs) lifts. For some women the walls of the vagina expand and the lower anterior vagina domes. The nipples become erect.

When a woman is close to orgasm, her body becomes rigid and her breathing turns to panting. When she experiences orgasm, the clitoris vibrates at a rate of .8 second. The muscles and tissues of the genitals contract rhythmically. Sometimes the vagina contracts, as well as the uterus and anus. During orgasm, most women prefer a cessation of stimulation. However, if stimulation is gently begun again after orgasm, the woman can experience more orgasms. This pattern can continue until the woman has experienced as many orgasms as she wants.

HOW WOMEN MASTURBATE

Manual Stimulation

One sage 84-year-old woman said to me, "The hand should be celebrated as the best sexual organ!" Most women masturbate using their hands and fingers on the clitoris and labia. A few also touch the vaginal opening and anus. Typically, a woman lies passively on her back and rubs her clitoris with one or two fingers of one hand. This style of masturbation is relaxing, easy, and effective. At 23 Kristie has been masturbating only three years. She states, "I use my fingers, and I stimulate the clitoris area. It is not a grinding touch. It's a lighter touch than during intercourse." Sanura says: "I stimulate my clitoris. I rub it in a circular fashion. I'm usually in bed lying down on my back. Sometimes I stimulate my nipples by slightly squeezing them." Cheryl Jean is heterosexual and 43. She says: "I seldom use penetration when I masturbate. My nipples are sensitive, and I touch them. I also touch my clitoris. I do a soft pressured movement over the clitoris, and just lightly touch my nipples. The time I take varies. It's not usually very long, maybe ten or fifteen minutes. For me, masturbation is usually just a release." Tina is a 36-year-old lesbian: "I stimulate my clitoris by rubbing it with my right index finger with different speed and stimulations. Every once in a while, I touch my asshole and kind of open up my vagina." Trina, a 24-year-old heterosexual, describes her style: "I use my three fingers to rub up and down and put pressure on the clitoris and the hood and the outside of the labia. I do it pretty fast." Josie is a 58-year-old lesbian who had her clitoris removed years earlier when she had a rare vaginal cancer. She still masturbates "with my hand manipulating the area that was the clitoris, since I don't have one now. It still is the same thing. If I put my hand there I have an orgasm. It may be partially mental." For Guadalupe, masturbation is a simple routine: "I usually lie in bed by myself. I like to be nude as opposed to any clothing that would bind me. With my left hand I hold my labia apart and I use my index finger on my right hand to stimulate my clitoris. I relax. I like the house to be quiet, and I like to nap 20 minutes after it. I feel relaxed, hungry, and invigorated. I eat an apple and then I'm on my way!"

Not all women enjoy direct clitoral stimulation. Forty-two-year-old Nicole says, "I don't stimulate my clitoris but the vaginal opening. The clitoris hurts, it's too sensitive to stimulate. I use fingers to stimulate the vaginal area." Rebecca, at 25, states, "I use my fingers on my clitoris. I can come pretty quick. I'm my best lover—I know what I want. I'm better with not quite direct stimulation, not touching the clitoris directly."

Some women like to take their time and massage their breasts, or stroke their bodies. Others take just a few minutes to achieve a simple release. Eileen, who is 30, says, "I use my fingers on my clitoris and on my nipples." Laura at 35 states, "I like direct clitoral stimulation, but that is not the only part I touch. I touch my breasts, the vaginal opening. I put my hand on my pelvic bone." June is a 28-year-old bisexual: "I stimulate my clitoris with my hand or a vibrator." Karen, who is 28, says, "With one hand I stimulate my clitoris. With the other I play with my nipples, or I put my fingers in and out of my vagina."

Vibrators

Some women who masturbate with their hands have found pleasure in adding toys to their self-love interludes. Vibrators are very commonly used. Peggy stated, "Every time I use the vibrator, my favorite sex toy, I give thanks to Nicola Tesla, who invented it. He could never have imagined when he experimented with vibrations that he would give so many women so much pleasure! I think every woman with a vibrator should know his name."

The preferred way to use the vibrator is to place it directly on the clitoris or with a towel in between as a buffer to soften the intensity of the vibration. Claire, is 37 and bisexual, says, "Usually I masturbate with a vibrator. I put my hand in between the vibrator and the vulva area. All I have to do is turn it on and I have orgasms, several of them. It can take seconds or minutes." May, 30 and bisexual, has similar sentiments: "I use the vibrator, a magic wand. I hold the head of it against my clit until I come in two to five minutes."

Heather is 26 and bisexual. She says, "I use a vibrator on my clit. It's fast and very intense." Cath, 45 and lesbian, says, "Usually I have the vibrator on the pubic bone above my clitoris. I tighten and release my thighs. Other than that, I don't have to do anything. It's very fast, intense, and purely physical." Heterosexual and 22 years old, Roseann uses the vibrator and strokes her body: "I use the vibrator on my clitoris. I don't move it around that much. I touch my breasts initially. I touch my stomach a lot. I might grab a thigh."

Vibrators are powerful stimulants, and women have mixed reactions to them. Leah, 45, who took classes to become orgasmic, found success with the vibrator. But her reaction to it is mixed. "When the vibrator got too intense, then I couldn't come at all. I built up to bigger and bigger vibrators. I got aroused, but I couldn't get a release. I used it often during sex with my husband.

"I used to keep pushing and pushing it. Try it and force it until it happened. Sometimes I'd give up and feel bad, both physically and emotionally. I felt frustrated and powerless, and the vibrator was not good for me. I hated to be dependent on it. I tried to take a break from the vibrator for a few months. But I went to a smaller vibrator and it works some of the time. I put the vibrator on my clit and the dildo inside my vagina."

On the other hand, some women find that the intense stimulation of a vibrator is too extreme, and orgasm is delayed because the clitoris reacts by becoming insensitive. Star, bisexual and 48 years old, has set aside the vibrator: "I like to use my hand to stimulate my breasts and my clit. I don't use the vibrator because it numbs me out."

Masturbating with Water

Women who learned to masturbate while bathing still prefer the massaging shower head with the spray directed at the labia and clitoris. Carla, who is 23 years old, says, "When I first started to masturbate, I didn't touch myself. I positioned myself so the water coming out of the tub faucet ran against my clitoris. Sometimes I still use the water massager on the shower attachment." Carla ingeniously found a way to masturbate and still obey the command, "Don't touch yourself down there." Robin, 26 and heterosexual, like Carla, states: "I use water stimulation. I aim the spa jets toward the vaginal area, or I use water coming out of the bathtub spout aimed at my vaginal area." Linda, who is 41, explains, "I lie in the bathtub with my legs propped up and I run the water from the faucet onto my clitoris." Barbara, who is 51, says, "The first time I masturbated was in the shower with water, so I still often masturbate with water. Sometimes I use the Jacuzzi. I let the water pulse on me. I kneel right next to the jet. Hinging on who is around depends on how blatant I can be. It takes me just minutes."

Dildos

Eleven women mentioned that they used dildos. Rene is a 39-year-old lesbian: "I do clitoral stimulations with a vibrator. Then I put a dildo in my vagina and move it up and down." Skye is a 35-year-old bisexual who did not start masturbating until she was 27. She states, "I like to masturbate with a dildo, and a vibrator on my clit. I put the dildo inside for my vaginal muscles to clamp down on. I stimulate my breasts, nipples, and I rub my whole body." Barbara, 51 and heterosexual, sometimes uses a dildo: "I have a silicone penis-like dildo. A lover gave it to me. He drew a little smiling face on the head. He opened me up to my sexuality, so using it gives me special memories of what he meant to me."

Peggy, 48 and bisexual: "Sometimes I use the dildo that my lover uses with the harness. I pull the dildo gently in and out, and I use the vibrator on my clit, or rub it with my fingers. The dildo takes on a more erotic meaning since I use it mostly with my lover. In a way, it adds her presence to my masturbation, and makes it more exciting for me." Julie is a 58-year-old heterosexual: "I just can't masturbate with my hand! I use a dildo but not a vibrator. I like to feel my vagina grab onto something." Many women do not like to visit sex stores, so they used candles, carrots, and chopsticks as dildos. The diameter of the object was not important; it is used as an extension of the hand to reach the inner walls of the vagina. Rachel, bisexual, at 35 says, "I like to use a vibrator on my clitoris. Sometimes I put a finger inside my vagina. I use chopsticks or a toothbrush as a dildo sometimes, while I stimulate my clit with a vibrator."

A few women described a more active type of masturbation. They lie on their stomach and rub the clitoris against a pillow. Tamiko, who is 36 and heterosexual, states, "I lie on my stomach and I rub

against something." As a teenager, Annie, now 43, found she could orgasm by "humping the pillow I had. It was a round pillow with edges. I propped up on the pillow for leverage," she laughed. "It wasn't a very thick pillow; the edge fit right between my labia. It worked best doing this on my stomach. I need the pressure of my body against the pillow."

Some women can masturbate by squeezing their thighs together. This movement also tightens the muscles in the pelvic platform and the labia and vagina. These are the body parts that experience the sexual excitation. For some, this technique works well with a tight seam of jeans against the labia.

MASTURBATION FANTASIES

Only nine women talked of sexual fantasies as part of their masturbation activity. Kate, who is 31: "I touch my clitoris with my hand while I read erotic literature, or I watch movies." Cath, 45 and lesbian, "Sometimes I fantasize making love to a woman's body, thinking about the last time that I had sex because that's the freshest thing in my mind." Sanura, 32, describes her imagery: "I fantasize about other couples. I'm watching them. Sometimes I fantasize three or four people, men or women. Usually one woman with a couple of guys if I'm fantasizing about more than two people." Claire is 37 and bisexual: "My fantasies involve male penetration. I think of women, too, but more than half would be with men, sometimes a combination. Sometimes I read sexual stories."

Peggy

Peggy, 48 and bisexual, states that she likes to "lie on my back in bed and begin by stroking my body, my breasts and thighs. Then my vulva and my clitoris. I like to rub the legs of my clitoris through the labia and sometimes the glans of the clitoris but gently. I let my imagination go wild. I keep changing the fantasy until I have one that excites me. At one point I did a series of fantasies of all the men I had sex with but wasn't orgasmic. The losers. But in the fantasy, I changed things so that I came. Now I usually fantasize a man and a woman, at least two people making love to me. I make love to them, too. If I have trouble getting off, which happens sometimes when I'm really stressed, I keep adding more and more people to the fantasy so that all the parts of my body are being stimulated simultaneously. I bring in all the people I've known who I wanted sex with but which for some reason never happened. Sometimes I try to masturbate as though it is an exercise in self-love, as Betty Dodson suggests. But even then I begin to imagine that my own hands belong to someone else. Fantasies are definitely a big part of my masturbation practice. I never masturbate without a fantasy."

Shaniqua, 25 and heterosexual, states: "Occasionally when I masturbate, I think about exotic far-off places that I've never been. I am there secluded with my mate. Jamaica, the Virgin Islands, Australia. I think it's because I'm trying to put a past experience right. Once, I went to the beach with my current husband in the car. We found a shaded tree and thought no one would see us until the cops came. They shone the light on us and said on the megaphone, 'Put your clothes on and go home.' It certainly spoiled our mood!"

In their sexual fantasies, some women use erotica, others imagine a present or past lover, or a celebrity. Their fantasies involve an element of romance. For some it is redoing a sexual experience that was disappointing and using the act of masturbation to improve the memory. For others it is a way to achieve the sense of greater physical stimulation by imagining more hands on their bodies.

We have seen that some women have internalized the concept that masturbation is not right. These women do not find it easy to just take the time to enjoy themselves. Fatima is a virginal 23 year old raised in a household where sexuality is completely hidden. She says she masturbates about twice a year: "Seventy percent of the time I wake up from a dream when I'm having an orgasm. My shirt rubs against my body in my sleep. When I masturbate, I stroke my body to excite myself. Then I touch my pelvic area and my hips, then with my hand I stimulate my clitoris and my vulva." In these rare dreamlike states of partial wakefulness she has permission to enjoy her body.

CONCLUSIONS

Sexologists view masturbation as a healthy positive way to enjoy the body. Masturbation is recommended for women who are pre-orgasmic. Many women do not have orgasm because they do not understand their own anatomy, and they have no idea of the kind of stimulation that excites them past sexual arousal into orgasm. Practice with masturbation is the first prescription for women who have never experienced an orgasm. Every woman is different and enjoys subtle variations in the part of the clitoris that is most responsive to touch, the amount of pressure needed, the kind of circular rubbing or up and down stroking, and the sort of vaginal or anal penetration or stimulation that feels best. After a woman has learned her sexual response by masturbating, she can share these techniques with her lover.

Women younger than 25 years old who have had fewer sexual experiences are more embarrassed and more conflicted about masturbation than older women. They are still unsure of themselves as sexual beings. They have not shed the cultural taboos against women touching themselves "down there." Most have been punished for their youthful excursions into self-pleasures. At the least, they know to keep it a secret. Privatizing their sexuality gives them no opportunity to validate that masturbation is a desirable pursuit and essential to the experience of one's sexual life.

These women are at the beginning of their personal sexual journey. They are unaware of their own sexual response cycle. Most of the women who are pre-orgasmic do view their inability to experience orgasm as a problem. But they also accept it as being unsolvable, at least by themselves. Heterosexual women are likely to be waiting for a male lover who will provide the magic touch. Instead of claiming their bodies for themselves, they are waiting for the competent man to direct their journey.

This attitude is a result of conditioned personal and sexual passivity. These women are cut off from their own bodies. They do not feel in control or that they can steer their own course. Many harbor an attitude that sexuality belongs to men. In the silenced world of women's sexuality, all the voices belong to men. This is what women know and accept. Heterosexual women have had to passively wait for a man to be interested in them and to initiate sexual activity. Attitudes of sexual passivity and alienation from one's own sex drive can be classified as a sexual dysfunction. But because women's sexual journey is so intensely cloaked, they are cut off from the knowledge that they can create their own delighted sexual fulfillment.

Younger women who do sink themselves into the pleasure of their bodies have a sense of self that strongly embraces their right to enjoy their physical existence. Their sexual independence and personal assertiveness make them a minority among their peers. After the age of 35, women are more likely to masturbate and to view it as simply another way to experience and enjoy their sexuality. They have dropped the worries about its "normalcy." Many of them have developed several different styles of masturbation. They may incorporate whole-body self-massage, vibrators, other sex toys, and erotica as well as different positions into their self-play. Masturbation is safe sex, clean fun, private and uninvolved with the interpersonal risks of partnered sex.

A SEXUAL REVOLUTION

The stories that women narrate about their process of discovering masturbation are evidence that there has been no sexual revolution on this front. When we map the terrain of masturbation, we see that there are several courses that women take. There are little girls who discovery their bodily pleasures and secretly enjoy themselves into contentment. These children learn that masturbation is a mysterious territory because no one mentions it. If they are fortunate, it may be an innocent secret. They have discovered a valley of private pleasure.

If a girl has been punished for self-touch, masturbation may become a guilty secret. Parents who are negative and reproach their daughter for masturbation are a terrible pitfall of the first childhood explorations of the body. The guilt and blame associated with the experience becomes an unnecessary pain that may be difficult to shed. These girls often grow into women who cannot freely relax with their own sexuality. Self-pleasuring becomes a confused combination of physical pleasure and guilt and shame for feeling good.

Some strong-willed girls who claim their right to good, sexy feelings see their parents as alien, old-fashioned, and wrong about masturbation. They keep their secret and build a wall between themselves and their parents. These parents will never understand or know about their daughter's sexuality. These rebellious young women transform themselves into stronger individuals by claiming their right to self-pleasure.

Masturbation is also sometimes spontaneously discovered in adolescence. Teenagers are allowed more privacy, and thus parents do not discover them in the act. This spares the young woman any parental reprobation, and so she may feel less guilt about it. However, it is still a secret. Since it is never discussed, there may be something wrong about doing it. Unless she has access to information on sexuality, her adventures in masturbation may be shrouded in shame and fears that she is abnormal.

Women who do not explore masturbation until their twenties or later are women who have understood sexuality as a partnered activity, usually with a man. The American sexual script is still one in which the male has the active role and the woman is "turned on" by him. These women believe that nothing sexual can happen when she is alone. Adult women discover masturbation from reading novels or sexuality books, in a college course, or after experiences with sexual intercourse. When a woman is enlightened about masturbation in adulthood, she experiences less shame and embarrassment. She is in charge of her own body and has already experienced sexual choices. Masturbation, for her, can be a joyful discovery because it gives her complete control of her sexual response. She is transformed into a self-sufficient and sexually independent woman.

A true sexual revolution would change a women's path to masturbation in many ways. Masturbation would no longer be a guilty, shameful secret but a commonplace and simple pleasure. Children would be taught the names of their sexual anatomy. When they touch themselves their parents would smile and say, "Yes, that feels good, and it is best for you to explore your special places alone in your bedroom." Older children would be told about orgasm as a wonderful feeling everybody can create. Girls would learn at a young age that they own their bodies and the pleasure they can generate. They would learn that this is one part of the mystery of sexuality that is always available to them. It would never happen that women first learn about masturbation as adults. Women would masturbate as the mood strikes them, with no need to connect this activity to a sexual relationship. Gone would be all the concepts that masturbation is nasty or sinful. Instead, women would celebrate the joy of the clitoris, whose only function is to give her pleasure.

chapter five

SEX WITH MEN

SEXUAL PARTNERS

Sixty percent of the heterosexual women interviewed were or had been married. However, only three women confined their sexual adventures to the marital relationship. Women explored sex with male partners before and during the marriage and after divorce. Ninety-eight percent of the women had experienced relationships with men. Two percent were virgins and had very limited dating experience.

Four of the heterosexual women were virgins. For the 100 sexually active heterosexual women, there was an average of 16 male partners. Two women had had 200 and 300 partners. As might be expected, younger women had had fewer partners. The age group 18 to 25 had an average of 16 partners. Women aged 26 to

35 had had an average of 20 partners. Those aged over 35 had had an average of 25 sexual partners.

Like heterosexuals, lesbians began their sexual careers with men at the average age of 17. Eighty-seven percent of the lesbians had performed intercourse with men. The average number of partners was 15. One woman had been a prostitute for a time. She had had 500 clients. Another woman was sexually experimental in the 70s and had had 200 partners.

All of the bisexual women had performed intercourse with men. Like lesbians and heterosexual women, the average age of first intercourse was 17 years old. Bisexual women had an average of 27 male partners. As a group, they had more male sexual partners than either lesbians or heterosexuals.

SATISFACTION WITH SEXUAL EXCHANGES

Some women do not achieve orgasm with a partner. They participate in sexual acts with him in order to satisfy his desires and to experience affection. Younger women are more likely to participate in sexual intercourse that does not include their orgasm. Sixteen percent of the heterosexual women aged 18 to 25 were never orgasmic with a partner. This was true of only one woman aged 30 and of three women who were over 35. Overall, 7 percent of heterosexual women had never experienced an orgasm with a male partner.

Women have various explanations for what prevents them from orgasmic experience. Leza, 24, says simply, "Something within me keeps me from it." Justine is also 24 and has had several partners. She says, "When I get excited I start thinking about being bad. You gotta stop thinking and just feel. The men know I don't orgasm, but we don't work on it. It's my issue." Jennifer is 21 and implies that it is her mental outlook that prevents her from orgasm. "If I can smoke pot I can forget the rest of the world, but I guess it's not enough to let me come." All these women indicate that their negative feelings about sexuality and/or themselves as sexual beings prevent them from losing themselves in a physical experience. They take responsibility for it, but are not concerned enough to seek sex therapy. It appears that their partners are not bothered by a nonorgasmic sexual partner.

Evie is 21. She states that sexual exchange is satisfying to her, even though she is nonorgasmic. She has had two sexual partners, one satisfying and one not. "I don't know what made sex satisfying to me. It was more how I felt about the person. I was in love with one man and everything we did was great. Whether or not I had an orgasm didn't matter. I didn't have feelings about the other man, so the sex didn't seem important or meaningful to me. The acts were similar. I didn't do anything different. But the way I felt about each of them was different." Evie makes it quite clear that she is seeking emotional closeness from the sexual exchange. In a way she is closed to the experience of intercourse as a part of her physiological sexual response cycle. She is unaware that sex is a dance that leads to a physical climax. She has no sense that she can choreograph the physical and emotional closeness to a leap into orgasm.

Leanna

Leanna, 20, expounds on the value of nonorgasmic sexuality. "With my first boyfriend I did have orgasms. I haven't had one with my last three partners, so it's difficult to think about what goes on. It just kind of happens. I think I'm not concentrating on having an orgasm. Instead, I'm watching what's going on. It doesn't bother me not to be orgasmic. I still feel the pleasure of intercourse when I'm finished.

"I think with the first boyfriend we were basically one, and with the others I feel separate. It's like I'm going through the motions of having sex. The whole scene is completely different." Without a certain emotional connection, Leanna is unable to relax with a partner to be orgasmic. She admits that, for her, sex is going through the motions. What is not clear is her motivation to be sexual. Why isn't she waiting to be sexual until she finds the man with whom she can connect? It seems likely that she is being sexual to keep the man around for status or to keep from experiencing loneliness.

In Chapter 4 we saw that Kim, 37, had never experienced orgasm, either alone or with a partner, until late in life. At the age of 37, when she was without a partner, she searched and discovered that she needed the stimulation of a powerful vibrator to achieve orgasm. It was only with the self-esteem she raised in her adulthood that she developed the drive to explore her own sexual response. She expects to bring the vibrator into her sexual exchanges with men.

Some older women have maintained a curious element of denial and confusion about their sexuality. Like the younger nonorgasmic women, they have not explored their sexual response cycle even though they have been sexually active for over two decades. They are not doing sex for the physicality and erotic pleasure of it. But they are not clear about their true motivations. Beverly is 47 and has had a number of male partners. She continues to be sexually active even though she finds the sexual embrace satisfying only 5 percent of the time and she never orgasms. Yet she rhapsodizes about the experience. "I use music as a method to visualize my orgasm energy as flowing up my spine to my head. But I don't know how to orgasm with a man. I've been told by men, 'You're built wrong.' A few men have known how to stimulate my clitoris but not enough to bring me to climax." Beverly is lost in her mental images. Though lovely, they do not increase her physiological arousal. In addition, she has accepted the ignorant suggestion that there is something wrong with her physical structure rather than looking into the fact of the matter that no man has worked with her on understanding her physical process. She has never openly communicated with a partner about exactly what kind of touch arouses and excites her.

Charlene is 48 and enjoys sex only 1 percent of the time. She is never orgasmic. She states, "I like oral stimulation: kissing and touching any place on my body. I don't need to have my clitoris stimulated." Since she is not sexually satisfied and she never orgasms, it seems that Charlene does indeed need to have her clitoris stimulated. But perhaps she does not want the vulnerable experience of orgasming in the presence of another. She is unconcerned that she has never experienced orgasm with a partner and does not view herself as having a sexual dysfunction. She is complacent in performing sex without physical satisfaction.

Women who never orgasm with their partners are on the extreme low end of the scale of sexual satisfaction. But it appears that few heterosexual women are sexually satisfied with their partners consistently over time. It is difficult to find a sexually fulfilling sexual partner.

Failure to achieve orgasm during intercourse or sexual exchanges is considered to be a sexual dysfunction. It is also a sexual dysfunction to consistently participate in a sexual exchange that is not sexually satisfying. Heterosexual and bisexual women are reporting a distressingly high number of sexual exchanges that reflect this dysfunction. Only 20 percent of these women report consistently satisfying sexual exchanges with men over their lifetimes. In contrast, we could not imagine American men stating that they achieve orgasm only 53 percent of the times that they have sex with a partner, as these heterosexual women report. Men become concerned with their sexual potency if it is not 100 percent of the time. Amazingly, these women do not see themselves as having a sexual dysfunction. They accept their low rate of satisfaction as normal and even inevitable. These nonorgasmic women do not have a physical problem that prevents orgasm. The reason for their sexual dysfunction is ignorance about how to stimulate their bodies to orgasm, an inability to tell their male partners what they want, and partners who are unconcerned with their sexual satisfaction or who are also ignorant of the female sexual response cycle.

Some women stated that their percentage of sexual satisfaction of orgasm changed significantly over time. They found that their early sexual experiences occurred with no knowledge of what created their orgasm, and their part-

ners were equally ignorant. Often their younger lovers were unwilling to cooperate in doing the sexual activities that brought them satisfaction. After they learned through experience and after they found lovers who were interested in their sexual pleasure, their sexual satisfaction jumped to a much higher percentage of the time.

Carmen, 42, is one of these women. "Sex was zero percent satisfying in my marriage. In my present sexual relationship I had to do a lot of learning. Now that I know, I'd say I'm orgasmic 80 percent of the time. I like to be on top with intercourse, and I rub my clitoris with my hand."

HOW WOMEN ACHIEVE ORGASM WITH A PARTNER

Women expect all kinds of sexual foreplay as a necessary prelude to orgasm in the sexual embrace. Kenya is 25 and says, "I like foreplay, cuddling, being caressed, talking, kissing. Then I can achieve orgasm." Even so, she only achieves orgasm 24 percent of the time. Shelley, 34, achieves orgasm 40 percent of the time. She is more specific than Kenya: "I just let go when my breasts are stimulated. That's where most of my sexual feeling is." Julia, 38, is orgasmic 90 percent of the time. "I like a lot of foreplay, cuddling, and nongenital touching. I like having my breasts and neck kissed. Anywhere on my body, if everything is working right: fingers, toes, skin." Candy, 34, achieves orgasm 45 percent of the time. She defines foreplay differently: "I need emotional stimulation to start with. I want to hear that I'm beautiful and that he loves me." Julie is 58 and is orgasmic 90 percent of the time. She uses her imagination to add to her arousal. "As I start to become sexual with a man, I run some of the physical stimulation of foreplay through my head before it happens, so I don't need long to be ready for intercourse." Aloha is 37 and orgasmic 60 percent of the time: "I like a lot of stimulation. I need a lot of foreplay. I like for a long, slow build-up to intercourse. I like my breasts touched and sucked. I like candles, rituals. I like the smells of sex. I like to watch films with eroticism in them." Camille, 40, is orgasmic 90 percent of the time. She describes her shift in consciousness around sexuality: "I let all the barriers fall away. I allow myself to receive the energy. It's similar to when I do art and dance. I go into a higher consciousness. I'm really with that individual. I don't preconceive."

Clitoral Stimulation

Women do not limit themselves to one sexual activity. They stimulate their partners' bodies and receive full body stimulation themselves. Intercourse is generally always a part of their sexual interaction. But by far, the majority of women state that their way to orgasm is clitoral stimulation. Doubtless, it is the absence of clitoral stimulation with some of their sexual partners that lowers their percentage of times of orgasm.

Carla, 24, orgasms 45 percent of the time. "I don't have an orgasm while

making love, I mean with intercourse. I get turned on with kissing and him touching my breasts, neck, face, side, and stomach. We watch each other masturbate. Sometimes we add vaginal stimulation with his hand or his penis." Janelle, 30, is orgasmic 70 percent of the time. "I get clitoral stimulation from him orally or manually. With vaginal penetration, he or I manually stimulate my clitoris and simultaneously stimulate my breasts. Sometimes we use a vibrator on my clitoris. I can come with my partner breathing and rubbing bodies. When I stimulate him, it can give me an orgasm." Eileen, 30, is orgasmic only 20 percent of the time. "It depends on how worked up I get with masturbation or foreplay. The sexual position makes a difference. Sometimes on top is better. Sometimes I masturbate myself; sometimes he does it to me."

Sanura, 31, is orgasmic 50 percent of the time that she is sexual with a partner. She takes an assertive attitude. She does not talk about sex as something that just happens. Instead she describes what she has her partner do for her. She is directing him. "I need to have cunnilingus or manual simulation. I have him lie beside me and use his hand to stimulate me while we kiss. Or I have him put his hand between my legs and gently explore the whole area from vagina to labia and clitoris. He stimulates and rubs the clitoris, starting slowly and increasing the pace while he kisses me and kisses my breasts. I have my partner use his tongue to stimulate my clitoris. He explores the whole vaginal area. Sometimes he fondles my breasts at the same time."

Paula, 44, has been happily married for 27 years. She achieves orgasm 95 percent of the time with manual stimulation of her clitoris and full-body stroking. "I orgasm with his hand. It is the only good way. His hand stimulates my clitoris. He has wandering hands, I never had to tell him. I expected him to check me out. I read sex books and talked about the books with him. I learned about sex with him."

Cunnilingus

Women who need direct clitoral stimulation love cunnilingus: The partner kisses and licks the woman's labia, vagina, clitoris, and perineum. Lesbians and bisexual women also state that cunnilingus is their preferred sexual activity with men. Robin, 26 and heterosexual, is orgasmic 90 percent of the time. "Usually I get clitoral stimulation by rubbing it with his finger or mine. He may rub it with his penis. He stimulates my clitoris with his tongue and he also kisses my vaginal opening. At the same time he might gently rub my anus with his finger in a circular fashion." Roseann, 22, is orgasmic 30 percent of the time, primarily with oral sex. "What he does varies. He goes in phases of different things. He can tease, flick my clitoris with his tongue and stop and then go back like a tease. Sometimes from beginning to end he won't stop or sometimes he does it harder, presses with his tongue harder. I would be on my back with his head between my legs. But I move around a lot. I'm energetic."

Taneisha, 23, has two reasons to prefer cunnilingus. She is orgasmic with it 80 percent of the time. Second, she is a virgin and does not want to perform vaginal intercourse until she is married. She is strongly Christian. The restriction of her sexual activities to oral sex is how she resolves being sexual without being married. "When I first date someone I let him know that we're not having intercourse, and they choose if they want to date me. Paul, my fiancé, was the first sex partner I had, and he was kissing my body, and that's how cunnilingus happened. It wasn't planned in advance, and I never said 'yes' to this and 'no' to intercourse. It took almost a year for that to happen between Paul and me."

For most women, however, cunnilingus is combined with other sexual activities. Mitzi, 32, is highly sexual and is orgasmic 99 percent of the time. "It depends on the man. I've had a different way of orgasming with every one. Mostly it's been oral sex. One guy I dated wasn't that good with oral sex, so it was with intercourse and my vibrator. He was on top, and I held the vibrator while he was on top of me. He sat up in an upright position, sat back a little bit and he'd rub my breasts. My favorite way is getting to the point where I can orgasm by oral sex and then getting on top of him and having intercourse." Rachel, 35 and bisexual, is orgasmic 60 percent of the time, and she prefers cunnilingus, with her partner's finger in her vagina stimulating the g-spot. Sometimes she is close to orgasm in intercourse. Intercourse is exciting and arousing, but she is not orgasmic with it.

Some women cannot allow themselves the receptive and passive position of cunnilingus. Lily, 20, is orgasmic 60 percent of the time. "I won't allow cunnilingus. I like to give pleasure. I can't imaging lying back and enjoying it." Kenya, 25: "I don't like cunnilingus, but I do like fellatio. Cunnilingus doesn't seem sanitary." Contrary to Kenya's belief, cunnilingus is quite sanitary. When the vagina is healthy there are fewer dangerous bacteria present in it than there are in the human mouth. Kissing a woman's vulva is more sanitary than French kissing her mouth.

A rare woman does not like cunnilingus for a different reason. Pam, 31, says that "cunnilingus is too intense, it's almost uncomfortable." Pam does not like direct clitoral stimulation, and finds she orgasms best through intercourse.

Intercourse

While all heterosexual women say they enjoy intercourse, few can achieve orgasm with intercourse alone. The most successful position is with the woman on top, with either her partner or herself using a hand to stimulate her clitoris. June, 28, is orgasmic 80 percent of the time with this method. "I come the usual way through intercourse and masturbation at the same time. He or I manually stimulate my clitoris." Jody, bisexual, 25, is orgasmic 97 percent of the time with men. She has her preferred pattern. "I like foreplay of manual and oral stimulation to my clitoris, followed by intercourse with me in control. Otherwise, if I don't come that way he'll usually help or hold me while I masturbate." Piper, 22, is orgasmic 90 percent of the time she is sexual. She says, "Usually anything works. The quickest way to orgasm is oral stimulation. Or if I'm on top during intercourse. Being on the bottom works the least."

Trina, 24, is married. She is more orgasmic with her current husband than she was with other men. She has been orgasmic only 10 percent of the times she's been sexual. She has found exactly what works for her. "I usually have to be on top in a sitting position. I have to be able to control the amount of pressure I put on my genitals. I like to press hard, my mound against his pelvic area above his penis. Sometimes we start slow and get faster and faster until I find the right spot to orgasm. I don't have orgasms from intercourse very often. I touch my own clitoris in doggy-style sex and he plays with his hands on my clit and with my anus a little bit. All the parts of my vagina, not just the clit, inside the lips and my hair." Shaniqua, 24, is orgasmic 65 percent of the time and finds she, too, needs to be in control of the movement. "Usually if I'm on top I can come because then I can control the direction of the clitoral stimulation. It's a lot easier for me to move around and know exactly what spot to hone in on than it is for him if he's on top."

While the female superior position is preferred, some women are able to orgasm while lying on their backs. Lily,

20, is orgasmic 60 percent of the time. "I guess it's clitoral stimulation. I get it a lot when we use the missionary position. I know he is enjoying it, and it gets more intense, and it brings me higher emotionally. When I'm on top, it doesn't stimulate my clitoris." Heather, bisexual, is orgasmic 75 percent of the time and also is orgasmic with intercourse. "I like all kinds of positions: top, bottom, missionary. I guess I like a lot of hands and tongue. But I can get off with vaginal intercourse."

Thrusting

For some women, the thrusting motion of intercourse brings them to orgasm. Most positions are satisfying. Kristie, 23, who is orgasmic 65 percent of the time, is one of these. "For me it's intercourse. It's not really the clitoris area, but a thrusting against the pubic bone." Skye, bisexual and 35, is orgasmic 90 percent of the time. She is one of the few women who reach orgasm through intercourse alone. "Through intercourse, I can come with only that. I like that thrusting. My clit seems to be up higher. I can't achieve orgasm from behind, rear entry position. Easiest is on my back. Cunnilingus can work. I don't come with manual stimulation."

Vibrators

Several women stated that they need the intense stimulation of a vibrator to achieve orgasm, so they bring this toy into their partnered sexuality.

Barbara

Barbara, 52, has learned to pay attention to her body's reactions. "I need a lot of clitoral stimulation. I used to be more easily orgasmic than I am now, but I always needed clitoral stimulation. One boyfriend was a master with his tongue. Others were good with their fingers, but for the last few years I just use a vibrator. It used to be a source of stress for me. I felt I had to have an orgasm more for my partner's ego than for my own satisfaction. So there was a certain amount of pressure involved and anxiety. Then I met one partner who simply said, 'Why don't you massage yourself?' And I said, 'Thank you!' It was so much easier than having to give directions. So that's what I've done since then.

"Sometimes I use a vibrator. One of my early boyfriends bought me a vibrator. It was great. That was one that fit over your hand. Now I have a big one with a disk head and a long handle. It's a vibrator and not a dildo. I just use it myself and they can stimulate other parts of my body, holding my breasts, kissing me, or caressing me. I like to have a hard cock inside me. I like to be stimulated all over. I like a finger in my ass sometimes. I have used a dildo for masturbating sometimes with a partner. I decided that I could introduce the partner to the toys. There was some other intimacy involved with it."

Molly, bisexual and 35, has been orgasmic only 60 percent of the time she was with a male partner. Now in her marriage and using a vibrator, she is more likely to experience orgasm. "I usually use my vibrator after we've made love for a while and he's come. He fucks me with his fingers, and I use my vibrator on my clitoris. Once or twice he masturbated me to orgasm, but I know so much better how to get myself off. I use the vibrator. I'm more comfortable with that. Frequently he stimulates my nipples with his hands."

Leah, 45 and bisexual, has been orgasmic 20 percent of the time with men. She also needs the vibrator to achieve orgasm. "I usually come with the vibrator. With a few men, I've come with intercourse. But rarely has oral sex worked, or finger play. I like to have a finger inside me while he performs oral sex. Or if he is just using his hand, I like one finger in the vagina and one on the clitoris. I like having him inside me with rear entry. Then I use a towel between the vibrator and my clitoris. If he has already come, I use a dildo and a vibrator with him next to me. Then he can kiss and stroke me, have a hand on my lower abdomen, or nibble my neck and ears. Men's reactions to the vibrator can vary. Some are uncomfortable. They don't like the noise or the intensity as a distraction. But anyone I've been ongoing with as a sexual partner has been okay with it. I've been with a lot of open-minded men."

THE SEXUAL DANCE

Sex with a man is not limited to a script of outercourse or foreplay, followed by penetration, thrusting, and sleep. What women do with a partner can vary depending on the couple's enthusiasm for experimentation and play. Trying many sexual positions and practicing with different kinds of stroking and kissing can keep sex interesting and exciting. Star, a 48-year-old bisexual, is orgasmic 80 percent of the time: "I can come different ways. I like to have men finger fuck me. I like my g-spot stimulated with his fingers. I can get clitoral orgasms from my nipples being sucked. I cannot come from fucking alone. I like cunnilingus. I like my breasts and clitoris stimulated at the same time. While his tongue is on my clit, his hands can be massaging my breasts and gently squeezing my nipples. I like foreplay: making out, back-and-forth stuff where we take turns exciting each other's bodies. I'm usually active in order to have an orgasm. I'm not a pillow princess."

Cheryl Jean

Cheryl Jean, 42 and heterosexual, has a wide repertoire of favorite sexual activities. "First off, I'm really sensitive orally. I really like to kiss. My nipples are also really sensitive, so I like if someone kisses me and is gentle with my nipples at the same time, gently touching them. I'm just as turned on by caressing the man. I like to touch his nipples and move around. Once I am aroused by caressing, kissing, and touching each other, I like the feel of the penis. I like fellatio, and I really like just to feel how everything progresses, the changes the penis goes through. My whole body is sensitive. I like to be with a man who can hold off his orgasm for a long time. I like to have one encounter last for one and one-half hours. I like to move in different positions. I want to have an orgasm in all the positions I like. I don't want to be rushed and I don't want to have to pick only one position for an orgasm. I like them on top of me, my legs on their shoulders; squatting on top of him; and leaning over a bed with rear entry penetration. Once there is penetration I like a steady rhythm. I think my clitoris is exposed enough that it is stimulated by movement and the different positions affect the feelings. I like the larger penis, I really do. If someone is a sensitive, careful, involved lover, I can have a good experience, even if he has an average-size penis. But if I can have all the factors, a large penis is one of them. I think it makes a difference because the deeper penetration seems to touch areas that aren't affected by a smaller penis. If someone has a larger penis and we move into different positions, I don't have to worry about it slipping out. I think men with a larger penis are more confident and are not so traditional and try different things. You can feel more with a larger cock. There are more sensations. You can feel that more often and longer. However, a large penis can't help a poor lover.

"I do like anal sex but not with a man who is large. That is not fun. That hurts. But with a man who's average-size, I like it. I can have an orgasm from it. Sometimes I touch myself. During anal sex I masturbate more." It is clear that Cheryl Jean has been inventive, adventuresome, and creative in her sexual adventures. She has discovered her sexual responses to a wide range of sexual activities. She knows how her body responds and how to move along her sexual response cycle. It is also obvious that she know how to direct her partner into the activities that will excite and please her the most.

Ryfka

Though once married, Ryfka, 47, is now a lesbian. She says on rare occasions she will be sexual with a man just for the fun of it. Ryfka is highly sexual and enjoys her sex play with men. "I orgasm easily. Men love to fuck me. They think the ultimate goal of sexuality is orgasm. They see it as proof of their sexual prowess. They say, 'How many orgasms can I make you have in an hour?' But it's no great feat. I can orgasm from playing with my nipples; pinching my nipples; my breasts being manipulated; having my hair on my head pulled; my clit slapped; fucking me in the pussy; fucking me in my ass; clitoral stimulation by tongue, fingers, mouth, hip, knee. I feel blessed. I have this body that is responsive. I get excited easily, and I respond positively to all stimulation. If it's someone I'm emotionally involved with, I don't let them touch my nipples or my clit because I don't want to have an orgasm too fast. I like to keep the sexual tension high. With men in general, once a woman has an orgasm they think you're done. So I don't want to have one right away and be done. I want to delay it. I like to have my fingers sucked. That can give me an orgasm."

Tsuruko

Tsuruko, 33 and heterosexual, has a variety of possibilities when she decides to be sexual. The first step is to find a man with certain qualities. "I want a man who is gentle and sensitive in terms of kinestheic qualities. I like touchy-feely men. They are more in touch with their senses, and they notice my responses that aren't verbal. I expect them to sense things, like that when I take a deep breath during sex, it's a good sign. Then I don't have to say, 'That's wonderful.' I need a partner who is communicative. I learn by example. It makes it okay for me to say, 'I want to do this.' It's so hard to be intimate with someone. I've learned that you owe yourself a certain responsibility for being active with a partner. If you're not, you won't be satisfied. And you'll be pissed, resent him, and cut off the relationship."

Tsuruko has learned that there are phases of getting comfortable with a new man. "When I am with a new lover, I have found that we're both shy about sex. We sleep together and do a little of mutual masturbation, but it takes a while before we're comfortable enough to really do sex. It could take two weeks to a month of sleeping with him. It can't be too much, too fast. There has to be more trust built up between us. We talk about it, but we don't want to risk the emotional consequences."

Once she has decided to make love, she begins slowly. "I like there to be a mutual amount of passion. A good place to start is to notice if the man is responsive. I start biting on his neck and hopefully he would respond and bite me on the neck. I like kissing, and I like it when his kissing roams over my breasts and thighs. I like to grab his rear and legs and stomach and rub his hips a little. We kiss on the mouth for a while: a little bit of sucking on my tongue, and I suck on his tongue while our hands are on each other's bodies. We have started with our shirts off, but not my bra. He rubs me through my bra. Then, my bra and pants come off and we rub each other's genitals through our underwear.

"Then I straddle him. We rub our pubic bones together and grind our pelvises together. I straddle his leg and rub his leg against my pubic area. I don't want to rush to jump on top of him. The underwear comes off at this point. I go down on him and with my hands I stimulate his balls and between the balls. Underneath the balls there is sensitive skin—the perineum. I stroke him there and have my mouth on his penis while I cup his bottom with my other hand and get him very excited. He's erect, and I get excited by getting him excited.

"Then he gives me oral sex while I lie on my back. He eases his tongue into my labia at a certain angle. There is a thin vertical angle that feels the best. With the tip of his tongue he stimulates the clit and the outside of the lips. Then he goes in a little deeper with his tongue and then back to the clit. He uses his finger to stimulate the clit and his tongue is inside the lips and I melt on the sheets right there if it's done right. It's different than if he puts his penis into the vagina. It's a lot softer. Many men fumble around with cunnilingus, and it's a nightmare. It's hard to tell them what I want. One lover knew his way around. He was just amazing. We had nothing else in common, but he was great with his mouth.

"At this point I have different scenarios of postions. I don't usually do all these things in one session. One scenario is that I want to insert his penis into me. He lies on his back and I straddle him and ease him into me slowly. It works better if I control it because my muscles are tense. So the penis is slowly inserted just a little bit, getting my muscles ready for deep insertion. That goes on for a while until the vaginal muscles are eased up. He thrusts with his hips gently, waiting until it is comfortable. He has to be somewhat passive. Then as I get loosened up, I am ready to go. Once he is mostly inside, I lean over on his chest and we roll over so I am on the bottom and he can be more aggressive. I am more passive, but I'm actively thrusting as well. Then we switch to another position because the angle gets old, and there are so many angles that feel great. We sit up together. I straddle him; he is sitting upward and I am somewhat on my knees for leverage so I can go up and down. We can kiss in as many of these positions as we can. The kissing and the fondling of my breasts is a nice side dish; it keeps it rolling along.

"Another scenario and one of my favorites is to stimulate the g-spot. We spoon on the same side. We lay on our right side. He and I together guide the penis in from the rear. He can kiss my back or shoulders and cup my breasts if it's possible. Or grab onto the hips and thrust a bunch. It feels real good. This position is logistically different depending on how he is built. If his penis is bigger, he might be able to touch my body better. If it is smaller he has to use his hand to hold it in more.

"The beginning of the scenario when I am on top gets me going and excited. I don't have an orgasm, but it really feels good. In all these positions, I don't get tired of the feeling because we keep changing things. The rear entry is really satisfying because it stimulates that spot you can't get to through most of the other positions.

"I can have a really strong orgasm from the rear entry position. But eventually any one of the positions gives me an orgasm. At that point I am ready to keep going until he has his orgasm. At the end I like to hug and he can fall asleep. I might be keyed up and read for a while. I would be cuddly and happy and if he fell asleep I rub his back and it's okay. I lie there and enjoy how I am feeling.

"I'm not comfortable with more than one orgasm. It's too much stimulation. All the synapses are firing, it feels like . . . I can't explain it. I seem to think I get more out of the friction of intercourse than the orgasm. It's more satisfying to get in there and have the friction, like an itch getting scratched. It's as satisfying as an orgasm. Sometimes it's better to just have the friction and not the orgasm with all my nerves firing. Sometimes it's nice to just have that. I don't have to get off every time."

Tsuruko has learned from experience how to conduct her sexual exchange to guarantee her satisfaction. She has found that getting started with a new partner must include communicating sexual styles and interests. Despite her awareness, it is still sometimes difficult to immediately talk about what she wants sexually. Mutual trust and an emotional comfort are also a necessity for her sexual experience.

Lelah

Lelah, 22, is married and has had several sex partners. She admits that it sounds shallow, but physical appearance is important to her when choosing a sex partner. "Physical attractiveness does count. He has to be fit, in shape, not overweight. He cannot have a belly. I like nice hair. He must be clean. I want him showered and smelling good. He has to have a butt; something I can grab and there'll be meat in my hand. He also has to make eye contact. When he speaks to me he has to look in my eyes." She says of his personality that "I don't want an aggressive man. He shouldn't mention sex because then I'm not curious. I don't want a man who brags about sex."

As she thinks of an ideal sexual encounter, Lelah reminisces of one particular evening with her husband. "We went to the living room. (I don't like sex in the bedroom so much.) We pushed all the furniture against the walls so the middle of the room was empty, and then we laid blankets and sheets down. Then Brian went to get Chinese food while I made a hot pot of tea. I put candles around the living room and we were both showered. I put plates out and when he came back with the food, I poured the tea. I was wearing lingerie—a white lace teddy, g-string, black spike heels, and make-up. Brian took all his clothes off by the door and came in the room naked. We just sat and talked and ate a little bit with chopsticks. Then Brian leaned over and gave me a kiss on my cheek and told me that I looked really nice. I said, 'Thank you.' He began by giving me little kisses across my cheek and worked his way to my lips. We gave little kisses and started to French kiss. I put my hands on his cheeks, and he kissed my ear and nibbled and licked my ear and earlobe. We exchanged kisses across the face. I like to kiss his eyelids and kiss his ear and put my tongue in his ears.

"Then he pulled the straps of the teddy down and pulled it off. He put his hands on my shoulders and pushed me down. Then he put some of the Chinese beef sauce on my nipples and started licking it off. I closed my eyes and arched my back. Then he cupped my breast while he was licking it and cupped the other breast. He alternated from one breast to the other. He pushed both breasts together so he could lick both nipples by sticking his tongue out. I asked him to bite my nipples. He did it gently, and I asked him to bite harder. He finally bit hard enough and I got a whole vibration through my body almost like an orgasm. Because it was so overwhelming I wrapped my legs around his waist and squeezed. Then he moved back up to my mouth and started kissing me. He trailed down to my ear and from my ear down to my breast.

"We rolled over. After that one shock of vibration I was energized, and I got on my knees. I was on top, and I love kissing his eyes. I moved down his chin, his neck, and his ear. I like to stick my tongue in his ear and flick his ear until he starts to shudder a bit. Then I moved down his chest. He has a hairy chest, and I licked around his nipple. When his nipple was erect I flicked his nipple with my tongue, and then I started to suck on it. I rolled his nipple between my teeth and he just shook and groaned. Then he pushed my head away from his nipple, and I sucked and bit the other one. Then I did little kisses down his chest till I got to his penis. I kissed around his penis and around his thigh. I did little kisses from the base of his penis to the tip. I got more of the sauce and put it on the tip of his penis. I sucked the very tip of his penis and licked the sauce from his penis. I twirled my tongue around his penis while my finger was in his anus going back and forth. He said, 'I'm going to come.' I kept my finger in his anus and he came. It turns me on to stick my finger in his anus.

"He said, 'That was so nice!' I washed my hand with soap, and then I had something to drink. He said, 'It's my turn now.' He took my shoes off. He kissed me on the lips and moved down my chest and kissed my breasts as he motioned me back to the floor. Then he laced my hands with his and lifted my arms above my head and kissed my breast. Then he moved over to the side of my breast, then to my armpit, and then up my arm. He then

came back down and licked across my armpit. The side of my breast is sensitive and he flicked his tongue back and forth there. He worked his way with kisses and licks down my rib cage and to my vagina, then to the side of my thigh. He wrapped his arms under my legs and lifted them. He kissed my thigh past my knee and down my calf to my ankle. I had my head back, and I closed my eyes. I cupped my breasts and played with my nipples. He worked his way down my leg with kisses and licks. Then he came up again and licked across my vagina back and forth. He opened my legs apart and put more of the beef sauce on my vagina and on my clit and licked it off. He moved to my clit. He flicked it with his tongue and sucked on it. My legs and everything felt numb. I started to shake and he stopped and sucked on my outer lips. He licked up my vagina and my clit. I like it when he sticks his tongue in my vagina. He did it fast, and I moved my body forward and backwards. He held the hood of my clit back with one hand and sucked on the glans. He stopped when I was close to an orgasm and went to lick the vagina. When he licked my clit, he finger fucked me with one hand. I asked him to roll my clit between his teeth. He sucked on it until I had an orgasm, and I ejaculated so his chin and chest were wet. He told me I tasted good."

When Lelah continues the interaction to perform intercourse, she enjoys all the sensations but she does not expect an orgasm. She feels aroused from the ongoing sexual activity and excited when she experiences her ability to pleasure her husband. Here she describes the second act of the evening.

"After we have eaten and talked about what we just did, we start kissing. Without a lot of foreplay, he got on top of me. I like to hold his hands next to my shoulders and he inserted his penis without using his hands. He inserted really slowly and all the way as far as his penis would go. Then he came out and then in again real slow. I put my arms around him on his back and his arms were under my shoulders. He moved faster and not so deep and then another deep stroke when I didn't expect it. I wrapped my legs around his waist while he moved in a circular motion and I moved in the other direction. We created a pattern. In the deep stroke he French kissed me. He asked me, 'Can I come?' and I said 'no,' and he took it out. I turned him over and I got on top and used my hand to insert him into my vagina. I straddled him and rocked back and forth. He had his hands on my hips and rocked with me. I moved in a circular motion, and we found a pattern. I propped up on my feet and squatted and supported my upper body on my elbows so I could move up and down. Again he said, 'I'll come.' So I stopped and kissed him. He was weak. I turned around on the penis so my back was facing him. And I arched my back while he put his hands on my ass. I rocked back and forth. Then I squatted and moved up and down hard and deep. Again he told me he's coming. He grabbed my hips and pulled me down, and it felt so erotic to feel his penis pumping. He grabbed me and held me there. He told me how good that felt. Then I lay next to him, and we talked a little bit. We always comment on the smell of it. Then I fell asleep in his arms."

For Lelah, the completion of her sexuality includes sharing the eroticism of her husband, the pleasure of the sensuality of intercourse, the companionship of the act, and the comfort of sleeping together.

Artemis

Artemis is 53 and found that her sexuality improved as she approached menopause. The first element required for this change was to become assertive. "In the first years of my sex life I would say, 'Oh, I don't know. Oh, anything is fine.' And basically I'd be like the carpet that you step out of the shower onto. This sexual energy didn't come until I was 47. Sex became unbelievable. It also became 'I'm gonna do it, and it's my way,' 'cause I wasn't afraid or intimated by any male."

When she decides to be sexual, the quality Artemis wants in a partner is a psychic connection and the knowledge that the man is not in a committed relationship with someone else. "The first part of the sexual act is in terms of the man. I know him in a moment. It's an eyeball connection. It's emotional and there are no words for it. In my younger years, if I had that eyeball connection I did not have boundaries, and if the man was married I still would go for it, which brought a great deal of suffering. Now I refuse if he is not unattached."

With these qualities ascertained, Artemis describes a romance. "One of the nicest affairs I had was with Douglas. There was no commitment, so there was freedom in the sexual expression. We had a date, and I drove over to his apartment. I found that thinking about a man who I want to be with . . . thinking about being with him sexually helps a lot. It's the anticipation. I walked into his place, and we never made it out of the living room. We made that eye connection. He walked up to me to kiss me, and we stood there kissing and feeling. I was quite surprised that we didn't melt a hole in the floor! The kissing at that stage was so magnetic, so unbelievable, energizing. He removed my clothing, one piece at a time. We kissed and rubbed against each other. Then I removed a piece of his clothing. We continued kissing, and I never gave a thought to how tired my legs might be. It was a good 30 minutes. It was so intense and so vivid. And no guilt. I came there with the full intention of having a full affair with him. And the nice part was, he was waiting with the same intention. While we were standing there, he knelt down and he gave me oral sex. It was all very gentle and enjoyable and flowing.

"He was an active type. He took full responsibility for being a lover. He did not just want to get fucked. And he loves women, he loves the female body. After we were finally both disrobed, he carried me into the bedroom, which was just wonderful—the damsel and the knight. It was very romantic. The sexual pleasure of his penis was wonderful. I like to be on the bottom and I like to have my hips elevated somewhat with him on his knees, and he just knew that. When I was nearing my climax he moved forward on top of me, undulating his body over mine and embracing me, creating an effervescent orgasm. When he fell forward on me, his pubic bone massaged my clitoris. There was something about his penis. There is a place inside my vagina that he just knew to zing, and I climaxed. It's a spot that has to be reached with a large penis. The size of the penis is important. It has to be thick enough to massage the walls of the vagina and its long enough, say 8 inches, and a thrusting little dickens.

"When I had sex with him I had wonderful climaxes. He always had enough endurance to wait for me, to be patient and enjoy mine before he would have his. His orgasm was not at the same time as mine. It closely followed. He would massage my back afterwards in a loving, wonderful, kind way—like he really cared; he nuzzled my neck.

"He was a nuzzler. Later during our relationship, if I would be in the kitchen, he would come and give me a kiss and touch me in my warm spots and get me fired up. Get me cooking while I was cooking!"

For Artemis, the attitude of her lover, his endurance, and the size of his penis are all factors that contribute to how memorable the tryst will be. She repeats her preference for a certain type of penis. "With a different lover, I was in a hot tub. I was on top, and he was sitting on the bench in the spa. We were making love, and I just had one orgasm after the other. I was doing the movement up and down, and he was thrusting. It was a situation of fitting. We just fit, my vagina and his penis. It just kept going like firecrackers! I must have had 15 orgasms. I thought, 'Hey, this is fun!' And then we decided to rest. I don't know why!" Artemis has found that the person, the environment, and the position of intercourse all contribute to creating unforgettable sex.

May

May, 30, traces a development in her sexual experiences with men that has been affected by acquiring a sexually transmitted disease and altering her sexual activities so that she always practices safe sex. "How I obtain an orgasm has changed over the years. When I was younger, the most effective way was oral sex and penetration of the vagina with his fingers. That has changed somewhat because one lover eventually gave me genital herpes from which I've had a few outbreaks. Because of him, oral sex has not been an option for me for several years. With a recent lover, it was from manual stimulation or using the vibrator and his hand, or I rubbed against his stomach and straddled him. We didn't have oral sex and no intercourse because he didn't want to use condoms because he couldn't keep an erection well while wearing one. And he disliked latex. Intercourse wasn't an option without condoms, so we didn't, and it wasn't a big issue. He didn't care about having intercourse. He was 20 years older than me. I don't have an orgasm with men whose penis is large, like his was. It's uncomfortable, so then I'd orgasm with his hand." When May became more active in the bisexual community, she found a male bisexual sex partner. Interacting with him opened an opportunity for more variety in her sexual life. "Currently my orgasm is with intercourse or his hand with three fingers in my vagina and some on the clitoris and thrusting motions. And also if I wear a teeny vibrator in a harness over my hips and another harness with a dildo and I fuck him in the ass, I come from the sense of the vibrator on me and psychologically fucking him. Or I come when he sucks on the dildo and it vibrates along with the other vibrator. I really like dating bisexual guys; straight men don't want to be fucked."

May has a different opinion about penis size than Barbara and Cheryl Jean. She does not enjoy a large penis. This is another example of the individual differences among women regarding preferred sexual activities. In addition, when she became a bisexual she met bisexual men in activist groups. These men encouraged her to expand her repertoire of sexual activities into exercising more role reversals. Her sexuality with men took on a different dimension with these partners who brought new activities to the exchange.

In contrast to May, Rebecca, 25, found that bisexuality opened her to new expectations about the sexual interlude after she had experienced sex with a woman. She had been orgasmic 10 percent of the time she has been with men when she was heterosexual.

Rebecca

"I only had orgasms with one male partner. I had orgasms with him without intercourse. I don't have orgasms with intercourse. Cunnilingus is my favorite method. Fingers are okay. I never had an orgasm just from penetration. After being with a woman, when sex doesn't mean penis-in-vagina, it all changes. Boundaries get blurred if one is sexual without intercourse. What constitutes sex with men changed for me. Being sexual is simply anything that turns me on. It could be sitting in a restaurant with our feet in each other's laps. But having sex has to include orgasm or genital contact with hand, mouth, or penis." Rebecca touches on an aspect of sexuality with men that shifted after she was sexual with a woman. The usual heterosexual procedure of all activity focused on the approach toward intercourse was altered. Intercourse was no longer the centerpiece of the sexual interaction with a man.

THE SEXUAL REVOLUTION

The sexual revolution in terms of sex with men will have happened when all women learn as they begin their sexual activities with men that there are certain elements that make for a better and more fulfilling erotic encounter. The first element for a woman is to create in her mind an outlook that removes guilt and shame about her sexuality and to replace it with a positive desire and intent to enjoy pleasure with this particular man. For some women, this means developing their self-esteem in order to know they are deserving of a completely satisfying and deliciously pleasurable sexual life. The quest of a successful sex life is a woman's own responsibility, in cooperation with her lover.

A strong sense of self-awareness can make a woman a better communicator when she is expressing her sexual desires to her partner. Barbara is a woman who believes that her self-assurance is the key to her ability to genuinely enjoy sex. When she achieved a high level of assertiveness and self-acceptance, her sex life became ecstatic.

Barbara

"Lately I care less about what men think of me. They have to accept me for who I am. I have had some men react negatively to using a vibrator in our sex play. Some men felt that they weren't adequate for me, that they couldn't satisfy me. I would try to assure them that this was my own personal sexuality. For many years I was more concerned with their feelings, of being a good lover to them. Somehow I've evolved more to accepting who I am, and they need to accept who I am. Also, sex is very important to me. I enjoy the sensations and the intimacy of it. So it is a matter of finding lovers who are accepting of me. One lover recently, we screwed day and night and we each had a dozen orgasms. He was so proud of himself. He said he tied his record!

"Orgasm is an indescribably sweet feeling and pure pleasure, a funny sensation. It is too bad it is over so quickly. It seems rare that I've been with men who like the whole act. There is so much pleasure to be derived from all of it: the touching and talking and the anticipation."

Barbara is confident and relaxed about the woman she has become. As a result, her sexual experiences are intensely fulfilling.

The second element for a woman is to understand her own sexual response cycle: to know how to stimulate her own body to orgasm and to be able to inform her partner of what sort of touch works best. Women need a partner who is understanding. They need to have developed a sense of intimacy and trust in order to fully relax with him. There is a feeling of vulnerability in sex, and women want to feel safe and secure with their male partner. This emotion of companionable closeness becomes the first stage of arousal

for many women. They also need a mental attitude of readiness for sex with the forethought that time is being set aside for the erotic encounter.

Women search for a desirable and willing male sexual partner with whom they feel safe when vulnerable. Most women begin this search as a teenager. Communication skills, exploring emotional intimacy, listening and being listened to, all these are only learned from exploration. The woman must learn to trust her intuition and to assess a man's receptivity to intimacy. This is an ongoing process that is developed by making attempts to connect with someone and evaluating its success.

When women have unfulfilled sexual liaisons, they are all too ready to blame themselves. It takes experience with several partners before a woman can judge whether her needs are being met. If a woman has a string of uninspired and selfish partners, she has no way of knowing when sex is unsatisfying, because she has no positive experience to relate it to. She may come to believe that sex is simply overrated.

Annie found that "the transformation to a good sex life came from having a sex partner who really wanted to please me. That changed me. At first it was so hard to accept, since I was so used to jerks. I used to try to get what little pleasure I could while they were doing their thing. My husband was the main influence in my transformation. One man before him tried to encourage me as to how I could come. But now I feel like I deserve it. Finally after years of being treated well in my marriage, I realize that is the way it should be."

Annie had the necessary knowledge to engage in great sex. She was aware of how to achieve her own orgasm and was knowledgeable about the male sexual response. But she had a series of sexual liaisons where both she and her partners were trying to achieve sexual gratification but not concerned with each other. When she was with a man who was unconcerned about her orgasm, her sexual assertiveness was seen as conflictive and communication was futile. Finally, she became involved with a man who was willing to give her pleasure and orgasms. Her husband approached her sexually with an attitude of cooperation and enthusiasm. With him, she found a partner who valued her and her sexuality flowered.

If, like Annie, a woman develops a successful and committed partnership when young, the life changes that happen as a result of maturity will lead both herself and her partner to deeper intimacy. For other women, dating can be a lifelong process, consisting of relationships of varying duration. Each relationship marks a level of growth. The strong and confident woman needs to choose her own direction with her partner and not passively follow his lead.

Regardless of age, women who demand certain responses from their mate are happiest with the relationship. A woman with high self-esteem and independence is able to leave a man who does not meet her needs. She takes the risk that she can be alone for a time and can wait for a man who welcomes an equal relationship.

The third necessity for good sex with a man is to unlearn sexual passivity and to become sexually active. Only 25 percent of heterosexual women stated that the most important aspect of their relationship with a lover was sexual. Companionship was the main reason to have a partner. Younger women admit that they engage in sexual intercourse to comply with the man's request—believing that if they refuse, he will leave them. For some women, this becomes a lifelong pattern. They feel lucky and happily surprised if a man is interested in satisfying them sexually, and they do not expect to achieve sexual satisfaction. Of course, many women do expect that a sexual exchange should include orgasms for both participants, but most heterosexual women state that most of their satisfaction in sexual exchanges are derived from cuddling and affection in bed. Although these are real human needs, they are not sexual needs. Such women are foregoing their sexual needs because they have a resistant partner, a man who is not interested in satisfying them. Or, they lack the ability to be sexually assertive and to tell their lover what they like or need. The reason for this may be their upbringing in a culture that encourages women to be passive. Or worse, it may mean that they are unable to accept themselves as sexual beings. Sexually aggressive and expressive women are called "sluts," "whores," and "castrating." It takes inner strength, self-awareness, and acceptance of one's sensual self for a woman to present herself to her lover as a freely sexually expressive woman who knows what she wants.

How does a woman travel from sexual passivity to erotic expressiveness?

Some women do not seem interested in making the trip. All of the women with whom I spoke saw themselves as sexually open (this quality was what allowed them to volunteer to be interviewed). Yet, most settled for a low rate of sexual satisfaction. What causes this acceptance of low erotic stimulation? Either they have low standards of sexual satisfaction or they are unwilling to risk communicating their needs with their male partners. They are afraid to move from a passive sexual object who meets her lover's needs, to a sexually assertive woman who knows how to ask for and receive erotic pleasure within the sexual exchange.

Eight percent of the heterosexual women describe themselves as sexually passive. They allow their partner to initiate and direct the sexual exchange. It is this sexual passivity that creates the situation where a woman is denied her orgasm. Even if her lover desires to bring her to orgasm, without feedback from her, he may fail. A passive woman only allows herself the role of satisfying her man's desire and creates a situation where there is no room for her own expression of her sexual needs.

Sixty-two percent of heterosexual women describe themselves as both sexually active and passive. For some women, this means a give and take of sexual activity. But for many women, being sexually active means that they will give their male lover the stimulation that he requests. It does not mean that they will direct him in how to make love to themselves. Thirty percent of heterosexuals see themselves as sexually active. These are the women who

are comfortable with and enjoy the sexual exchange. They understand their sexual response cycle and are familiar with the male cycle. They experiment with what feels good, and they communicate their needs with their partner in order to elicit cooperation in bed.

It is possible to move from sexual passivity to become actively involved in the sexual process. Sanura relates how she made this reversal in attitude. Sanura's first experience with sexual intercourse was limited and unsatisfactory. However, she was able to evolve from unsatisfactory teenage experiences to a sexually fulfilled woman. She began with a self-searching analysis of her past experiences.

Sanura

"I started looking at things that detracted from my having the total sexual experience. What I found was that my participation in the process was oriented around the gratification of my partner. I found that he and I both were working toward his gratification. I started a gradual shift toward learning to pay attention to my needs, my desires, what I wanted. I began to take the initiative in going about getting those needs met. What I found out during that process was that a lot of the things I was doing to please my partner were not necessarily contributing to my own arousal. In fact, they were somewhat distracting.

"I immediately started focusing on the things in the sexual relationship that were stimulating to me, instead of what was stimulating to my partner. I started doing things that were going to turn me on. Not that I wasn't concerned about my partner's gratification, but I think that men know how to take care of their own needs. It's just that when I did something like oral sex [fellatio], I shifted my focus from thinking what would feel good for him. From, 'How could I do this?' to 'How does this feel to take this penis into my mouth?' And, 'What areas on his penis do I want to explore? What do I want to do with it?' So basically I was shifting my focus from 'What will turn him on?' to 'What will turn me on?'

"The reason that experiencing sexual fulfillment is so difficult for me and other women is that we are trained to take care of other people's needs first. Nowhere does this become more prevalent than in a sexual relationship. We're taught that the sex act is intercourse and that we are supposed to climax at the same time as the man. When we start to focus on ourselves we feel very selfish. I know so many women who tell me they don't like oral sex performed on them because they can't stand the focus being on them. That's all the training of being a woman in society, that it's not okay to kick back and let someone else take care of your needs. The irony is that your sexual relationship is going to be so much better if you're stimulated, too, because your partner is going to have a much better time with someone who is getting their needs met.

"As a teenager, a lot of the things I thought were part of the preparation for having sex—a negligee, my hair fixed, my makeup ready—I discovered these things were just distractions because they're all part of creating some kind of an image at the expense of the self. To truly get to know your sexual being, you have to be in connection with that self."

Sanura made a transformation from male-focused sexuality to female-focused sexuality. Her metamorphosis involved more than taking the initiative. It included a psychological evolution from male-influenced sexuality to a deep confrontation with her self and body. It required Sanura to explore her own sensual and sexual experiences, to revel in her physical experiences, and to allow another person to respond to her needs as a complete, physical being.

Women have to overcome the idea that male lovers are the sexual experts. Since women's sexual responses are so unique, even a knowledgeable man cannot always predict what kind of stimulation will be effective. The woman has to be the one who teaches him about her sexuality. A satisfying passionate exchange requires that both partners have an understanding of one another's sexual response. Since many men have no comprehension of women's, it is the task of the woman to thoroughly inform her partner about the kind of stimulation that she enjoys and that leads her to orgasm.

Women learn from childhood to silence themselves about their sexuality. They hide their sexual explorations from their parents. As children, they secretly exchange information and misinformation. As teenagers, they talk to their girl-friends about boys. They may tell their special girlfriends that they are having sexual intercourse, but they usually do not talk about explicit sexual activities and how to achieve pleasure. After years of training not to talk about sex, how do women suddenly move from silence to open communication with their lovers about their own sexual pleasure?

Talking about sex with a lover is something a woman gets better at with time, practice, and conscious effort. Cheryl Jean felt used and unsatisfied in her first experience of intercourse, which lasted a very short time. Her sex partner made no effort to please her. She had achieved orgasm first while masturbating and knew that there could be more to the sexual exchange. She found that when she learned to communicate, she was able to transform her sexual experiences for the better.

"When I was younger, sex wasn't always satisfying. Some of it was me grow-ing up. Some of it was practice. Some of it was asking for what I wanted and not expecting the man to know what I wanted. Also, asking men what they wanted and getting comfortable with what worked for me, being able to say 'yes' and 'no.' It was important to me to be able to feel good about sex and to feel good about myself. It was conscious work to make efforts to improve myself.

"I feel that way about other things, too. I was jealous 20 years ago, and I'm not jealous today. Once I could accept myself, I didn't need to be jealous anymore. It goes back to taking charge of your own life."

Cheryl Jean thinks that her ability to communicate about sex is part of her personal development and maturity. As an insecure adolescent, she did not have the strong self-esteem necessary to conduct herself sexually as she does today. Her sexual transformation did not simply mean learning to express herself. It also meant self-reflection, as well as conscious changes in her personality. She learned to lead a purposeful and more fulfilling life.

When all these factors are in place and the tryst begins, a woman discovers that she enjoys all the massage, stroking, and kissing of the erogenous zones of the body. She also gets turned on by arousing her male partner. For many women, this sensuous movement and caressing are the most enjoyable aspect of the sexual meet-ing. Cunnilingus is the favorite path to orgasm for most women. When women perform intercourse, they like to take control of the insertion of the penis. It is most erotic to wait until she is full of desire for this connection and actively moves onto the penis. Women also feel that this allows them to proceed at a pace that enhances their pleasure and coincides with the relaxation of the vaginal muscles. Most women prefer the female superior position of sitting on top of the man so that they can create the movement and level of penetration that is the most stimulating. They also communicate with their partner about the rhythm of thrusting that is most pleasurable. Experimenting with different positions is important to keep arousal at a high level. Some women find it essential to use vibrators with their partners, and this toy is introduced into their sex play.

As the sexual encounter comes to an end, women need to communicate with the partner about the closing acts. Most women want to cuddle and talk and bask in the afterglow of a shared orgasm. They appreciate massage and caring touch. If the encounter is during the day, a shared shower and meal may be a way to continue the feeling of togetherness. If it is at night, the pleasure of sleeping with a trusted lover provides a restful completion.

The sexual revolution will be made when all women have a receptive male partner who is considerate of their needs. When women understand their own bodies and sexual responses and can communicate these easily to their partners and when mutual sexual satisfaction is the norm, the revolution will be complete.

chapter six

SEX WITH WOMEN

Because lesbianism is hidden in women's day-to-day lives, women vary widely as to when they first unearth in themselves a sexual attraction for other women. Twenty percent of the lesbians interviewed in this book had never been attracted to men and believe that they are innately lesbian because they were aware of being attracted to women from an early age. At the other extreme are lesbians who perceived themselves as totally blind to this option until much later in life and not before adulthood. The average age for being aware of the first sexual attraction to a woman was 17 years old for lesbians and 18 years old for bisexuals. Ten percent of the lesbians were first attracted to women after the age of 30. The average age for the first sexual experience with a female is 20 years old for both lesbians and bisexuals.

Being sexual with another female does not necessarily mean that a woman will label herself a lesbian or bisexual. It takes some time for women to come to terms with the idea that being sexual with a woman means that she should identity as a lesbian. Many lesbians, when they are involved in their first sexual relationship with a woman, say that they are not lesbians, they just happen to be in love with this particular woman. The women in this survey had been identifying as lesbians for an average time of 11 years. Women who were bisexuals had taken the label for an average time of 8 years.

SEXUAL SATISFACTION WITH WOMEN

Lesbians and bisexuals vary widely in their experience with women sexually. Most lesbians fell in the range of 1 to 30 part-ners; one woman had 100 partners, and another had 200 partners. If these two extremes are dropped from the sample, lesbians had an average of 8 female sexual partners. Bisexuals had an average number of 5 female sexual partners.

Interestingly, lesbians had more male sex partners than female sex partners throughout their lifetime. The average number of male partners was 15. Since most lesbians found that their connections with men were unsatisfactory on many levels, they went through a succession of male partners. Lesbians had fewer female sexual partners because they tend to form relationships with women and because women are more hesitant to form purely sexual liaisons than men are.

Bisexual women also had more male than female partners. On the average they had 27 male sexual partners—more than heterosexuals or lesbians. Bisexual women state that they would like to have had more female partners, but they find that it is easier to meet and date men. Many lesbians do not wish to date bisexual women, so they are less available as sexual partners.

Both lesbians and bisexuals are much more sexually satisfied and orgasmic with women than with men. Lesbians' state-ments about sexual satisfaction and orgasm with each other are also higher than what heterosexual women report about their sex with men. Lesbian sexuality is oriented around the clitoris. Intercourse, which does not produce orgasm for most women, is not the central focus for lesbian sexuality. In addition, the enhanced communication styles of women to other women make it easier for women to tell one another what they need and want sexually. There is no fixed sexual script of foreplay, intercourse, and afterplay, as there is for heterosexuals. Each lesbian couple invents the progression of their sexual activities. Since they have to communicate about what they want and since each encounter can be unique, lesbians are more likely to receive the stim-ulation that will give them satisfaction.

HOW LESBIANS ACHIEVE ORGASM WITH WOMEN

Lesbians and bisexuals view themselves as involved lovers. Only one lesbian stated that she was sexually passive, and only 6 percent of bisexuals said they were sexu-ally passive with women. Twenty-eight percent of lesbians and 25 percent of bisexuals said that they are active in their sexual play. Sixty-nine percent of lesbians and bisexuals stated that they can be both sexually active and sexually passive or receptive.

The sexual activities that lesbians do with one another are very similar to the activities that they did with men. One lesbian stated that her sexual expression with women was identical to what she did with men. Yet with men she was never orgasmic and with women she always is orgasmic. She believes the essential differ-ence is her deeper emotional involvement with women and her sense of safety and love with women. A number of lesbians were very orgasmic with men and contin-ued to be so with women, doing the same sorts of activities.

There is no difference between how bisexuals are sexual with women and how lesbians are sexual with each other.

Women like to begin their sexual exchanges with the activities that heterosexuals call "foreplay." This word is an awkward term for lesbian sexuality since foreplay means play before intercourse and intercourse (with a dildo) is not always a part of lesbian sexuality. Lesbian sexual activity does not easily divide into the progression of sexual behavior with a predictable arrangement of beginning, middle, and end. Women begin with kissing, stroking one another's bodies, undressing one another or themselves, and lying down side by side or one on top of the other. Women spend a long time in cuddling, massaging, and stroking the torso, arms, and legs. Kissing moves from the mouth to the face, ears, neck, and breasts and other parts of the body. Lesbians rub their arms and legs and torsos together in full body contact and stroking. Love talk, breathing together, kissing, and stroking the bodies can be the longest part of the sexual exchange between women. Women can take turns in giving and receiving this attention, or they may be simultaneously active with one another.

Lindsay, 22, describes her activity: "First there's kissing, then touching and rubbing our bodies. Then I lie on top of the woman or on the bottom and explore with the hand on the clitoris and rub myself against her."

Rudy

Rudy, 44, gives some details about kinds of sexual play she enjoys with women. "I'm more likely to achieve orgasm with direct manual stimulation of my clitoris. I don't have orgasms with oral sex. I take a long time to have an orgasm. That was a source of conflict in one relationship. I like kissing and touching and licking and sucking. I like penetration, usually a hand. I'm not into devices. So many of the dildos look like penises, and I don't find penises attractive. I like the control of the hand rather than a piece of rubber. Some of the best sex I had was goofy wrestling. I like to suck and bite, but I have to control myself. I don't want to inflict pain. I like long sessions. I had one partner, we made love all day and all night. We'd stop and eat and smoke cigarettes. One time we sat in a bathtub 12 hours. I like water and soap and stuff. I used to always take baths with lovers. My preference is to be with someone who is open sexually and free. When I take the lead I'm often very caretaking in the process and not particularly focused on myself. It's hard for me to shift the focus from them to myself. If I'm with someone who is uptight or sexually shy, then the role of caretaker comes out in me. I feel like I'm a good lover, but if I'm with someone who is free, I don't have to caretake. I can focus on myself and get looser as a result of it. The best lovers I've had really loved sex and loved themselves being sexual."

Lesbian sexuality takes the form of women taking turns giving one another orgasms. Since women are capable of many orgasms, a sexual interlude can go on for several hours as each woman brings the other to orgasm repeatedly in the manner that is usually successful or in a different way if the woman can be orgasmic from different kinds of stimulation. Rosalie, 46, says, "I get so wrapped up in her reaching orgasm that I come, too. It has to be continued, I'm not into taking turns on different nights. We can make love for hours. I'm multi-orgasmic. We keep playing. It's fun." When touching and kissing proceed to the vulva, lesbians use their tongues and fingers on the clitoris, in the vagina, and occasionally playing with anal stimulation. After one woman achieves orgasm, the sexual play may return to the same kissing and stroking that preceded the genital touch and the cycle of lovemaking continues again.

Cunnilingus

Cunnilingus is a favorite sexual practice of lesbians. Most women achieve orgasm through cunnilingus and find it to be the most exciting sexual activity. This is reflected in a response one French-American lesbian made to a heterosexual woman who wanted to know what lesbians did in bed. She said, "It's the difference between an American rabbit and a French rabbit. The American rabbit goes 'hippetty hop,' and the French rabbit goes 'lickety split.'" Tina, 36, describes one of her ways to achieve orgasm: "She has her mouth on my clit and fingers in my vagina or her finger on my anus and the other on my vagina. The clit always has to be stimulated. I like my asshole licked, too."

But some women find that their clitoris is too sensitive for direct stimulation. Molly, bisexual and 35, says, "I have a hard time with people going down on me. I stiffen with fear. They hit my clitoris dead on. I can't have it touched directly." Molly prefers indirect simulation. In addition, she likes to masturbate to orgasm when she is with a partner. She prefers to be in control of her final release.

Mutual Masturbation

Lesbians take turns touching and rubbing the lips, vagina, hood, clitoris, and anus of one another. This can include finger fucking—the penetration of the vagina with one or several fingers. Penny says, "I prefer to be penetrated with fingers in combination with her rubbing my clitoris." But genital contact can done while the rest of the body is being stroked. Josie says, "I like her to have one hand on my genitals and the other caressing my body." Star, bisexual, finds that her sexual activities with a woman are the "same as with a man. I like to finger fuck, cunnilingus, and breast stimulation. I get aroused by giving, so I'm more assertive, and that turns me on."

Some women like the final control of their own orgasm and will masturbate themselves when with a partner. They feel that they know best which pace of rubbing and depth of pressure will assure their release. However, most lesbians trust their partner to ask, know, or experiment enough to learn what works the best for them. Rebecca, bisexual, says, "I never stimulate my own clit with female partners. They know better what to do than a man."

Lesbians can also use self-masturbation in their sex play. Guadalupe says,

"My partner stimulates my nipples or holds my hand while I masturbate, or she penetrates me with her fingers while I masturbate. I know what to do with myself. She is there breathing in my ear; talking to me; telling me how my heart beats. She penetrates my vagina with one or two fingers, usually not moving. Or, it depends: I let her do as she pleases, not saying anything. She's not rough, but gentle. Some women have a wrestling match. I like it better if wrestling is a prelude to sex. Then there's not so much tension with sex."

Vibrators and Dildos

Lesbians have no reluctance to use vibrators and dildos with one another. Sex toys are commonly used, especially by women who already use them for private masturbation. The subject of sex toys will arise when women exchange information about how they achieve orgasm. They are incorporated into the sex play in the same way that they might be used in masturbation. Jolene, 40, says, "After full body contact and oral sex, I finish myself off with the vibrator, or she'll use the vibrator on my clitoris."

Dildos can be used instead of fingers in the vagina during cunnilingus or with manual stimulation of the clitoris. Some dildos can be strapped onto the body using a leather or cloth harness made for this purpose. When lesbians use a strap-on dildo they can perform intercourse in all the positions that heterosexuals might use. Like women in general, some lesbians like vaginal penetration, and some do not. Personal preference will determine if only one woman is penetrated or if they take turns. When lesbians use dildos for intercourse, they also use manual stimulation of the clitoris to achieve orgasm or they use a vibrator on the clitoris. Some lesbians use a strap-on flat vibrator with the harness so that the wearer gets clitoral stimulation. Some long, two-ended dildos are available that allow both women to wear it in their vaginas as they rub against each other.

Ryfka

Ryfka enjoys the use of sex toys in her sexual exchanges. "I don't have just one way to achieve orgasm. I like oral sex, using a vibrator and a dildo, and mutual tribadism. One way we use the dildo is: I am on my hands and knees. She's fucking me with a fist up my pussy and a dildo in my ass. Or, it's reversed. She's on her hands and knees and I'm in back of her. I have a dildo on, pressed into her ass. My fist is inside her pussy. I have a vibrator pressing on the dildo which my clit is pressed up against so it's vibrating in her ass and also against my clit. It doesn't matter which position I'm in. It's very exciting. I get awfully wet. Sometimes I fuck myself on a rocking chair with a double dildo. She comes in and climbs on top of the other end of the dildo. Or she kneels down and starts sucking on the other end of the dildo pushing it into me with her mouth." Ryfka's description illustrates that some women like rough sex with a great deal of intense penetration, pressure, and vibrations. Her tough form of sex play is not painful, as many women who prefer soft and gentle sex might think.

Tribadism

Tribadism is the sexual act of lying on top of each other and rubbing one's clitoris against the other woman's clitoris. Tina, 36, refers to tribadism as "humping abdomen to abdomen. It's not rubbing." Alana, 44, describes this: "Sometimes if I'm on top I can stimulate my clit on her pubic or hipbones, and my vagina may be also stimulated." She continues, "I like to straddle my lover who is lying on her back. I spread the lips of my labia open so that my clit is more exposed and I press it against her pubic bone. I ride up and down, finding just the right pace that turns me on, I lean forward and squeeze her breasts and play with her nipples. She will play with my breasts, too, or she will stroke the sides of my body, press her hands into my waist or grip my ass. She arches her back to press her mons up to meet me. I can reach behind my ass and press some fingers into her vagina. Sometimes I will push her arms up over her head on the bed, restraining her from touching me. I put my fingers in her mouth for her to suck while I ride her."

For Ryfka, "rubbing on a hip, or riding the hip are some of my favorite things to do while she is playing with my breasts." Rubbing the clitoris against another woman's pubic bone is a vigorous hip movement similar to the rocking motion of intercourse. Depending on the location of the clitoris, this sex act may not be successful in producing orgasm. A woman with a more recessed clitoris may be unable to obtain good stimulation from tribadism. For women who like a more active sexual activity, tribadism is an exciting full-body and energetic experience.

THE SEXUAL DANCE

Sex between women takes on a unique quality. The softness of a woman's body, her sensual nature, and her attention to the other, based on her training to be nurturing, create a flowing exchange. This gentle, yet arousing, sexuality is newly discovered by Reanna, who is 30 years old and had been married five years. She and her husband had been together ten years from the age of 16 to 26. Today Reanna is bisexual.

Reanna

"I would probably have sex with a man again. My first sexual experience with a woman was in the last year."

The first turn-on for Reanna is the personality of the woman. "I am very attracted to women who are very sensitive, emotionally sensitive, and very strong. A confident woman with a strong sense of identity but who can also be very vulnerable. This vulnerability is a melting thing where there are no boundaries. It requires someone willing to be completely real and honest. Being honest and open and sharing what is going on for me and for me with this person, that makes an energy connection. She should be willing to be seen, not be hiding any feelings. I want to be completely open with her, sharing my intimate feelings, my intimate experience of myself, the hidden things about myself."

Physical appearance is also important for Reanna. "I like an attractive woman, slender and fit. And I like breasts and a nice abdomen and butt. I don't go for butch. It's cute, but I like the feminine energy more. The energy of the woman, how she carries herself is more important than how she looks."

When she describes her sexual exchange with a woman, Reanna speaks of the interchange and a psychic or energetic quality as the element that contributes to her arousal. "We start out by lying in bed, dressed and sharing the energy, talking about our lives. The energy builds. I lie on top of her, and the energy gets electric. The first time this happened, we were quiet because there were other people in the room. I had my body propped up on her. My mouth watered and I wanted to kiss her. I let that feeling build. She was so soft and knew exactly what to do and how to handle me. She is usually the initiator. She kissed me, and it was perfect. I was melting. Our noses were rubbing, and she started kissing me, and I got so aroused. It's in the desire that I really get turned on; the wanting it and the burning. While there were people there, we couldn't really do anything, and that turned me on. She always knows when to pull away and create more of a longing in me. There are no boundaries. I lose sense of self in kissing. The ultimate orgasm is to completely disappear and become as one. I felt that in just kissing her.

"It wasn't a physical orgasm. I'm petrified of that experience. I'm totally gone, and I get afraid, and I'm right back. That is way better than an orgasm. I would rather have that all the time than

have an orgasm. An orgasm is over and dissipates the energy. Especially with her—we can be in bed for hours and keep going. It can fill my body with that energy and I feel it all over. When that first exchange was over, I thought it was this love. A real sense of love."

As Reanna developed a relationship with this woman, their opportunity to expand on the sexual interaction created a longer and more fulfilling sexual dance. "The best scenario is to be making out while lying in bed, talking, kissing, touching. I love stroking her hair and playing with her ears, face, and breasts. I love breasts. I know how to turn her on with touching, how to touch her breasts. And when she's turned on, I'm turned on. It builds the energy, and she gets me going when she touches me. She is not aggressive. She initiates. She knows when to touch, when to stop and pull away. I get turned on because she is so turned on. She loves my breasts, it drives her crazy.

"What turns me on is the constant foreplay. She gets all heated up and desirous. She touches me genitally with her lips. She likes it and gets her energy going. She likes it so much that I feel her being turned on, and I get more excited. She is soft, and I melt. It's hard to describe.

"She kisses me on my neck and my breasts. She'll spend an hour just going down my body and kissing me all over. She is just totally present to me. I express a lot more with her than I did with men. I make a lot more noise. I express more verbally than I ever used to. I can't stop it. She'll move my hips and turn me over and lift my leg up and lick the back of my leg and behind my knee and eat my foot. She uses her lips and her tongue. It's an energy thing. I can feel her totally loving it. She'll lick my whole foot, each toe all around it. Then go on to the other leg. Then she'll come back up to my face and kiss me because I get afraid of the vulnerability. She is sensitive and caring. Over time, knowing that she cares and is present with me has allowed me to open myself. By then I'm crazy and then she touches my vagina with her lips.

"We want to have orgasms, but we want to do the ultimate with our energy, to move it to the higher chakras when the whole body is vibrating and burning. I give her orgasms. She'll touch me first in the way I just described. Then we'll lie together and talk, sharing. Then the energy changes and I'll start kissing on her; kissing her ear with my mouth and tongue. Making love to her ear turns her on. And then I might turn her over and I'll lie on her and kiss her neck. I salivate a lot, and I kiss her breasts. I'm much more nervous about that and I'm learning slowly to open to that. She has her navel pierced, and I love to kiss her there. I love her abdomen and the hair line; that's one of my favorite parts after her breasts. I'm not as slow as she is. I'm the first person that she's opened her legs to. The more connected we are, the more she allows me in. As she opens more, I can tell because she allows herself to be turned on. I move her legs around and I tease for a long time around her leg and the crease of her hip and crotch area and lick behind the knee. I bite a lot with my teeth. She likes it. It seems like a natural thing. She really gets wet, and that

turns me on, too. She doesn't use toys and gizmos. I like it that it's just us. She'll put her fingers up me, so I started doing that to her. My other hand on the inside of her leg or reaching up to her head. I tease as long as I can and gently go in with my mouth. I don't put my fingers up her vagina right away. That comes later. I'm really gentle at first, and then pull back. She moves with it and enjoys it and gets into it and moans.

"By the time she has an orgasm I'm so turned on, so I work my way back up, kissing and licking. I lie on top of her or at her side; I kiss and play with her hair and her ear and depending on what time it is, start all over. We lie there for a bit and eventually get up. It's hard to be in that space of total union and then go back to the real world."

Jane

Jane, 55 years old, has been a lesbian for 24 years. The new thrill of a woman as a sexual partner has been replaced by a quiet confidence in knowing her favorite way to make love. "I am a femme. So after many years of following a line that lesbians don't play femme/butch roles and after finding that I was coupling with other femmes who didn't give me a lot of satisfaction, I now look for butches. With regard to sex, one of the questions I ask a prospective lover is, 'Do you like to start on top or on the bottom?' Because when I start making love I like to be on the bottom. So I look for someone who likes to start on top. I think that is characteristic of butches.

"I identify a butch as someone who has a kind of a 'butch burr' in her voice. There is a distinct sound in butches' voices that I don't hear in the voices of femmes. I can't describe it, but I recognize it when I hear it. I look for someone who is a grown-up tomboy. I like someone who is a soft butch, someone who is sensitive and who likes, for example, the beauty of nature and someone who is gentle. I would love to find a butch who loves to talk about her feelings, but I haven't yet.

"The first thing I discovered when I started relating physically to women was I felt this tremendous passion that I never felt with men. I felt very, very grateful that I could experience that kind of passion. I came out in the context of the women's liberation movement when there was a strong lesbian separatist strain, and women were writing feminist utopian novels. I believed I could achieve feminist utopia. Part of relating sexually to a woman was to get to a point to where we would be so strongly connected while making love that we could feel each other's physical sensations and communicate without speaking, read each other's minds. But I was never able to do so.

"But I did find early on that I could feel their feelings, their sensations, as we were making love. So if we were kissing and the electricity went straight down to her cunt, I could feel it in my own before she told me. What I like to do is to touch her very gently and try to sense her reactions and what she is feeling. And then as she becomes excited, I become excited and I feel very strongly connected to her.

"I like a lot of gentle physical stroking for a long time, to stroke and be stroked so lightly at the beginning that it's almost like tickling someone's back. Not in a teasing way, but very light touching. There is no part of my body that doesn't like to be touched. I especially like the soles of my feet tickled in that way. I like to start out by stroking her very lightly to see which areas of her body want to be touched. One of the things I discovered about women's bodies is that certain parts want to be touched at certain times. That is where the sensations are focused at the moment. And then it goes from one place in the body to another place in the body. So it might be that a woman's neck or shoulders are sensitive at first. And then, after a while, another part of her body wakes up and says, 'Now I want to be touched.' It might be her breasts. The focus moves from one part of the body to another part of the body.

"Eventually, when she's really turned on, the focus of sensation centers in her vagina and clitoris. Then I like to touch her vagina and clitoris with my tongue. I feel if I'm very careful and tuned in, I can tell how and where she wants to be touched there. I try to concentrate on how her body is reacting to the way she is being touched. Usually I can feel her tightening up as she gets closer to having an orgasm. I really like performing oral sex on a woman. So I don't mind if it takes a long time—at least 15 to 30 minutes. I am happy to do it a second time, if she is able to have a second time.

"I like to be touched very gently for a long time, and I like to have someone stroke my hair, back, neck, and shoulders. If she kisses my breasts, I like it done very gently. I also like to have her use her hands to stimulate my clitoris with her fingers. But I don't like penetration. I like oral sex best of all. I give instructions about oral sex, if necessary. One partner and I were having difficulty learning each other's bodies, and at one time I got out a mirror. We looked at me in the mirror so I could show her where exactly it felt good and exactly where it didn't feel so good. It's hard to use words. It's usually just 'Down. To the left. There. Harder.' But the mirror really worked. It turned our relationship around.

"We end by cuddling and drifting off to sleep. Often we make love in the mornings, but still I like to cuddle and take a nap before we get up and face the day 'cause it feels so good to drift off to sleep after making love. Making love with a woman feels completely natural to me."

Elizabeth

Elizabeth is 58 and has been a lesbian for 44 years. When she seeks a lover, she wants "someone who is strong. I don't care about looks or size. She should be sensitive, trusting, loving. Someone who likes to share the same things that I do: the coast, movies, plays, being out of doors, reading, music that is older, classical 1940s to 1960s, and dancing.

"The way I make love now comes with age. It is softer and gentler and seems more loving. It's real comfortable. I usually start by kissing her upper lip, the side of her face, down her neck and gently touch-

ing her breasts, kissing her breast. I like to lie on top of her and to move around on top of her. I prefer oral sex to any other kind. I like to make love very slowly. I usually lift her hips on a pillow, so it is a little elevated. I fold my arms in front of me so my head doesn't get tired and I can do it a long time. It's up to the woman if there is any penetration with my fingers.

"I like the same thing. I prefer oral sex to anything else. I don't particularly like penetration. I see it as a male thing. It's more of a turn-off now. I like a lot of touching—my head rubbed and my back rubbed as a prelude. I usually make love to her first, so that gets me turned on. When she starts making love to me, it moves a little faster. I like to lie back on top of her at the end and just cool out for a while."

Peggy

Peggy at 48 has been a bisexual for 18 years. When she identifies a potential lover, she looks for a number of characteristics. "My female sex partner should be relaxed and open and honest about sexuality. And experienced. I am not interested in the bi-curious. I want an experienced lover. She should be fit and not more than 10 years younger than I. I have never had an older lover. She should be smart, funny, and adventuresome and should like the outdoors because I like to have sex in the outdoors. She should be confident and independent. The essential ingredient is the magic, the smell of her, the turn-on, the sexiness, whatever it is that generates the feeling of 'I want you!'"

Peggy prefers variety in her sexual interludes. "Sexually, I like to find a woman who wants to try everything. There is a yin and yang to sex. When I am yin, I feel open, and I allow my lover to touch me and go with the changes in my body. I feel that I draw her energy into me and when I do, I experience a charge, a rush, a shaking, a flow, or a deep sucking in of who she is into my gut. I want her to take a turn at being yin. That means I can be yang. I touch her and push my energy into her. It's not just my touch of her. I visualize that something of my substance goes into her and changes her in a way that she feels exquisite pleasure. I like to take a long to time to have sex. All day or all night if possible! If we are indoors, I want a nice quiet bedroom, so I can scream or make other noises without it being a problem. I like to have lots of candles, incense, tasty massage oils, and sensuous foods that we can feed each other in between the sex. Purified water is essential. I get so thirsty! And perhaps some wine. We might also have toys, like vibrators, dildos, and a harness. I won't do anything painful, no bondage. I don't want to be tied up. The society does enough of that to me, and I don't like it. I won't tie her up either. So I guess I don't do everything.

"I like to start by lying next to each other and looking into each other's eyes. Up on my elbow while she lies on her back or her side. Then I slowly touch her cheek and trail my hand around her head and her ears. Then I proceed to her neck and shoulders, down her arm to her hand. I lightly hold her hand and circle her palm with my index finger. I lace our fingers together and then push against her hand.

She pushes back, and that is her chance to let go of my hand and start touching me in some way. My ears and neck are really sensitive, and so are my nipples. So if she starts touching these areas I become quickly aroused.

"We continue touching until we have covered all the parts of the bodies, including a back massage. That can be accomplished by switching positions until one of us is on top of the other. I like to trade around. I don't want either of us on top the whole time. But whoever is on top can have her back massaged by the one on the bottom. In that position, we rub our legs together, so the legs get touched, too. It is fun to sit up then and massage the legs, to see what parts are exciting, to see how she reacts to strokes and tickles and maybe having her toes sucked. It can be a lot of fun to suck each toe and each finger, too. Apparently not too many people do this because women are usually pleasantly shocked by how good it feels.

"Then it's time to start kissing. Everyone kisses differently, and I am always ready to learn a new style. Sucking the upper and lower lip can be a turn-on. I can run my tongue along her teeth and gums and then penetrate her mouth forcefully with my tongue. It can be really exciting if she sucks my tongue hard. Then we can get into a duel of tongues in my mouth or hers. I like to lick a woman, too. So after kissing I will lick her cheeks and eyelids. I use just the tip of the tongue on the lids, very lightly. Then go to the ears and lick around and penetrate her ear with my tongue. While I'm doing that I might pull her hair lightly with my hand and gently push my index finger of my other hand into her other ear. I hope she gets the idea that I'm doing these things because I like them, too. Then it's her turn again.

"By this time we are both hot for each other, and one of us will approach the genitals. Maybe she would straddle me as I lie on my back. Not all women can get stimulated this way. I don't. But it's wonderful to look at her body while she rocks against my pubic bone. We might spread our labia open and lay them against each other to get a better connection. She can rock like this until she comes. While she is doing it, we play with each other's breasts and nipples. She might lean forward so I can kiss her breasts. She could put her fingers in my mouth after she has wiped some of our juices onto them. And I'll suck her fingers and smell them. She could pull my hair a little. When she is exciting and concentrating on coming, I put my hands on her hips or her buns and enjoy feeling her vibrations. I almost get a sympathetic orgasm when a woman comes with me. I love for her to make noises, panting, grunting, or yelling. And then that moment of orgasm is so sweet. She goes limp and smiles. If she is capable of multiple orgasms then it's time to see how long it can be prolonged. When you have practice with a woman, you can go on and on.

"Then it's my turn to come and I love cunnilingus. So I can just lie there, and after she catches her breath and recovers, she can eat me for a long time. If her tongue is talented, I'll get off. I'm multiply orgasmic, so I want her to keep on so I can keep on coming.

"Then we might rest, drink, talk, or eat, and it's time to start again. I mean it when I say I like to go all day. I'd rather make love fewer times in a month, but take longer each time. We start again with the kissing and stroking but perhaps don't take so long to get to the genitals. We take turns using our hands on the other's labia and clitoris until we both orgasm, never at the same time. I go down on her. If she likes, I penetrate her vagina or anus with my fingers. Some women like the thrusting and fullness of fingers. They have no problem saying 'Add another finger!'

"If she's into toys we might start again with a harness and a dildo and lots of k-y jelly. We move into intercourse in much the same way as I do it with a man. We might switch into lots of different positions. I like intercourse, but I don't orgasm that way. So after a while we stop, and she can bring me off with her hand. Then it's my turn to see how she likes intercourse.

"Then we might nap or walk around a bit. Eat and drink. It's so great when you feel like you can't get enough of each other. A shower or bath with bubbles might be nice if we're sweaty. Then it's back to bed to see what else we can think of. Try again the things which you noticed before were a real turn-on. Women do get into favorite positions and touches. We might use a vibrator with one another if we're getting tired.

"If we each come about five or six times, that is pretty good. If we can sleep together and have breakfast in the morning, it's so tender and sweet. It's exciting to be waked by someone who wants you! But I still need my eight hours of sleep!"

THE SEXUAL REVOLUTION

The sexual revolution for a woman who loves women happens when she overcomes all the obstacles in both herself and the environment that prevent her from being sexual with another woman. It seems amazing that someone would not be sure that she is feeling sexual attraction. When women see only stereotypes of lesbians as the extremely butch or the outrageous women in gay parades, it is difficult for them to identify with the lifestyle. The many lesbians who are living ordinary lives are not the ones who warrant photographs in the media. One woman told me that she had been married 20 years and had five children. She felt herself going through a transformation, and she began to wonder if she might be a lesbian. She told her closest male and female friends. Both of them told her that she could not possibly be a lesbian because she had a good marriage that had lasted so long. She took their word for it. But three years later she fell in love with a woman and left her marriage. If she had been able to trust her own experience of herself, her transformation and its accompanying joy might have come sooner.

Once they have found a suitable partner, most women recognize that the sexual acts flow naturally. Like all sexual techniques, lesbian sexual techniques are learned and practiced. With time and interest, women discover that it is easy to become a good lover to another woman. Their communication around sexuality is relaxed and complete, and they are very sexually satisfied with one another.

Other researchers have observed that an issue that arises for lesbians in relationships is that after about two years, the sexual activities may disappear from the relationship. Often, one woman is dissatisfied with this arrangement. The lesbians and bisexual women who want to keep making their personal sexual revolution need to continue to value the pleasure and intimacy that is available solely during sexual activity. They have to find ways to foster the dynamic process that occurs only in sex.

chapter seven

MEN AND WOMEN AS SEXUAL PARTNERS

Women who have had sexual experiences with both men and women can compare men and women as sexual partners. Heterosexual women are the least likely to make these comparisons since their experience with women is very limited. The 10 percent of heterosexual women who did perform sex with women had single, or fleeting and interrupted liaisons. Therefore, they had little basis for making comparisons. This is also true for the 20 percent of lesbians who had never experienced sexual intercourse with men. Therefore, this discussion is contributed by lesbians who were once heterosexual and by bisexual women.

LESBIANS

Since lesbians find that their sexual experiences with men are usually not sexually satisfying, they tend to be critical in their evaluations of men as sexual partners. But their comments reveal their perception of the differences between how men approach sexuality and how women do. Not one lesbian said that sex was better with men. Fifty-five percent of lesbians said that women were better sexual partners. Ten percent said that women and men were the same as sexual partners. (Thirty-five percent did not answer this question.)

Lesbians are critical of men for being more concerned about their own sexual gratification than with their partners' satisfaction. Roselle, 32, says, "There is more caring and sharing with a woman, more concern about the other's needs. There is more caressing and closeness with a woman. Men are more centered on the genitals and on getting off. It's a better all around feeling with a woman; with a man it's more a cold thing." Maggie, 35, found the same attitude from men. "Men are oriented to their satisfaction and only temporarily attended to my needs. With women, sex is longer and more mutually satisfying. Women are more sensitive to my state of arousal and have a willingness to match my pace. Women's bodies are more exciting, with more places to play!" Spring, 43, is more cynical about men and sexuality: "Women are so giving and interested in my pleasure, and men are interested in their own. If you derive anything from it, it's a by-product." Penny, 49, agrees: "Men are demanding, self-centered, and unromantic. Women are more sensitive, gentle, understanding, and patient." Danielle, 42, is more compassionate toward men: "Men are not in touch with the sensuous part of sexuality. They haven't been taught."

Rudy

Rudy, 44, sees men as emotionally disconnected partners in sex. "I have been with insensitive men and insensitive women. Insensitive men are off the scale regarding being aware of what is going on. The insensitive woman is somewhat aware, conscious of your presence but not aware enough to do anything about it. The worst woman is not as bad as the worst man, and the best man is not as good as the best woman.

"I think I know what an orgasm feels like for a woman, but I have no idea what an erection feels like or what it feels like to ejaculate. So when I'm with a woman I think I know what it feels like to be her. I don't think men are trained to respond sexually at any kind of sensitive level. I never had a woman make love to me and go to sleep. I never ended a session with a woman with silence and snores. We cuddle and talk. There is a real connection. I had to train my best male lover not to roll over and go to sleep. He was a good lover, but he'd give me a kiss and then turn his back to me."

The problems of relating to men and their bodies are also a factor when lesbians draw their comparisons. Danielle, 42, finds these issues are both physical and social. "There's no comparison! Men just don't taste or smell right. That's physical chemistry. They are hard enough to deal with on a social level, or on a level of equality." Sandy, 41, makes this summary: "Women are hotter and more loving. Women smell better and feel better than men. You don't get razor burn when you kiss them!"

Most lesbians talked more about what they like about women, than what they didn't like about men. Marion, 57, explains: "I like women's bodies. That's why I'm a lesbian. I'm more attracted to women's softness, both physically and intellectually. A woman's body is much more appealing. I don't like the roughness of men's faces." Jolene, 40, finds "women are softer, more romantic, more exciting. Men are too fast. Women are slower, and thus are more satisfying, creative, and passionate. Women are prettier. I don't like the hairiness of men. Women have breasts and nicer bodies. Men's muscles are nice to look at, but I don't like to touch them." Ryfka relates what she likes about women sexually and how men fall short: "I like women's bodies more than men's. Men's are hard, rough, and hairy suckers, don't you think? I like touching women and being touched by women. I like breasts. A lot of my male lovers tended to just focus on their dick, but the last couple of men lovers I had were not that way at all. They were good lovers. I could be satisfied being fucked by a man, but I never got satisfied fucking a man. In contrast, I do get satisfied fucking a woman. It's a physical difference in satisfaction. Men like to be on top all the time figuratively and literally. They want to be in charge. They don't like to be passive."

Lesbians like the quality of the sexual exchange with women, which they see as more emotionally expressive. Cleo, 28, notes how women's bodies and attitudes make sexuality different. "Women are softer physically, not as rigid. A man can be experimental, but it is always 'cookbook sex.' It's never spontaneous. With a woman you just do it spontaneously. It's easier to say what I want to a woman and for her to react instantaneously. With a man, he will stop and say, 'What?' Women are more gentle and tender. Men have to work at it."

Some lesbians describe sexuality with men as purely physical. Sex between women is a more emotional experience. Nokomis, 28, sees it simply that "with a man, it's more of an act. With a woman, it's an actual way of being. With a man, it's a linear process and has a beginning, middle, and end." Minette, 38, develops this theme: "Women are satisfying emotionally, spiritually, and physically. Men are satisfying physically. Women are more creative. I lose myself in a way I didn't with men. I prefer a dildo over a penis. Penetration with a penis is a distraction from pure pleasure. I like penetration when it's a female with a dildo. It's not pleasurable for me to touch a man's body, but I like touching women."

Rosalie

Rosalie, 46, finds that the physicality of male sexuality is fascinating but secondary to the experience of sex with women. "Women are slower, more gentle, more willing to please each other instead of looking for self-pleasure like men are. I get more sexual satisfaction from women. Sometimes I miss what guys have to offer, but it's totally based on the physical. There is a different aura with men—there is something magical in that big dick. In some sick sort of way you feel taken care of, and there is an illusion that a guy will do that for you. Something about the strength of men that makes you feel safer. I only miss it about once every ten years. There's something different about sex with men—ramming everything together. It's not as sensitive as it is with women."

Rudy

Rudy, 44, was one of the few lesbians willing to admit that not everything is perfect in the lesbian sexual world. "Some women are not good lovers. I've had some relationships with women where we weren't able to communicate. The sexual relationship suffered over not being able to talk about what pleased us and what didn't please us. The quality that makes a good lover, besides an adventuresome spirit, is sensitivity. Being in tune to where the other person is. You want to be with someone you don't have to spell it out to all the time. Where you don't have to say, 'Don't do that' or 'That hurts me.' Now a good lover is someone who, when they are making love to me, is in tune with my needs. Some women are good with that, and some women aren't. When I make love with a woman I like to do it one at a time. I like making love to someone and let them receive. With men you are doing it at the same time, and I find it distracting. That's the difference."

BISEXUALS

Since bisexuals accept men as sexual partners, we can expect that they would be more sexually satisfied by men than lesbians are. Twenty-two percent of bisexuals found men to be better sex partners than women. Molly explained how her male partner was more satisfying than a woman. She draws her comparison between her two female partners and her male partner, her husband. She discounts her early fleeting sexual adventures with men. Her comparison of her husband and her female lovers is a reflection of all the personalities. "Roy is much more sexually generous and imaginative than my female lovers. When I began my sexual experiments, I picked incompatible lovers with men. I find women more physically attractive than men, but my husband, Roy, makes up for being less physically attractive, by bringing humor and fun to lovemaking, much more than my women lovers did. My experiences in bed with Roy overcome my stronger attraction to women's bodies. He has a positive attitude about sex that is refreshing and overcomes my performance anxiety. He's in it for the fun of it. Neither of my woman lovers were."

May, 30, also finds men more exciting, but she thinks that with more experience this could change. "So far sex with men is more satisfying. That has more to do with the particular women I've been with. Neither of them had much experience with women. There's been an intensity coming from the men I've been with that I've enjoyed and that so far I haven't found with women. I've thought I should find a lesbian or a bi woman who is more out. I feel I'm going through adolescence as far as women go. I feel I'd get along better with strong and butch women, but I find femmy women less threatening."

Thirty-nine percent of bisexual women say that men and women are equally sexually satisfying. Men and women as sexual partners are enjoyed for different reasons. Heather, 26, explains:

"Women have breasts. It's pleasant being with someone of my own size. Women are generally lots of fun. With men, I like the penis. Men can be too big and heavy in overall body size. Sometimes they are too quick to orgasm and then won't continue."

Star

Star, 48, considers the personal connection in sexual encounters to be an integral part of the total experience. "I have never been a victim in the world. I don't set myself up with bozos, so I've had good experiences with emotionally available men who are not afraid of their feelings. Because the men have been emotional and vulnerable, the sex has been intense and satisfying. I've had more experience with men. It's the chemistry and the spark that turns me on. It's fun to explore the differences between men and women. It's wonderful to be with men who love women and women's bodies. Men don't have to be the driving sexual force, they can be passive, too. Men like to be on their back as much as women do. I have a woman friend who won't go to bed with a man who hasn't been fucked by a man. She only wants to be with bisexual men, because they understand the psychological experience of being entered sexually.

"With women it's erotic because of the sameness. There's a comfort and a familiarity that is exciting. There's a language I already have with a woman's body. With women I give myself more permission to be assertive and to get more of what I want. Yet now I have less hesita-tion about going for what I want with men. Being with women allows me to understand myself more as a woman.

"Now with AIDS we have to talk more about sex and what we want and need. In the past this was not considered romantic. Now we have to be in touch with our bodies and what we can do. It helps to break down the gender roles, which keep women from being sexually fulfilled and keep men from responding to them."

Claire

Claire, 37, finds that women and men both offer something that is sexually unique. "One soft, butch woman's sensuality was intensely stimulating sexually for me. Just lying in bed with her, being close to her was exciting. It was great. I haven't had that experience with a man. Intercourse with a man is very focused and is exciting, but is different from this sensuality. Men are more intensely sexually exciting, but women can be that way, too. Men direct things, they take you along step by step. If they're too directive, that's a problem. If a woman's not directive, then I have to take the initiative and deal with my fears of being rejected. But I can do it. Depending on my mood, I can like being directive with a woman."

Peggy

Peggy, 48, does not like the idea of comparing lovers along gender differences. Instead she thinks of sexual skills as a better measure. "It's easier for me to compare skilled lovers and unskilled lovers, than to distinguish between men and women. In my experience, the vast majority of men were unskilled and selfish. There can be this moment during intercourse with a man when he is very excited and about to come that he seems to completely forget that I'm there! He just mentally goes into his physical sensations. He might as well be masturbating. At that point, when he's spacing out, I whisper, 'It's me. It's me you're with,' to draw him out of a masturbatory mode. Sometimes men get angry that I spoke! They say it breaks their concentration. For me, the point of sex with another person is the contact with them on all levels, so this is an ultimate disappointment. I feel I should have been paid for my services. With a man like that, the first time is the last time. I've learned to be more discriminating with men. The men who were skilled, interested, and passionate lovers were my best sex partners. My wildest and most thrilling sex partners were men.

"It is less possible to be sexual with a woman who is using me to masturbate, which is different than with men. At that same stage of excitement, say when a woman is humping my hip or pubic bone and is about to orgasm, she will share it with me. She says, 'Oh, honey, I'm coming!,' and brings me into her experience. She lets me know that I am part of it. It's me and my body that excite her. This is a major difference between men and women.

"Women who were unskilled lovers were still interested in learning to satisfy me. Some women who were poor lovers were sexually passive, which is boring. I want a passionate thrill to develop where we both can't get enough of each other and where we stimulate each other's body to a higher and higher peak. I've certainly had that with some women, and it was wild! Some women want to be in control the whole time. They want to make love to me, but they won't let me make love to them. At first, that situation is great. I get all the orgasms I want. But not being able to reciprocate ultimately makes sex unfulfilling. I want to make love to my partner. I want to create that exquisite pleasure in her."

Twenty-eight percent of the bisexuals found women to be better sex partners than men. Their comments reiterate the opinions expressed by lesbians. Devorah, 25, describes her discovery about differences between men and women sexually when she had her first experience with a woman: "I met her three weeks earlier at a party, and I'd decided to make a trip to see her for the weekend and to see some other friends. The whole night there was this strong sexual energy, and I wasn't sure what would happen. She was involved in a nonmonogamous relationship. We went to her apartment, and I was so nervous. She invited me to try out the hot tub. Afterwards, we went inside, and I said, 'What about sleeping arrangements?' And she said, 'Even if nothing happens, I'd still like to sleep with you.' So we got in bed and started making out and then had sex. I found I was more interested in exploring her body. She asked me, 'What would you like?' And I said, 'I want to lie here and be with you.' I wasn't comfortable enough to communicate what I would've wanted. But she asked, and my male lover never did. With him, I would just lie back, and he would fuck me. I've never had that experience with a women."

Amity and Rebecca blame penis-centered sexuality for the lower ranking of sex with men. Amity: "Sex with a man centers around the penis, and with two women it is more equal. Women are more attentive. With a man, it is not a mutual centering on each other. Men are too ready for their own satisfaction. My female partner is less interested in only her satisfaction. With a woman, it's so much like your own body, that you can feel what you're doing. But with a man, he can't feel what you feel and you can't feel what he feels." Rebecca agrees: "Women are more tuned into other women's pleasure. It's different. Women have more creative definitions of what sex is. There is a broader range of eroticism that includes the more emotional aspects of erotic life. Some men just think of sticking it in and getting off. There's a certain level of equality in having the same genitalia. Safe sex with women is harder to negotiate. That part with men is simple—use a condom."

Jody, 25, focuses on what it is she likes about women's bodies. "Men are less in tune with my needs. Women are aesthetically soft, and their bodies are sexually exciting. Everything is so different. Kissing a woman is better. It is very arousing to fondle and kiss breasts and vaginas. They have the smells and textures of my own body. But the equipment on men, their penises, small buttocks, can be stimulating, too."

The element of nonscripted sexuality with women is one that bisexual women find more exciting. Rochelle, 26, "I don't know how to begin! There's something awfully exciting about giving pleasure to a woman. It's 500 times more exciting than with a man. Sex with women is not predictable. It can be predictable with men. The outcome is predictable. Women are more cuddly."

Alexa, 33, thinks women are more sexually skilled. "A woman knows how to make love to a woman better than a man does. Women know how much pressure to use." Denise, 39, concurs: "Generally, women are more intuitive about what I like and need less training. You need to find out by trial and error what works. Just to see a lady bending over and touching me is so much more a charge than seeing a man do it!" Phoebe, 46, also believes that women know more what another women wants: "Women intuit more of what is pleasurable, due to having the same female body, needs, and wants. There is more acceptance of the female body. There is a mutual emotional connection with women, and more time is invested in sexual pleasuring."

COMPARING MEN AND WOMEN AS EMOTIONALLY SATISFYING LOVERS

Heterosexual women form deep loving and fruitful friendships with other women.

However, since sex is not a component of these relationships, they do not think of their female friends as lovers. Nor do they demand from them the kind of sexual intimacy they desire from men. Some heterosexual women may be deeply committed to one another in friendships. They may be more emotionally intimate with a female friend than they have ever been with a male lover, but the loving friendships between heterosexual women do not have the volatile component of sex. Therefore, heterosexual women cannot compare men and women as lovers on this factor.

Lesbians do not find men to be emotionally satisfying lovers. Consequently, they do not expect to form an emotional bond with a man as a lover. Their comments about a man's capacity to be emotionally responsive are faultfinding. None of the lesbians stated that men are more fulfilling emotionally than women.

Bisexual women seek both sexual and emotional connections with men, and 17 percent of them found that men were more fulfilling emotionally. Fourteen percent stated that men and women were equally satisfying in terms of emotional connection.

Peggy

Peggy, 48, explains that these comparisons are not as simple as they seem. "If I say that men and women are equally satisfying emotionally, I have to qualify it. Some people are skilled emotionally, and some are not. By emotionally skilled, I mean open, assertively affectionate, funny, and also receptive to my emotional communications. As a group, men are not as emotionally skilled as women. In fact, many men seem to be emotionally retarded! So the average male is not emotionally satisfying. When I click with someone emotionally, we can communicate what is happening to each of us, and we can even anticipate each other. I have had that with a few men, but it happens more commonly with women. Women criticize men for being emotionally remote. But when I have established an emotional bond with a man, I experience the remoteness as a nice boundary of privacy from one another. I have my own desire for silence and secrets. All the men I've had relationships with were independent and respected my independence. If you appreciate independence, there can be both an emotional closeness and also freedom and separation.

"With women, there is this intense, emotional joining that can be an ecstatic way to lose yourself. I crave that in the sex act. But in day-to-day life, I find it to be like a big hook, trying to drag me out of my self. A woman's dependency on me can be a huge, demanding pull. It can feel like a constant need for attention and reassurance. I resist that. Because of this emotionality, I find women to be more demanding than men. I find this to be draining and irritating, and I resist. I have to be with independent women. Women are trained to be dependent, so the truly self-sufficient woman is hard to find."

Sixty-four percent of bisexuals said that women were more emotionally rewarding partners. Claire discovered that her sexual experiences with women brought a novelty she had not expected. "I've had more sexual experiences with men then with women. I remember after I came out as a bisexual, I had sex with a few women. It was exciting and I liked it a lot. But I began to feel that if I were sleeping around, I shouldn't do it casually with women, because they were more emotionally vulnerable. Then I realized it was more my feelings of vulnerability that were coming up with women! I was less defensive emotionally with women, and so it wasn't as easy to have casual sex with them without feeling hurt. I don't separate the emotional and the physical part. I had more casual sex with men than with women, so the comparison isn't exactly equal."

Claire goes on about her discoveries of the emotional differences between men and women that she learned after she accepted the different level of intimacy with women. "With women in a relationship there is more emotional closeness and less differences to bridge. There is a feeling of being in a similar place; a mutual understanding of ourselves. I can have good connections with men, but there's a quality that feels different. There's more energy in men's personality. They are bigger and noisier. It's more relaxed with women, more quiet."

Alexa, 33, finds that women's emotional availability far outranks that of men. "Women are definitely more nurturing, more giving, understanding, and communicative. Men are more self-centered and less aware of my needs. But some men have been very insightful." Amity, 18, thinks of love as the emotional component that most separates men and women as lovers: "I think the love you get from a woman is different than from a man. It's more intense, more serious in terms of planning for the future. Women are programmed to be emotionally expressive, so two women tend to be more intense."

May, 30, finds that the emotional possibilities with women allow her to take a position with females that she never considers with men. "With women I tend to be idealistic. When I've had strong emotional connections, it's been an understanding of each other's souls. This doesn't seem to happen with men. There are some men I have been able to get close to, but it takes more work. I don't demand the emotional connection with a man in the same way that I do with a woman. You can say it's a double standard. I expect women to be more perfect, sexually and emotionally. I'm trying to be more open about being purely sexual with women and letting that connection develop. But I'm a little scared of the intense connection with women. I worry about getting taken over."

When bisexuals compare their reactions to men and women, they find that their varied responses mean that they want and expect different sorts of things from men and women. There is a social, emotional, sexual, and mental aspect to every relationship. On each of these levels men and women offer different aspects. Consequently, some women do not feel that the label *bisexual* accurately reflects their feelings. Bernice, 46, says, "I'm innately sexual," as a way of sidestepping the label bisexual. She explains, "I feel myself equally drawn to men and women sexually. I feel myself drawn almost exclusively to women emotionally and mentally. I feel I am homo-emotional and unisexual." This comment illustrates the complexity of sexual attraction that bisexual women experience. All women desire a physical and an emotional attraction to their partners for the best sexual interaction to occur. Their decisions about their partners and their reactions to them are not readily divided up into these components. Instead, men and women are seen holistically. They offer different sets of characteristics in the role of lover. Bisexual women are able to appreciate the unique strengths and weaknesses of both men and women as lovers.

THE SEXUAL REVOLUTION

In the perfect world after a sexual revolution, men and women will have learned to be skilled lovers to each other. Today many men fall short as lovers because their social conditioning makes it difficult for them to develop characteristics that are erotic. When women visualize an ideal lover they see someone who wants his partner to be turned on and is interested in giving her pleasure. The eroticism of touch and sensuous, gentle, and subtle stimulations of the flesh is something that few men have mastered. The ideal lover pays attention to all the minute changes in her responses that signal her enjoyment of the sexual activity. He is spontaneous in the sex play and is not compelled to follow his own script that leads to a culmination of ejaculation in her vagina. Instead, he is open to pursuing any activity that feels good to both of them at any particular moment.

If this change in men is to happen on a widespread level, it must begin with men who are interested in becoming good lovers. They need to be open to hearing women describe what they want sexually, to trying new activities, and to developing sensitivity and skilled touch. Fortunately some men are already relating to women in this manner, but apparently their numbers are still too few.

Most women want an ideal lover to be emotionally available, open, and vulnerable in the sexual exchange. Since women are socially trained to develop their emotional selves, this is a regular feature of their sexual exchanges with one another. But for men, this is an area of their sexual selves that they need to develop. The privacy of the sexual connection may make it safe for men to allow themselves to experience the sexual vulnerability, sensuousness, and intimacy of the sexual act accompanied by emotional openness. Still, this kind of sexual responsiveness is contrary to the dominant gender conditioning that men learn. When men have the option to experience sexual activity with the completeness of emotional abandonment that women have discovered, another step in the sexual revolution will have been taken.

chapter eight

RELATIONSHIPS WITH MEN

Heterosexual women desire sexual experiences with men, but, more important, they seek relationships with men. The heterosexual woman's sexual tour begins alone, but her erotic travels are foremost a search for a suitable man who is willing to be in a sexual relationship with her, not just a sexual affair. For the young woman, almost every sexual partner is part of the quest for finding the man who will make a monogamous commitment. Nonsexual relationships with men will usually end up involving a sexual excursion as a test of erotic compatibility, if both the woman and the man are sexually available. Once a male friend becomes a lover, a woman's hope is that he becomes a life partner.

In their twenties and thirties, women concentrate on a course of acquiring a male companion. This is the stage in which women have the most relationships.

For some of the youngest women, almost any man will do. The fear of being alone is too great to endure. With time and maturity, women more easily reject men as incompatible sexual partners, or as lacking in qualities desired in a committed companion. Some women find, marry, and settle in with an intimate and trusted man by the time that they are 30. Their erotic journey is focused in a safe haven of a familiar, predictable, and reliable partner. The discomfort of searching for the perfect companion is over for them. A commitment allows them to center their sexual energy into one secure outlet.

However, some women will remain with an unsuitable mate because they are unable to embrace the freedom of the single life. They sink in and settle for less because they dislike the alternative of renewing the quest for a man who will meet their needs. Searching for a mate can be laborious and time-consuming. It demands an outgoing and confident personality. It may mean entering new social situations. And it involves a dating game that still demands that women remain both available and nonassertive, a delicate and conflicted role. For many women, it is easier to stay with the familiar than to venture into the mysterious and difficult territory of dating.

It is only single, heterosexual women in their 40s and older who put less energy into the quest for a male companion. When they are comfortable with their own company, when they are economically self-sufficient, and when they are sexually self-sufficient by practicing masturbation, they demand higher standards for a male complement. He must add a richness to her life with a minimum of conflict. He must be emotionally available, sexually proficient, financially secure, and single. In other words, he must have the same qualities that she has developed in herself. Where is he to be found? She is not going to return to an energetic journey to search him out. He must stray into her fully active world of work, family, creative endeavors, and maybe children. If he does not, she can live without him.

NUMBER OF RELATIONSHIPS

Women make a distinction between men who are sexual partners and men with whom they define a relationship. There is a wide variability in women's concepts of the nature of a relationship. What one woman defines as a relationship, another may say is an affair. Women did not label every sexual liaison a relationship. Heterosexual women had considerably more sexual partners than relationships with men. Young women aged 18 to 25 stated that they had an average of four sexual relationships. Women aged 26 and over had an average of nine relationships. Compared to the older groups, the younger women had had significantly fewer relationships. This is to be expected, as they have had a shorter period of time to explore the sexual world. Forty-two percent of these women had been or were married. But most of the sexual relationships were not marriages.

Bisexuals had an average of six sexual relationships with men. The average length of time for a relationship with a man was five years. Forty-six percent of the bisexuals had been married.

Over 80 percent of the lesbians interviewed had had relationships with men. Since at the beginning of their sexual awakening, many lesbians considered themselves to be heterosexual, just like everyone around them, this should not be surprising. At this time in their lives, lesbians were indistinguishable from their heterosexual peers. They were serious about their relationships with men. They were looking for Mr. Right. They lived out the traditional feminine role and tried to be happy in it. The average number of relationships with men was five and the average length was three years. Thirty-nine percent of these lesbians were married at one time.

WHAT WOMEN WANT IN A RELATIONSHIP

Monogamy

Most women expect to be monogamous, and they want their partner to be monogamous. Fifty-eight percent of heterosexual women, 47 percent of lesbians (who had been with men), and 50 percent of bisexual women stated that they practiced serial monogamy. Monogamy is a basic requisite for a relationship for the majority of heterosexual women. It reflects an attitude that only one person is allowed to see the sexual self. Dale, 21, expresses this belief: "Monogamy is important to me. To love and trust someone with everything about you, that's the person I want to be with." Camille, 40, has similar feelings. She is monogamous, even if her partner is not. "I always choose to be monogamous. Sometimes my boyfriends haven't been, but I always am."

Women feel that monogamy permits them to trust their partner with intimacy. Evie, 21, ties trust and monogamy together. "I think of it as cheating and breaking the trust of the relationship and not respecting the other person and not viewing the relationship as the same as I would view it. So if I'm in a relationship, then the bottom line is monogamy." Shaniqua, 24, is married and childless. For her, trust means responsibility around safe sex and pregnancy control. "For me monogamy means being close with one individual. I've never been comfortable with having multiple partners at one time.

There is also a higher likelihood of sexually transmitted diseases. Some of my friends who had multiple lovers became parents at a young age. So it doubles the chance of getting pregnant, especially if you're not careful with each person."

Women who are monogamous believe that they would only feel the need for an affair if there were problems in the relationship. For them, it is better to practice serial monogamy, end the unfulfilling relationship, and begin a new monogamous one. Nicole, 42, finds that "monogamy is usually fulfilling for me, and I see no reason to venture out. It's not because of the sexual relationship that the relationship ends."

Women who are married take monogamy for granted as a part of the commitment. Paula, 44, was a virgin when she married her husband 27 years ago. Monogamy for her is a given. Yet she says, "Until five years ago I'd never even thought about an affair. I'm curious how I'd be with someone else, but I feel guilty about these feelings. I'm always sexually satisfied by my husband. My girlfriends say 'Don't bother with other men. Don't ruin a good thing.'" Paula's commitment to monogamy in her marriage will not allow her to test out a fantasy about other men.

Monogamy was not always so important for the 40 percent percent of the heterosexual women, 38 percent of bisexuals, and 23 percent of lesbians who stated that with some partners they were monogamous and with others they were not. Women who value their sexual freedom see monogamy as a loss. Rebecca, bisexual, 25, says, "I don't have any rules about monogamy. I don't like to box myself in. I want to explore my other attractions." Some bisexual women like sex with men, but would not limit themselves to one intense relationship with a man. Devorah, 25: "I will continue to be nonmonogamous. I haven't met very many men I feel I would want to be in a monogamous relationship with. Most men bore me so."

Some younger women take monogamy as a rule, but it is a rule they feel free to break if their relationship were sexually unfulfilling or if there were other problems. The game playing and insincerity in the relationships is evident in the dynamics of these young women. Sharisse, 23: "I have sexual contact with other men at times. Once I did so as revenge at a man for his affairs. Once I did so because it was fun. I think I should be monogamous if I love the man. But if I don't love him and he is screwing around too, then why shouldn't I?" Lynette, 21, shares the sentiment: "In my longest relationship, he messed around on me, so I did, too. So I felt the rules changed. But now I plan to be monogamous." Tamika, 29, is unapologetic for her lifestyle, which requires nonmonogamy. "I have been seeing a married man for ten years now and I have been seeing other men at the same time. I don't want to give him up, but he can't give me enough time. So I have another life with the men I date." Kyoko, 36, finds that monogamy goes when the relationship is not fulfilling. "I'm always monogamous to begin with, but as things fall apart I change."

For many heterosexual women, being nonmonogamous is equated with a dating relationship, being young, immature, or not being serious about the relationship. They feel that when they decide to develop a deeply intimate relationship, monogamy becomes essential. Cynthia, is 21, "Now I am monogamous, but at other times in my life, I wasn't. I'm more serious and committed now." Concha, 19, found that a particular man changed her. "I was not monogamous until I met my present boyfriend. I wondered if I was not the kind to be monogamous until I met him." The seriousness of a marital commitment changed things for Vicki, 35. "With some of the men I wasn't monogamous then, but I am now. I'm married now, and it seems a natural thing. I was looking for love in all the wrong places. In my previous marriage I wasn't monogamous. Now I have no desire to have other sexual relationships. In this marriage I'm happy and I feel secure."

Women feel that with age and maturity, monogamy becomes an important element of personal stability and reliability in the relationship. Eileen, 30, believes that maturity brought her to monogamy. "Some four or five years ago I started to feel I wanted a monogamous relationship. Prior to that I had no commitment. I found I wanted stability. I was tired of playing the game, and I wanted a dependable partner with no sexually transmitted diseases." Rachel, bisexual, 35, also feels that monogamy is necessary for a mature relationship. "In the past I was not always monogamous. Now I am monogamous. I am more mature, wiser, and serious. Now I realize the value to monogamy. It is easier to build trust. I feel it makes a difference."

For some women, monogamy is not essential to a serious relationship, nor is it a special mark of maturity. Instead it is negotiable with every man. Sanura, 31, explains: "I'm monogamous now. My present partner would prefer it that way, and I'm content with that. In the past I said I didn't want monogamy. There was an understanding that an affair was a possibility, but I never did have an affair. I had one relationship that was not a monogamous relationship." Leah, bisexual, 45, says, "Whether or not I was monogamous varied on various things. If it was open or short-term, I wouldn't be monogamous. If I was sexually satisfied, how often I saw them and what they wanted to do in bed were all factors I took into account."

Even within one relationship or marriage the issue of monogamy can change. Kristie, 23, renegotiated her arrangement. "I've been in a relationship four years, but we can see other people. I told him I wanted nonmonogamy so I could date other men." Robin, 26, states that for the "first four or five years of my sexual experience I was nonmonogamous. For the last two years of my current relationship we've been having affairs." Some women had a period of separation from husbands when there were problems in the marriage. They had affairs during that time. But they reformed the marriages into monogamous ones. Karen, 28, reports, "My husband and I opened the marriage for eight months. We both had sex partners but not affairs. That was the rule." It was a rare woman who made an arrangement

in the marriage that both partners could have affairs without concealing them from each other. Kim, 37, revealed that "most of the time my last relationship was an open marriage, and we were not monogamous." This marriage ended due to other reasons.

Some women feel that sex with multiple partners has nothing to do with loyalty and commitment to one primary relationship. Glynis, 37, sees her affairs as making the most of spontaneous opportunities. "My proclivity is to be monogamous. But occasionally people come into my life, and sex with them is irresistible! But basically I am monogamous, although the outside world might not agree. I'm very loyal. My affairs don't change that." Glynis's loyalty is a personal loyalty, not a sexual one.

Cheryl Jean, 42, has found that monogamy is not essential to a serious relationship. It is situational and serves as a prevention of sexual jealousy. She sees it as an agreement that two people may make in order to intensify the relationship. "The attitude I have is that I believe that I'm basically a very loyal person. When I'm in a full-blown relationship, I agree to being monogamous. To me it's not a sellout of my freedom and independence. But I believe people have a right to their own privacies. I remember that one man I was with told me that his father had an affair and told his mother. I told him, 'If you do that, don't tell me. That is your problem. You work it out and don't tell me and make it my problem.' I'm not jealous. I don't like liars, but I believe that people have their privacy. I would not be with someone who is not loyal and dependable. Men don't know how to react to these attitudes; it scares them and confuses them. Jim said, 'Now I can't trust you.' So I told him that I would tell him if I had an affair because I'm honest."

After 20 years of an active sex life that included marriage, brief affairs, and long-term relationships, Cheryl Jean harbors no illusions about sexual commitments, jealousy, and temptations for sexual experimentation from both herself and her lovers. She values communication and is prepared to hear the complete reality of her partner's sexual life and to share her own. It is only by conquering her own jealousy that she could bring herself to hear the full story of her partners' sexual lives without becoming emotionally charged.

It is clear that while the majority of heterosexual women prefer a monogamous relationship, there are no hard and fast rules. Women who are not monogamous are comfortable with making their exceptions to the rule. Still, when women believe that the relationship is "serious," they expect monogamy as a means to isolate the relationship and create an intensity as well as an atmosphere of trust.

The issue of monogamy with a man takes a different twist for lesbians and bisexual women. Of the lesbians who had affairs while in a relationship with a man, 21 percent had affairs with women and 8 percent had affairs with men. Nokomis, 28, was not monogamous with men. "I wanted the availability of other partners. I wanted to be with women." Lesbians ultimately resolve the conflict of wanting both men and women as sexual partners by choosing women and by ending their marriages and relationships with men. But many bisexuals struggle with the fact that monogamy means they are limited to a heterosexual or a lesbian sexuality.

Molly

This is a serious issue for Molly, 35. She is married to a man. Prior to this relationship she was a lesbian. "I went into my present relationship as a monogamous one. My husband has always been monogamous, so we both went into it from that viewpoint. But there's not a day that goes by that I don't think about sex with another woman. Roy told me that nonmonogamy was okay. But I believe it would bother him. So the rule I worked out is that if I sleep with another woman, it will include him, too. However, I only became good at hunting for a sexual partner just before I met him. I don't know how to hunt as a couple. Plus, I'm not sure I'd want to sleep with a woman and him.

"Before Roy, if asked, I would have said, 'Yes, I am innately monogamous.' But given that I wonder about women lovers, I'm not sure that I am monogamous. If Roy had lovers, I don't know how I would deal with my jealousy. His jealousy is a real issue, too. He never tries to push me around. It's just a sense of fairness. I think he'd have a difficult time dealing with it." It is obvious that Molly does not want to practice monogamy in her marriage. But she is emotionally faithful to her husband and does not want to create a strain on their connection. If she is to stay married, nonmonogamy is the only way she will be able to be with a woman sexually. She has no simple solution to her problem. The clearest issue is that both she and her husband will have to learn not to be jealous before she can be intimate with a woman.

Leah also is married. She wants to keep her peaceful, rewarding relationship with her husband, but she wants to be sexual with women. She is confident that her husband is understanding and not jealous. Together they worked out an option that she can have affairs with women and date them as long as it does not interfere with their relationship. She has dated several lesbians. But they very quickly found that they were uncomfortable with the arrangement and they ended the affairs. Recently, she placed an ad in the personals, hoping for a response from someone like herself.

For bisexuals, the issue of monogamy is complicated. It is not a matter of sexual fidelity to one person, as heterosexuals might think. If a woman feels that her personality is nurtured and strengthened in different ways by intimacy with a man and with a woman, monogamy will not open her to all the possibilities that might present themselves. Some bisexual women see monogamy as a personal limitation. Its only purpose is to create an illusion of security for those whose low self-esteem

or high level of jealousy require it. To be openly nonmonogamous requires a high level of direct communication and emotional support for all involved. It seems that few bisexuals can find those who can maintain this plane of consciousness.

Companionship

What do women see as their reason to be in a relationship with a man? Different from a friendship, a relationship implies a sexual partnership. But a good sexual partner was not the major reason for heterosexual women to enjoy a relationship. Overwhelmingly, women of all ages and all sexual orientations look for companionship. Companionship means different things at different ages. Younger women, especially if they do not live with the man, have simple needs. Dale, 21, wants a man "for security. I don't have to date anymore. I like to have someone there to talk to. I haven't found anyone I can talk to about everything, except maybe my mom." Leza is 24, and for her a relationship is "having somebody to be with, do things with. It's acceptable to spend time together. A sex partner is more likely to make the time than a casual friend. It's someone to tell secrets with." For Amy, bisexual, 25, a man offers "common ideas about life, physical attraction, a common sense of humor, similar interests in art, music, and travel—a sensitive person, not macho."

Young lesbians whose relationships with men never advanced beyond dating dated men in order to fit in with their friends. Lakeisha, 32: "I dated men basically because everyone else did. I didn't have any lesbian friends to lead me to the path of righteousness! So I did what my heterosexual friends did and talked about. It gave me companionship on a superficial level. I realize now it was a way of saying, 'I am a sexual being.' For Eve, 33, it was the same teenage lifestyle. "You needed a date to go places with the social group. So I had dates and was one of the crowd." Other teenage lesbians looked at dating as a way to gain acceptance from parents. Lucy, 30, recalls, "My mother stopped bugging me about having boyfriends."

Not all lesbians dated in order to melt into the crowd. They looked for companionship with men. Kameko notes that men offered her the similarity of interests which her heterosexual female friends could not provide. "The good stuff with men was companionship. Someone to talk to who was not just interested in going on about dates, hairstyles, and makeup like most of my girlfriends. We had more things to talk about and do with each other. We camped in the wilderness, cross-country skied, and snow camped." Nancy, 34, summarized the best of what her husband was to her. "He was my buddy. We laughed, played, had fun. We shared companionship, intimacy, communication, touching, and affection."

Emotional Availability

Perhaps the most important quality in a male companion is the ability to share his emotional world and for him to be interested in her feelings. Cynthia is 21 and expects "openness, sharing, a feeling of being needed by someone and needing them, too. The emotional part of it is very important." Leslie is 23 and wants "companionship and unconditional love and being able to share everything and not worry about how I'll be perceived and how it'll affect the relationship." Rochelle, bisexual and 26, expects intimacy to be mutual. "I want emotional closeness and sharing of common pursuits and goals. I like being so personally involved in someone else's growth: Their wins are my wins. I want someone who meets the need of their making up for my inadequacies."

Emotional intimacy can be all-inclusive. Rebecca, bisexual, 25, defines it as "being in love, physical attraction, affection, getting validation, intellectual challenge, feeling good about myself, sexually and emotionally. Chemistry, you know. A big part is self-esteem. It helps me to feel good about myself. It empowers me." Karen is 28 and has found that her partner's emotional openness means "we're best friends. He knows my inner fears and desires, and I know his. We enjoy each other's company; we want to be with each other. We get intense support from both of us in what we desire. We have fun, we laugh. I receive encouragement to live out my dreams."

Rudy

As an intellectual and a lesbian, Rudy, 44, found that companionship with men met this need. "I had great companionship in my relationship with Jeff. He was my first experience of falling in love. He was my first sexual experience. I learned about my sexual being from him. He was the kind of person who, no matter what, I had his 100 percent support, unconditional love. When I told him I was a lesbian, he came back a week later. He had gone to a male friend and tried to have sex with him. It didn't work. He said, 'We're so close. I thought if you were a lesbian, I must be gay.' He thought if he was gay, we'd stay close.

"Another relationship was with a professor. He gave me entry into a world I wouldn't have known otherwise, both literally and figuratively. We took trips to San Francisco. We went to films and to intellectual kinds of places it wouldn't have occurred to me to go. Figuratively, he was someone I admired, and being with him sexually was getting into his inner sanctum. There was this private world, and I was privy to it by him. Conversations in the classroom we finished in bed. I was privileged in a way other students weren't. It was like being the chosen one. But looking at it now, we were incapable of having a relationship. I was having an affair with a teacher. That is what he was to me."

Women see emotional availability as a process that involves conscious exploration of personal growth for both the man and woman. This exchange keeps the relationship vital and interesting. Sanura, 31, works as a provider in alternative health care. She is very self-reflective, and her long-term companion is her reference for personal development. "My companion is a resource for developing intimacy. I mean, by having to share more and more of yourself. When getting to know someone over an extended period of time, you discover new barriers to intimacy. You drop those barriers only to discover more. By doing so you really get to know yourself, your limitations, your vulnerabilities, your potential, discovering the depths of who you are. That's what I get out of a relationship. When you spend that much time with a good friend or a lover, you get confronted with your own demons as well as your potential."

Molly, 35 and bisexual, also thinks of her relationship as a route to deeper intimacy and a focus of growth. Molly likes the way her husband deals with her personality. "We have a very affectionate relationship. I regard myself as having a mercurial temperament, and I grew up in a combative family. When the blood spurts out of my ears in anger, most of my former women lovers couldn't deal with it and Roy can. So I've developed more of a sense of humor about my temper because he doesn't react combatively. Now I can overcome it in minutes and then discuss things rationally. I can't express how much that means to me to be with someone who can deal with my personality. It's great."

Security

Security is important for women who marry, want children, family activities, and marital stability. Laura, 35, wants a life and a home together: "I like shared physical activities, skiing, boating, traveling, talking in bed, making love, building a home together, growing food." Donna, 46, wants the security of sharing responsibilities. "I want somebody worrying about the bills; to be responsible so I don't have the whole thing on my shoulders. I like affection, having him put an arm around me; doing things together and having someone to share things with; sharing interests."

When women have a marriage based on the common values of the family lifestyle, they feel a completeness in their relationship. Paula, 41, describes her marriage: "For me it's communication: talking; open conversation; making sure we have time to do things together, minus the kids. We always had Saturday night together. Even when we had no money we'd take a bath, eat on the floor with an indoor picnic." Martha, 48, is happy to have found a husband who is in complete agreement on how to live their lives together. She remains blissful after 22 years of marriage. "The only thing we've ever argued about is money, not having enough or how to spend it. We agree on how to be parents and how we raised our son. We are unbelievably compatible. We only had four dates. I met him through the USO during the Vietnam War. When he was overseas we wrote letters to each other every day for two years. We still have the box of letters we wrote, and every now and then we read them."

Lesbians also enjoyed the financial stability granted through family life. Spring, 43, had practical motivations about her marriage. "He was the father I wanted for my children. And I have to admit that economics was important. I just didn't want to be poor again. He also gave me emotional support." Rita, 48, lesbian, reminisces, "I enjoyed the children, and I liked him all right. But during it all some part of me resisted the permanency of this." These lesbians have no regrets about this phase of their lives. They have continued relationships with their children and grandchildren. Through them they are tied to their heterosexual past. They are the treasured remnant of that period of their lives.

But the security that some lesbians sought in their relationships with men was a result of being afraid to be independent. Phyllis, 35, says, "I was being taken care of by the man in my life. I had such low self-confidence. I wanted to be out there doing things, but I didn't know how." Virginia, 35, was expecting the same kind of caretaking until she saw it to be illusory. "I was with men wanting to feel loved, protected, and taken care of. Security. Not that I got it!" These lesbians had low self-esteem and were raised to play the weak feminine role. They looked to men to take care of them. When they gained the self-possession to be independent, their relationships with men shifted. They did not need them as they had at the beginning, and they were free to leave and search for a singular connection based on intimacy, not need.

Many lesbians see their marriages as times when they had social acceptance. Union with a man gave her a place in the heterosexual world. There is a security in living in the mainstream that is more apparent to women who have left it. For Ryfka, 47, being married with a husband and children meant living a familiar lifestyle with its own rewards. She was learning how to communicate in an intimate relationship, and she was orgasmic with her husband. "My marriage got me social approval from family and friends and society. My parents quit bugging me about getting married. I fell in love with the guy. There's a level of familial approval that is important. We had kids and a family, making meals together, doing things as a family. I liked that."

Some bisexual women expressed similar thoughts about marriage as a refuge of respectability. A few bisexual women think about relationships with men as establishing their status in the world, making them legitimate and socially acceptable beings. Patricia, 37, believes that "there's a certain power that comes with having a man, in our society. It's the key to many doors." Margret, 43, puts a relationship with a man as a measure of her womanhood. "It meant I was successful as a woman and allowed me to be a little nontraditional. A woman must change her lifestyle if she doesn't have a man's validation. It is necessary for the social role. For me, I don't care to live alone. I like to have somebody there to share with."

Lesbians and bisexuals who were with men for social acceptance were not necessarily aware of this benefit at the time that they were involved with men. They were heterosexual because they were unaware of the option of being with women. Relationships with men were what was available when they wanted sex and intimacy. It is only after moving into a relationship with a woman that does not carry the benefit of being socially acceptable that this factor becomes salient to lesbians. They note in their sexual expedition that they have crossed over into a sector that is undervalued by the heterosexual mainstream.

Shared Values

The security offered by the shared values of the typical nuclear family is understood by most people. Women who want a standard marriage can expect that a man knows what she means. But when women adopt a radical philosophy, they need a more progressive man. Bisexual women want a more radical political perspective from the men in their lives. Claire, 37, discovered that the political ideology of her partner is a prominent factor. "The quality of the interpersonal connection is important. Part of that is his values, political and ethical: feminist values; equality, respect, affection. I want him to be the kind of man where I feel relaxed and can be myself. Where I can do what I want and not be judged and controlled. Not all men have all these qualities." Denise, 39, also claims that a man with leftist politics is a requirement. "Men in my life have to be smart, nurturing, caring, and empathetic. I like to get a lot of physical contact before going to bed. Having the same mind-set helps. I have been with doctors and nurses, and I like being with other health care workers.

I couldn't go to bed with a Republican, racist, or sexist man." Star, 48, also combines the personal, political, and sexual: "What I want from men is almost the same as what women give: intellectual and emotional clarity, a sense of humor. I don't have a physical type. I'm attracted to something beyond the physical being. They have to have a feminist consciousness and leftist politics, or it won't happen. Period. They also have to be comfortable with safe sex."

Older women perceive that their needs in a relationship have changed over time. What they wanted from men when they were young altered as they matured and became more complex individuals. They change partners when their values and interests change. Beverly, 47, now wants "honesty and integrity." But "when I was young I wanted a man with a certain physical appearance to create the genetic structure for my children. I succeeded in this. Now I want friendship; artistic inclinations, good health, and gentleness."

Cheryl Jean

Cheryl Jean, 42, has her own business in the fashion industry. After her early marriage that gave her two sons, she stayed single. She charts the changes in her life through the shifts in her relationships with men. "What I want in a relationship with a man has changed. When I was younger, having a boyfriend was about acceptance and security and feeling you belong because your friends have boyfriends. It validated my exis-

tence. It made me old. I had a lot of boyfriends in high school, but I also had male friends who were high school age. I did things with them. I had a '57 Chevy. We were friends and went out and raced the cars. I wasn't having sex then. My friends were the rich kids who had no responsibilities; and I wanted just to have fun."

"Then I got married at age 17, and it was about getting the hell out of my mother's house. I married a farmer who was three years older than I. After four years he developed schizophrenia. I had affairs when I was married. My husband wanted to control me, and the affairs were about being myself and having fun and playing.

"One affair was with my brother-in-law. I cared a lot about him. He was the only one who talked to me about how I felt when I was pregnant. We had fun. My husband was so involved in his work he didn't know what I was doing. I can't believe I did it. But I was only 18.

"After I got divorced, my relationships vacillated between trying to create a whole, well-rounded relationship, and a total lark. It depended on how I felt at the time. When it looked like fun, I did it. And when I felt total passion, I went for it, and that's probably the same today. I don't do too much of the lark stuff now.

"I don't look at some guy and jump his bones like I used to do. I'm not attracted to so many men as I once was. It's more about connecting to people and getting to know them. Connecting to men is being with somebody who has a good balance about what he does with his life and how he feels. He is not dependent on roles. He can talk about the logistics of things, talk about feelings, and have an independent lifestyle. Not someone who expects me to cook dinner every night; no role expectations. I don't want to have to be there all the time.

"Finding this is hard. The men I've had relationships like that with are friends. It doesn't quite go far enough. I think guys end up having a serious relationship with somebody else. I don't know why. Jim, a friend that I've had this sort of relationship with, is an example of this. We know deep personal things about each other. But he wanted to me to set him up with one of my girlfriends. He didn't see that we had a relationship. He can't hear it, it doesn't penetrate. Since we don't have sex now, he doesn't see it that way. So I need to keep going and doing other things. I think I was spending too much time with him, so I'm spending more time now with women friends. I'm finding support and closeness with them."

After marriage, two sons, and divorce at an early age, Cheryl Jean's life forced her to develop her independence. As she became more self-sufficient, her needs and demands from a relationship changed considerably. She describes her ideal relationship as one that embraces personal freedom for both parties. She has surprised herself to find that her concept of relationship moved from the traditional, secure, sex-role stereotyped marriage to a relationship that is both intimate and fluid and free. Her concept of this bond is so radical that the men in her life have not recognized it for what it is. For them, perfect freedom coupled with deep loyalty is too distant from the form of traditional marriage to be recognized as a relationship.

Sex

If sex is what makes the difference between a good friendship and a relationship, one would think that good sex would be high on the list as a requisite aspect of a relationship with men. But it is not. Only 25 percent of the women stated that sexual compatibility was an important aspect of their relationship with a man. Yvette, 25, emphasizes how companionship intersects with sexuality: "Getting along and enjoying his company is almost foreplay. It makes sex enjoyable. I prefer that instead of just wild sex." Eileen, 30, also combines sexuality and communication: "He must have the ability to touch without using words; to convey meaning; to be sexual or nonsexual without words." June, bisexual, 28, says that what she wants with a man is "feelings for each other. And incorporating all these emotional feelings into the sexual relationship." Another bisexual, Carolyn, 29, emphasizes the same emotional-sexual link: "I like being seen as an individual. Communication, trust on both sides. Lots of touching, sexual and not sexual. And the most idealistic one on my list: unconditional love." Peggy, 48, describes her concept of a partnership. "My ideal relationship is a sexual friend. Wild, passionate sex is essential. Sexual friendship is what I can offer a lover and what I want from her or him. Friends give each other security out of caring and trust and acceptance. Friends are not jealous of lovers, other friends, and time commitments to work and creative efforts. Good friends maximize understanding and minimize demands. That is my model relationship." For Skye, bisexual and 35, sex is the only thing she is desires from a man. "I want sex, their energy and intensity. I have a thing for young men aged 18 to 25. I'm trying to break that. The only thing I really can do with them is be sexual. But I want to be in love. I want my sexual desires to match my emotional ones. I want to broaden who I'm attracted to, such as older men." While Skye may fantasize about creating a relationship with a man, she has not been able to make it happen.

Barbara, 51, was married for eight years at an early age and has a grown son. She has a requirement list for a relationship: "A sense of joy; intimacy; a comfort. By comfort I mean relaxed, playfulness is probably like joy. And a big hard dick. I like the feel of a cock inside. And I like it hard. [sigh] I want sex in the context of a relationship. I don't think I could get turned on if I didn't care about the man." Every woman who discussed sexuality in a relationship linked it to communication and emotional fulfillment.

Seventy-five percent of the women did not mention sexual intimacy or sexual compatibility as essential to a relationship with a man. Sexuality is not their primary focus. In fact, women seem willing to forego a good sexual relationship in exchange for intimacy and companionship. Many heterosexual women remain sexually unsatisfied, yet they stay in these relationships. Mitzi, 32, says, "Every man I dated until my husband kept me sexually satisfied. We had sex every day or every time we were together. But my husband doesn't want sex as much as I do. We get along in every other way, though. I'd be a fool to give him up just over sex, wouldn't I?" Women like Mitzi are making a trade-off that they believe is worthwhile. If they have security, stability, communication, and emotional sharing, they can relinquish sexual satisfaction.

SEX ROLES WITHIN THE RELATIONSHIP

Thirty years after the beginning of the second wave of the women's liberation movement, can it be said that women have relaxed the traditional, stereotyped, feminine sex roles with their male partners at home? Most of the women I interviewed held down full-time jobs, some also attended college, many had children, and all had an active social life. They believe themselves to be equal to men in the public arena. Have they also demanded and initiated equality at home?

Traditional Roles

I asked women if they played a traditional feminine role with their partner. The traditional role was defined by women as a passive, nonassertive, compliant demeanor, coupled with taking responsibility for the typical female household tasks of cooking, cleaning, laundry, and childcare. Thirty percent of heterosexual women, 43 percent of lesbians (who had been with men), and 35 percent of bisexuals stated that they played a traditional feminine role at home. Most of the heterosexual and bisexual women had a sense of pride about being old-fashioned, conservative, and traditional. They also believed that this role made life easier. Both men and women could readily predict what was expected of them. They felt that it was a sign of respect for a man to open doors for them and to spend money on them. They are content to manage the home life and to interact in a passive way. If their own interests are the same as his, they will want to do what he wants. So they do not feel oppressed or controlled by him.

Sharisse, 23, talking about her fiancé, proudly states, "Yes, I act like a woman. I go to him for protection from other males. If I go out with him, I'm safe. Sometimes he cleans the kitchen and cooks for me." Betty, 22, is fine with the traditional role. "He is more dominating. I cook and clean and do little things for him. He fixes the car and does outside chores." Melanie, 34, sees more of the psychological benefit from the role. "I guess I still do play the feminine role. I kind of like being taken care of, and I don't really like being alone." Paula, 41, has never challenged the traditional marriage. She has never worked outside the home. "I do laundry, cooking, and cleaning. He does the outside of the house. I think we're pretty equal. Generally, I'll give in more easily than he will." Despite this role playing, Paula feels that as two individuals she and her husband communicate as peers. To her the division of labor is equal.

Some bisexual women embraced the traditional female role. Rachel, 35, "Yes, I'm traditional. I do the cooking, sewing, cleaning. I love it. My fiancé watches my son when I do it, and I appreciate the relief." Phoebe, 46, "Yes, I'm traditional. I believe in men pursuing women. I let the man set the stage for the woman. I follow the male definition of the relationship in regards to roles and expectations. He defined what was okay."

Women who accept the feminine role have been exposed to the critique that it fosters inequality with men and that it can be a reflection of low self-esteem in women. Therefore, some who embrace it struggle with trying to become more assertive. Carla, 24, "I cook and clean house. I serve him more. I'm more emotional. I cry. I wear frilly clothes to try to be sexy for him. But I'm not always submissive. I would like an equal relationship. I don't always give in. I practice being in the control position. I practice being the aggressor." Carla knows that her feminine posturing puts her at a disadvantage. So while she adopts the outer feminine role, she is trying to alter her personality so that she becomes more assertive. A similar awareness is there for Trudy, who at 49 has lived with the traditional role much longer than Carla. "I never take the aggressive sexual role. Even now I don't feel right. I won't make sexual advances.

It makes me feel weird. But lately, I've been demanding equal rights."

Most of the lesbians were relating to men in the 1970s and 1980s when they were in their twenties. They were trying to follow the heterosexual rules and the rigid standard of gender stereotyping was just then beginning to loosen. Lesbians who reflect on their years as submissive house-wives recall it with anger and resentment at being channeled into a hated role. Phyllis, 35, never confronted her husband but seethed inwardly. "I was dissatisfied doing the things that were expected of me. I didn't like doing the repetitious tasks. I never had the satisfaction of seeing a project complete like he did, building a deck. I had to structure my time around my home responsibilities. This was not argued about. I internalized it." Roselle, 32, remembers the painful time of being someone she did not want to be. "We fought about my role. They wanted to make me feminine, clean the house. I despised playing the role. They were sick relationships with alcohol and drugs. I hated myself. It was a way to cope with a world who condemned me for who I was, a lesbian."

Lesbians felt that they were sacrific-ing their personalities during their marriages. Virginia, 35, recalls, "I cleaned house, cooked, and was supportive of my husband as he explored his life while not doing anything for mine. I had his baby. I stayed home. I was giving, loving, supportive. I subjugated my needs for those of the man. It was my responsibility to be sexual when he wanted it." Roselle tried to conform her personality as well. "I

tried to be passive. I did subtle manipulat-ing to create what I wanted. I went along with society's expectations of make-up and feminine clothes. Being feminine, it didn't feel comfortable at all!" These lesbians felt constrained and oppressed in these relationships. They were glad to escape them. They left these men behind with no regrets. They were forcing them-selves to make a marriage work.

Many heterosexual women also fell into the traditional role when they were young and in their first relationships. This was how they saw the generation of women before them, and they imitated it. But as they saw that the feminine role was failing them and making them unhappy, they found themselves changing. Gayle, 25, is in the middle of this process. "Sometimes I'm the total little Miss Housewife. But as the relationship has matured, there is less emphasis on tradi-tional roles."

Personal assertiveness, speaking her convictions, and holding to them was the talent Beth, 38, had to develop. "I used to play a traditional role, but I don't anymore. When I was younger, the man would decide what we'd do. I didn't speak my opinions. Now I speak my opinion, I don't tolerate their things that aggravate me. I don't do things if I don't want to do them." Maureen, 38, also sees that maturity and experience with more partners changed her. "At times when I was young, yes, I played the role. But less so with each relationship. These days I'm not that way."

Some bisexual women say they were trained as girls to be passive and obedient to men, and their early relationships reflected this fact. Claire, 37, "I thought I was liberal and I had a modern feminist relationship. But when I look back, it wasn't balanced. I did most of the domestic work, and he earned the money." Star, 48, "That's what I was trained to do. I didn't think about it. I was raised to be a wife and mother. And I wasn't allowed to work because I'd have a husband to take care of me. That was how it worked. I was married young, age 19."

First Marriages

Women see the passive role they played in first marriages as one of the reasons that they were unhappy. They changed the second time around. Denise, bisexual and 39, "Yes, I did act traditional with my first husband, but I intentionally did not with my second husband. I was oppressed and abused by the traditional feminine role, so I made sure the second time that that wouldn't happen." Alexa, 33, realized that the wifely role conflicted with her feelings as a bisexual. "I was traditional in some ways. My first husband was threatened by my bisexuality. With my second husband, I played the traditional, bullshit, passive role. With my third husband, I was able to be an active bisexual without his participation. I didn't need his approval. I've had six or seven male partners. I don't always come out about bisexuality. I'm afraid they'll manipulate it and my sexuality is not for others to manipulate."

Carmen, heterosexual and 42, was married at 18 to a South American man

and she played the submissive role with him for years, as her mother had instructed her to behave. After her divorce, Carmen acquired a new self-confidence learned from working and raising her two daughters on her own. "At first, yes, I was traditional but not any more. It's different now. I speak up and say, 'I don't like this. You can leave any time. The door is always open.'"

Being submissive and a caretaker does not allow a woman to get her own needs met. May, 30 and bisexual, came to see that her training to behave this way did not serve her own needs. "My first year in college I felt my function was to make the other person happy and not to ask for anything for myself. It mattered that he was having a good time. But I wasn't bothered by the fact that it wasn't doing much for me. My second boyfriend was emotionally abusive. He broke up with me brutally. I went to therapy, and suddenly it occurred to me that I could be angry. It was a revelation. My family was anti-anger and it was exhilarating to be angry. I was in a pattern of being pushed around by men. That's when I started to become a feminist."

Even though women consciously want to redefine the role of housekeeper, their training from childhood makes it second nature. Glynis, 37, understands this. "I try not to be traditional. But sometimes I get caught up in it. Sometimes it's hard to define the roles. You do them without thinking. For instance, doing the laundry: I find myself doing 80 percent of the laundry. He works more, and I end up doing more housework." Violet, 37, has found that making these changes takes time. "I guess up to about three years ago, I was strictly traditional. I used to be chief cook, bottle washer, homemaker, and caretaker. I provided sex on demand. Now I ask for help and for what I want, either in the caretaking or sexual role. Sometimes I insist." Violet has found that her ability to be assertive in getting help around the house overflowed into the sexual part of the relationship. She became more active in all aspects of her home life.

Problems with role stereotyping come from the rigid separation of male and female tasks. Housework must be done, and the solution is to have it shared. Submissiveness keeps a woman in a child-like state. Her ability to form judgments and to establish her convictions is essential if a partnership is to be one of two mature adults. Taneisha, 24, has the benefit of parents married 30 years, and her mother is a working professional. She is beginning her first serious partnership with a sense of teamwork. About her fiancé, she says, "I like to cook. I cook dinner—not because I'm supposed to, but because I want him to eat healthy. Otherwise he'd eat Taco Bell or Jack in the Box. I think people see us as a typical couple. He's a football player, and I'm smaller. They think he looks like he could protect me if I needed protection. I don't feel I need protection. I had to learn how to take care of myself with my brothers.

"I don't defer to his opinion. We have decided that we'll split the chores in the household. We had a party and both got the house ready and both cleaned up.

He doesn't expect me to agree with everything he says or to serve him."

Taneisha is at a starting point that for older women has been the end of a long journey. Barbara, 52, now without a partner, describes the changes she went through beginning as a naive "model housewife" to a complex and mature personality.

Barbara

"Having been a part of the women's movement 20 years ago, I don't think that much about traditional roles. Some things that are traditionally women's roles I like and some which are traditionally men's roles, I also like. I like cooking, doing the dishes, repairing things in the house. I loved being a mother. I work for myself and enjoy that. I don't know what traditional women's roles are in sex.

"I went through a transition. When I got married at age of 20 in the mid 1960s I essentially became my mother, who led a traditional woman's life. I married a man I thought embodied stereotypic masculine traits. He was dominant. I was passive. He made all the decisions. I worked and completely took care of the house. When I had my baby, I took care of him exclusively, even though I still worked. I deferred to my husband's career and his job.

"In 1970 after my baby was three months old it began to dawn on me that I was getting the short end of the stick. After months of rage I ended the marriage. I decided it was time to figure out who I was. Thereafter I had a number of relationships with men who were more passive than I am. They moved in with me. I was the center of the home and the strong one. When I didn't like the way the relationship was going, I kicked them out. After my divorce it seemed so easy to end a relationship if it wasn't making me happy.

"It was an immediate and complete change. Some elements endured, like my attempts to be the perfect girlfriend and the perfect mother, but it felt radically different. It was a very exhilarating time. One of the things that I cherished was that I was feeling emotions. During my marriage I hadn't felt anything. Not happy, sad, or angry. I felt like I had been asleep for seven years, and I was very withdrawn. After my divorce every moment was an adventure. It took about 15 years before I realized that I liked myself and that I knew who I was and I like the person I had become.

"I notice as I get older, I care less of what other people think and am in tune with what I like. My taste in furniture and clothing are feminine. I wear a flannel shirt and jeans, but I have lace underwear on! I cover my house with flowers and with flowered wallpaper. I think that at this stage of my life I am a mixture of feminine and masculine traits, and I am drawn to people who embody those characteristics."

Cheryl Jean, 42, has come to see shifting gender roles as more complex. "In the traditional family, the female plays the support to the male. She takes on the secondary role of the two of them. She cooks and cleans and does the errands. He makes the most money, and that is a huge factor. That measures success. Women are there to make the guy look good. I am a loyal person, but I'm ambitious and I see support as equal. I don't follow the roles; we work together. I work on my cars and I also like to iron. I don't look for validation from the fact that I have a man in my life. I can get my own money. I don't want to reverse the roles. The nurturing is instilled in women, but I think men can learn it. Women can be nurturing at work. When women try to be like men at work, we are selling ourselves short. Staying at home and taking care of kids is a valid job if you make it a valid job. My grown sons can cook, clean, work on cars, take care of children. They are good friends to women."

Cheryl Jean and Barbara participated in traditional, young, first marriages and then refused to take on this role again. Making their way through the world of work as single parents made them self-reliant, assertive, and resilient. They would not trade this for the acquiescent gender role that was assigned to them. They exemplify women of all ages who discovered that they were trained to behave in a stereotyped fashion and did so, only to find that it was not rewarding. In fact, it was stifling or confining.

Assertive Women

Forty-four percent of the heterosexual women, 30 percent of lesbians, and 37 percent of bisexuals stated that they always refused to play the traditional feminine role. They constantly asserted their independence and control over their own lives. They initiated joint activities including sexual exchanges, managed their own money and career, and expected that household tasks would be equally shared. Younger women are especially critical of the traditional role. Dawn, 22, sees the "traditional woman as the underdog. It is a stagnant role, with no growth." Kenya, 25, also refuses this role and is angry that a man might impose it on her. "I am not passive. When I was younger I was passive. I have been told by men that I make them want to hit me because I expect things and am assertive. I see that as his problem. I am amazed that a college-educated man is still so macho. He thinks I should follow his career!"

Women see sharing gender roles as essential to an experience of equality in the relationship. Lily, 20, has dropped the special female training from her culture. "The traditional role in Japan is the submissive woman. We try to compromise and try to make it more equal. I like to do things on my own." Janelle, at 30, with several relationships behind her, has no patience for the dominating man. "I don't cater to men. I'm not at their beck and call. I don't subjugate myself to inflate their ego. I choose relationships. I don't sit and wait for a man to chase me, to sweep me off my feet and come in and run my life!"

When women refuse to relinquish their independence, they find that conflict is inevitable with some men. Jennifer, 21, says, "I don't put up with their shit. I don't need them. I'm independent. I don't report on where I am." Dale, 21, finds herself a modern woman among unchanging men. "I attract men who want me to sacrifice for them. I won't do that, so they find a women who does do that for them. I won't sacrifice feeling or beliefs. I'm independent; I don't want to be with someone who'll support me." Shaniqua, 24, is married to an accepting husband. But in the past, she says, "I've been told I'm too independent. I'm very confrontational, which for some men is seen as a threat."

Lesbians experienced similar confrontations with men when they claimed their independence. Those who were assertive endured conflict that rose from refusing to fit into a feminine role. Lakeisha notes, "I'm not a traditional female. I'm a confrontational person. I don't back down. I won't let them change my opinion." LaQuita, 29, found that her personality was the obstacle to harmony. "We fought over what my role was. If I was aggressive or too smart, it created a problem. I was supposed to play the dumb, helpful female. I didn't come from a traditional household. I think of traditional as the woman staying home and being wifely. I always liked working and being independent. I don't like to cook or sew. I like sports and being outside the home. My mom taught me the importance of being independent. She was dependent on Dad. Then he died, and she raised us alone. So I had to be prepared to be independent. I did my share of housework, but wouldn't be bogged down doing everything." Unwilling to alter their personalities, these women inevitably locked horns with men.

Relationships with men can work even though women do not play the traditional feminine role. Rudy, 44 and lesbian, came from a home where her mother was a traditional housewife. But her mother was everything she didn't want to be. "My mom was a traditional housewife. I hated watching her do that. But I took advantage of it. I never offered to do it for her. I saw my dad had power, and I didn't want to be like her. Although I never stayed home and did housework and cooking, I did traditional female stuff, such as emotional caretaking. I've always been more interested in intellectual conversations than cooking. When I was younger, I would be with a group of couples, and the women would be doing women things and I'd be with the men talking. Until I was 22 I didn't like women all that much. There were some I adored and admired. But I saw them as an exception. I saw the average woman as silly. She didn't have much to offer me. The women I knew kissed up to men, placated them, and stroked their egos. They made it harder for women like me to deal with men. So I detached from women." In a sex-role stereotyped world, Rudy saw the female role as the most confining and least interesting. Her friendships with men were the centerpiece, but she identified these as peer connections. She abdicated from the heterosexual female role itself.

Leotie, a lesbian, had an unusual marriage. She and her husband together developed an evolving marriage devoid of sex roles. "He was not a traditional man. He cooked a lot. He was very sensitive. I only cooked when I had to, if he was away. I worked and had a career." But a sexual incompatibility eventually became clear to them. "The marriage ended when we each came to terms with the fact that we were both gay."

Some women feel that they have reversed the typical gender roles. They see themselves as both the initiator and active director. Piper, 22, "I'm probably more the boss than him. I'd rather it be more even, but he's pretty passive. The traditional role is man being in charge. We're doing the opposite. Nothing gets done if one person doesn't initiate." Kate, 31, and her husband have shifted roles. "I work. I am the major money earner at times. I make household decisions. I'm not passive in the relationship." Hope, 40, has included in her shifting roles a sense of female superiority. "I dominate a lot of aspects in the relationship. I'm the emotional leader. I set the ground rules regarding honesty, monogamy, time spent together. I think it's because men don't know shit about what they want."

Sanura

Being aware of how to create equality in a relationship is not simple. It requires constant evaluation as Sanura, 31, explains. "I think that I define the traditional feminine role as not taking the initiative. It means being somewhat submissive. It means having the sex primarily revolve around the male sexual gratification. I don't think I've ever been in a typical traditional feminine role. I'm more assertive, more individual-oriented. There is more of a balance of power. The balance of power means to me having an equal role in decision-making. But that definition is oversimplified.

"Let me talk of what doesn't work. Relationships that I think are unequal. I have a lot of women friends who say they have a balance of power in the relationship. Their discussions occur with both sides giving their input. But ultimately, if there is a decision to be made, the man makes the final decision about whether something happens a certain way. He gives the final approval. So the dynamic seems to be that the woman is trying to convince the man that things be seen a certain way. His role is to decide that her opinion is okay. He gives validity to whatever it is that she wants.

"I acknowledge and see as valid my own perspective, independent of my partner's perspective. But at times I find myself losing sight of that. It's a process that I've had to be aware of. Being in a traditional relationship, a male/female relationship in this culture, and to try to do it differently is difficult. There are all these societal forces that are trying to put you in a certain role, to mold you into what is an acceptable relationship role. They are strong forces. It's really difficult. Sometimes I wake up and realize I've fallen into a trap that I thought I had a better handle on."

Housework

Altogether, 70 percent of the heterosexual women prefer to think of themselves as liberated and not tied down to the classic feminine stereotype of the passive housekeeper. For them, liberation means developing personality characteristics such as assertiveness, independence, self-direction, and sexual initiative. But what happens when it comes down to housework?

In terms of their self-perception 70 percent of the women saw themselves as nontraditional or endeavoring to be liberated. When it comes to household work, 55 percent are leading the liberated lifestyle. They have found partnerships with a man who is equally responsible for the household. Another 10 percent have found partners who take on more household tasks than the women do. This means that once they established a goal of finding a man who would cooperate in sharing the responsibilities of the home, the women were successful in creating this sort of relationship.

Traditional women's tasks are repetitive and constant. Cooking may mean three meals a day, including clean-up. Washing floors and laundry may be weekly. These chores are always waiting. Male-defined tasks such as mowing, barbecuing, and fixing electrical outlets are occasional and can often wait. If all household chores are tossed together in terms of time, equality means that the man must do chores that are typically labeled as women's work. Women who want to have a nontraditional household must find a partner who is willing to do his share of the so-called women's work. For the 65 percent of the women who shared tasks equally with their partner or whose male partner did more than they did, it is a case of the man taking on the traditional feminine tasks. For a woman, liberation means that her partner must transform also. He has to be willing to drop the traditional male role of man of leisure at home and become a working partner in taking on responsibility for the domestic environment. Increasingly, men are understanding this and changing.

CONFLICTS WITH MEN

Conflicts and arguments destroy the sense of companionship because they emphasize opposition. What are these arguments about? What drives women away from their partners?

Power and Control

It is widely thought that relationship conflicts center on sex, money, and children. This appears not to be true. These women, regardless of sexual orientation, repeatedly defined conflict with men as a struggle over power and control. These women believed that their partner wanted to control them. A few women admitted that their goal in a relationship was to control their partner. The issues of power and control inevitably led to a break-up. The deep issue was his need to exercise power and control over her. The content may be over childcare, sex, or money.

Younger women who are in dating relationships are particularly sensitive to issues of control. Dawn, 22, has found that her break-ups occur when the relationship reaches "a conflict when he has a need to control or dominate me. Which I won't put up with. Not being able to handle an equal relationship. Expecting me to meet their needs." Kenya, 25, has found the issue to be equality. "They think I'm too demanding. I want to feel equal, not powerless. Control is the biggest issue. So I'm always fighting for them not to be in control of me. I think two individuals should take care of themselves." Justine, 24, has found that "power over" is the conflict. "I'm a feminist and if the guy is traditional, he'll want to dominate. I won't let him. No one tells me what to do." Dale, 21, discovered that control issues ruined her relationships with men. "They belittle what I've done, my schooling. I'm just a woman, less than they are. They've tried to control me. I used to play the game. Let them think they were in control, but it's too much acting." Dale learned a role where because she is a woman she is supposed to pretend to be less intelligent than her partner and to turn control over to him. She found the strength in herself to drop the farce and to continue her quest for an equal partnership.

A controlling man attempts to determine certain elements in a woman's life. This involves creating a situation where the woman's life is centered on him. Kristie, 23, found that this established a direct conflict. "My problem with men has been possessiveness. He expects to be first, number one in my life. I should meet his needs and feelings. To me, my career and school is first. I have to take care of myself." Janelle, 30, also determined that meeting her personal goals precluded his concept of a relationship. "What ended my relationships was my unwillingness to compromise. I wanted to run my own life. Maybe selfishness is a better way to put it. I wanted to further my personal goals more than to further the relationship. I refused to be dominated to any degree. My vocal feminist attitude turned them off."

Shaniqua, 24, realized that the man's concept of sex roles imposed on her an inequality that she resented. "I hate his ideas about patterns of expected behavior. For instance, I was expected without being asked to do something like cooking dinner. He might say, 'I thought you would since we ate out the other night.'" Blythe, 34, has found that with various men the issues were different, but it was always power and control. "We argued about cooking, doing dishes, which in his mind were not shared tasks. I would have to ask him to do things. We argued about sex. He knew what I liked, but only did it at times or withheld it. I would get rewarded with sex when I was good. Another guy was so jealous; he wanted 100 percent of my time. One resented my education."

Several bisexual women looked at their former marriages as climates where they were emotionally abused by domineering husbands. Leanne, 41, says, "I was pressured sexually and physically manipulated. He is bigger and can just pick me up and move me. We had poor communica-

tion. I wasn't an equal, not a real person. He wanted me to stay home, not work. He expected me to cook all meals and houseclean. I had no help in childrearing. He held the fact over me that he made money and I didn't. I felt like a sex object. He was not concerned with my feelings and was unfaithful, breaking a promise."

Claire, 37, states, "I was intimidated. I learned to be intimidated from my mother, as well as my father. With my mother, I had a fear of speaking out. It would displease her. I brought this to relationships and was vulnerable to dominating men. We would argue about money, sex, being late, and my not doing what they wanted to do. Men have an unconscious sense of entitlement, and I was afraid not to go along with them."

Another bisexual, Toni, 50, states, "Our conflicts were about invasion of space. I did not feel that the other person heard me. I was getting lost in the relationship, not feeling dominant. The biggest conflict was losing track of my wants because I was too in touch with the other person's wants. I was caught in a role in which I can't be myself. I chose men who were drinkers and womanizers. I got tried of listening to them. It took much of my energy. The penis comes between us—it's the third party."

Phoebe, 46, describes her very unhappy marriage: "Life centered around what he wanted. I felt I should do something, but he defined what I should do. I strived to be more independent and not supported financially by him. Sexually, I didn't feel cared for. There was no time for what I wanted. There were verbal put-downs. He undermined my authority over the children and my intelligence."

Issues of power and control can be successfully negotiated if neither partner has the goal to dominate. When both people are giving as well are receiving, the couple can together weigh the trade-offs and strive for fairness. Sanura, 31, describes that the issue of one's own personal needs and goals versus the relationship is what arises in her relationship. But she and her partner are successfully resolving it. "There's been a lot of work in this relationship on what it means to meet the other person's needs without giving up yourself. Both sides feel unappreciated at times and feel that they've contributed more in certain areas. It's what's behind a lot of the issues. Who cleans the kitchen more often, who does the laundry. The bottom line was feeling your needs weren't being met, a deeper issue." Sanura and her partner have the communication skill and the commitment to an equal relationship that enable them to elevate this issue beyond the level of domination, control, and assigned sex roles. They have moved into a deeper sharing of the moods and feelings that underlie attempts at control.

Poor Communication

When women state that communication problems destroy a relationship, they are thinking on a number of levels. First, if there is no respect for the woman as an equal, conversations will not develop but will remain a power struggle. Second, most men experience difficulty in discussing their emotional lives. This leaves women feeling frustrated. Third, if the man holds to rigid sex roles, he will not be open to her demands for equality. All these issues surface when women say they have communication problems. Leza, 24, finds that miscommunication is her major problem with men, but it takes different forms. "Before my exposure to feminism I thought differently of conflicts. I found I couldn't talk to him, that he was uncommunicative. I had trouble with him not being interested in academic pursuits. I had to force him to do household stuff. Now I correct his sexist language. He feels that I'm angry all the time. I try to get him to understand what's important to me but he wants it only in small doses."

Time and again women mentioned men who are unable to talk about emotions. Vicki, 35, makes a generalization about all men: "Men are not sensitive or emotionally supportive. You can't resolve issues around simple things like housecleaning and bills because they aren't able to. Because they can't express their feelings." Mitzi, 32, had a similar viewpoint: "The major conflict is communication, that men don't open up about their feelings. That's been a big problem in a lot of my relationships." Edie, 36, sees men as both unemotional and weak. "They hold back their feelings and are not aggressive enough with me. I want a man to be as strong as me. I don't feel loved enough. I want unconditional love."

Money

Conflict over money revolves around not having enough, or how to spend what there was. Robin, 33, is very concerned about her financial status and her career. She's had conflict with men over both issues. "I've fought over work. I need to work a lot, and men don't understand that. They say they do, but they don't. I feel betrayed by men over money. I get involved with men who don't make as much money, and I get angry when they spend it foolishly. Mitzi, 32, found similar conflicts: "I used to date men who couldn't financially support themselves. I wouldn't give them a penny. I've always been financially independent." Both of these women felt used and put upon when the men they were with couldn't handle money.

Sex

Sex can be an issue in a number of ways. Sometimes the woman wants more sexual activity. Susie, 33, "I'd like to have more sex. He's wrapped up in his work and brings it home. He's uptight. He doesn't have energy for the relationship." Mitzi, 32, found, "We argue about sex. I want more sex with my husband than he does. He thinks I should talk to a counselor, but I think it's our problem. We might go to therapy together. Otherwise the relationship is good, and it would be stupid to end it because of that."

Men can try to limit a woman's sexual expression as Carolyn, bisexual and 29, complains: "In two relationships the men didn't like me being sexually active with them. They wanted me to be passive and wait for them to initiate. That drives me crazy!"

In some cases, the man wants more sex. Karen, 28, "We have conflict about sex. He's wanted me to be more sexual. I did not have a sexual awakening until I met my husband. Before him I was not orgasmic. I refused sex for long periods. I wanted Brian to love me, and not for sex."

Barbara

For Barbara, 51, her husband's desire for sexual variety in the early 1970s and her cooperation with him led to the end of the marriage. "In my marriage it was all give and no get. He wasn't my friend. He wasn't my lover. He was critical, and I was very unhappy. My husband said, 'Let's try swapping.' And since I was unhappy I thought it would be rewarding. One night we had dinner with another couple who were friends, and then we switched partners and went to separate bedrooms. As soon as I was kissed, it felt different from how my husband, James, kissed me. There was affection and sensuality, and when we had sex he was much more involved than James was. So I fell in love. We had an affair for nine months. His wife knew about it, and we were supposed to break up. But I was so enthralled. It was irresistible, and I continued to see him. I felt bad about hurting his wife. I told him I wanted him to choose, and he chose the marriage. So I ended the affair, and then my marriage."

Barbara was sexually naive and inorgasmic with her husband. Since she had no comparison, she accepted this sexual incompatibility. She assumed that there was something wrong with her. Open sexual conflict with her husband ensued when he initiated a sexually open marriage. She learned that her marriage had been seven years of sexual dissatisfaction. This precipitated its termination.

Janet, 43, found herself sexually interested in other men. "I was sexually attracted to other men, and I wanted to act on it. But in the relationship I was not able to." But her issues around sexuality and sexual incompatibility went further. "I had difficulty asking for what I wanted sexually. I had a religious conflict. I was taught that sex was for procreation and not for pleasure." Janet's sexual problems involved sexual contexts. She wanted to alter the agreement of monogamy. And she had her own private guilt about being sexually active that she had to resolve. Until she could shed her guilt, she would have sexual conflict with any partner regardless of his sexual openness.

Lesbians list sex problems as the second most frequent form of conflict with men (gender role issues is number one). Virginia, 35, recalls an unpleasant sexual style. "He wanted fellatio, but no cunnilingus. When he came, sex was over. I got pushed for sex when I didn't want it. He threatened to find someone younger and better. He said I didn't move right." Phyllis, 35, felt pressured into sex. "I'd go on strike, and he'd insist I provide services. I hated sex with men. No deep communication and little tenderness."

Jolene, 40, "I was dissatisfied sexually and felt he was out only for himself. I wanted more nurturing than I got. He wanted more sex. He was messy, not loving, not tender enough." For Maybelle, 50, "sex was completely unfulfilling. I expected him to validate me, and he didn't know how. So I retaliated by turning off sexually. Sex was so tense that he was a premature ejaculator." These sexual problems went unsolved. Most lesbians were not sexually fulfilled by men. They did not sexually bond with them in the way they later were able to join with women.

Priorities and Values

If women are looking for companionship, how the couple spends time together becomes an important consideration. The things that they do together should reflect interests of each. Shared activities bind the couple. Conflicts arise when they learn that different things are important to them. Angela, 24, "The most important conflict was priorities. That I had more priorities for us and he had more priorities toward friends." The issue of dividing time among the relationship, other people, and work is a large one for younger women. For some women, the problem is that the man does not give her enough time. Cynthia, 21, feels deprived: "I feel he's too involved with his job and doesn't have energy for the relationship." Taneisha, 23, has similar feelings of being left out. "We went from spending all our time together to three hours during the weekend. It was hard because I felt when he had free time, he didn't spend that time with me but with his friends. I felt unappreciated, and he didn't think I was important. So I dated another man at the same time."

For other women, the situation is reversed. They don't want to give the relationship as much time as he wants. Carolyn, bisexual and 29, "Men become angry because I don't want to spend my every waking minute with them. Most relationships have made me feel claustrophobic. I get accused of being closed and distant because I need private time."

Devorah, 25 and bisexual, rejected a man she was dating over serious differences in values. "I dumped him because he was laughing at feminism, and it stunned me that he was like that. I was looking for a reason to end the relationship. He wanted me to invite a woman friend over so he could have sex with both of us. I didn't feel like he was listening to me. He didn't care about what was important to me." Doris, 50, heterosexual, specifies that differences in priorities mean different values and lifestyles. "We didn't share enough common interests. I wanted to have space from him and do what I want to do. We had different point of views. I wanted to pick up hitchhikers. He wouldn't stop to help an injured man. I wanted to foster kids; he refused. This created too much pressure, and we divorced. He had an affair. I had a breakdown after all our arguing on lifestyles, and lost communication."

Differences in values are also a reflection of different personalities and personal needs. Rudy, 44 and lesbian, recalls her most notable male relationship: "Jeff was the most significant. We argued a lot about me having to be responsible for him. One of our biggest blow-ups was when my dad had an heart attack. I was going to school and going to the hospital, and I was on a thin edge. He said I wasn't giving him enough attention. He was a kid. He was great to play with, but when I needed someone to take the load off my shoulders, he wasn't there. He never had money and he was irresponsible."

After Jeff, Rudy found herself entangled in a different scenario in which she could only lose with the man. "He was married. When I first got to know him, he was separated. We had sex when he was separated. He decided to try a reconciliation and by that time I was hooked. It was a mistake. I spent a lot of the time of that year waiting for him. I couldn't make demands. I was afraid if I went out he'd call, and I'd lose my chance to see him. Now what I see is that you can't build a relationship with someone who's involved with someone else. Either it's dishonest, or someone is not finished and they can't give you their full attention."

May

May, 30, finds that she has fewer conflicts with bisexual men than heterosexual men, and she has been selectively dating bisexual men for this reason. Most bisexual have an open-minded attitude about relationships and nonmonogamy, an attitude that is essential to create the sort of companionship she desires. "I really like dating bisexual guys. A lot of it has to do with feminism. Straight men can be sweet but cannot understand what it's like to be a woman in this world. And because straight men have the power, a bi man is on the bottom of the totem pole. A bi man understands the experience of not having power. So I feel safer and more comfortable. I have anxieties about being taken advantage of by straight men. I'm uncomfortable with straight men who like to settle down with a bisexual woman. It feels like the stereotyped thing of straight men wanting to have a lot of women crawling over them. Other straight men are uncomfortable about nonmonogamy and my wanting to date women. Bi men are more likely to want the same type of relationship I do."

Childrearing

Women who said childrearing issues were a problem saw this as simply part of the relationship complex already described. Although conflict may exist on many levels, when his actions affect the children, tensions are magnified. Parenting requires a high degree of responsibility from both parents. These women did not see the man as doing his share.

Ryfka

For Ryfka, a lesbian, the problems with her husband did not emerge until they were married and trying to make a life together. First, he seemed to be just irre-sponsible. But everything escalated to a dangerous level. "The biggest conflicts were over childcare. It was presumed that I had total responsibility for them. For example, the kids would get presents. When they got presents from my relations, I made sure they wrote 'Thank you' notes. When they got presents from his relatives, he didn't take that responsibility. And I got blamed when I didn't enforce the 'Thank you' notes. He was diagnosed as manic depressive after we separated. He refused to acknowledge that he had mental illness. He became dangerous. I had to choose to protect the children or take care of him. I took the kids and hid." Following the termination of this disastrous marriage, Ryfka went onto other sexual relationships with men. But she "didn't get involved in a relationship where it would be intense enough to have conflict. They didn't like my independence, and that usually ended it."

Carol Ann, 43, says, "In my marriage the big conflict was communication. There was a lack of identical goals. What he wanted from life and what was important to him was not what I wanted. Our childrearing practices varied greatly. My ex-husband did not spend time with the kids. He was not communicative or patient with them. In the later part of the marriage, sex was a problem. We could never discuss his premature ejaculations." Emily, 32, had similar problems: "I wanted to be independent, and he didn't want that. He tried to control me. We argued about money, childcare, goals, what we wanted from life. We had conflict around sex. It was too infrequent for me. We discussed what makes people happy, and I was frustrated that he couldn't communicate about it."

Women want an active co-parent as a father for their children. Disinterested fathers and fathers who could not agree on childrearing practices were usually dominating men who were also emotionally abusive. Conflicts about childrearing were a major unresolvable difference.

Personal Problems

His Problems

Women left relationships with men when the men's personal problems created trauma or instability. One common problem of men is their inabiltiy to control anger. Thirty-six percent of the heterosexual women, 22 percent of lesbians, and 32 percent of bisexuals had been in relationships where they were physically battered by their partner. In these violent alliances, 23 percent of the heterosexual women, 8 percent of the lesbians, and 23 percent of the bisexuals stated that they hit the man in retaliation. A larger number of heterosexual women, 72 percent, were emotionally battered by men in relationships. Fifty-two percent of lesbians and 55 percent of bisexual women were emotionally battered by men. Forty percent of the heterosexual women, 46 percent of lesbians, and 30 percent of bisexuals admitted to emotion-

ally battering the man. Violent relationships usually escalate into more violence unless the couple involve themselves in intensive counseling. These women chose to end the relationship instead of trying to heal it. Being in a violent relationship with a man made heterosexual and bisexual women more careful in their choice of future male partners. For lesbians, it became another reason to avoid men altogether.

Cheryl Jean

Cheryl Jean, 42, as a teenager married a man who developed schizophrenia. "My husband was violent and beat me. I think he thought he'd have me under control when we married, and he wasn't able to do that. He wanted to isolate me; he didn't want me to be smart. He wanted me to be the wife of the farmer. I got a job and he didn't like it. I was scared to leave because I knew the violence would escalate when I left. I was afraid he'd kill me. He was dangerous, violent, and sick. He took me to court for 19 years. I had 100 custody hearings. He learned how to work the system. I changed my name and moved to escape him. He took the kids to court when they were 11 and 12 years old because they refused to visit him. He wanted them jailed." Surviving this brutal and destructive relationship made Cheryl Jean more determined than ever to preserve her independence.

Not all women experience relationships with these vicious extremities, but they found that men had different personal problems that made them undesirable. Crystal, 20, broke one relationship when his personality fell short. "I left him because he was 27 years old, but he needed to grow up. He was unsure of himself and boring. He was nonmonogamous, but he wouldn't let me be alone. He was competitive and tried to outdo me. He was irresponsible and didn't do what he said he would do." Jennifer, 21, had similar complaints: "He was too emotional and insecure. His jealousy kept me from talking to people. He broke plans without calling."

Julie, 58, found in her first marriage that her husband's problems drew in every issue: "He was a compulsive gambler, so we argued about money. For me, it became an issue of survival. There was no money to feed the kids. He was a bully, and he put me down. We had communication problems. Men in general won't talk about or express feelings. I wanted more emotional sharing and more communication. I was more sexual, and he rejected me sexually. He didn't want to explore more sexual variety." With her husband's refusal to take responsibility for any of this, the relationship was doomed.

Bisexual women define some of their problems with men as a combination of his personality and his attitudes and values. Molly's ongoing conflict with her husband centers around his passivity and lack of ambition. "He is too passive. We have had some arguments about sex recently. I'd prefer him to be more aggressive. We argue about who's doing more things. I feel I am, and it's getting tiresome. We have an ongoing thing about that."

Her Problems

Some women admitted that their own personal problems created havoc in relationships. One element of these situations is substance abuse. Thirty percent of the heterosexual women, 50 percent of the lesbians, and 25 percent of the bisexuals acknowledged that at some time in their life they abused alcohol. Another 28 percent of heterosexuals, 35 percent of lesbians, and 28 percent of bisexuals abused drugs. Substance abuse was a problem for Roseann, 22. "I used to drink and do drugs, and I could fight about anything. I was jealous of everybody. I didn't want them going out with their friends. I was furious if they had contact with other women and I wasn't there. As a result, in every relationship the guy cheated on me. I usually broke up as soon as I found out."

Other women unearthed that their conflicts were more closely related to their personalities. Gloria, 44, says, "I am susceptible to depression. I'd feel depleted emotionally. I'd lose interest in anything sexual. I'd become lethargic. We had conflicts about my career. I had trouble maintaining interest in his friends, and I'd lose contact with my friends. I tended to get sick a lot. I lost my identity. I wouldn't stay centered professionally." For Pam, 31, her personality problems pushed up against his problems. "I know that my jealousy and possessiveness led to arguments. I wanted all his time with me. Then his bad temper created conflict. He was violent. He felt his needs weren't being met. I wanted attention." These women, having done some healing and work to overcome their problems, can look at their past relationships to observe that they created the conflicts. When they were abusing substances, depressed, and insecure about their own identities and goals, they were unable to sustain a relationship.

But personality problems do not have to be so severe to become a source of problems in relationships. Being inconsistent, not knowing what they really wanted, and changing their attitudes made problems for some bisexuals. Alexa, 33, "I take the responsibility for some break-ups because of the power conflicts. Sometimes I go into a relationship being submissive, and later I want control, like over finances. Star, 48, wanted an equal partnership and felt comfortable in the traditional role, yet ultimately it did not serve her. "I become dependent in some way. I hold myself back. He would encourage me to go and be more. It was a conflict because of my training to be a wife and mother. We had no arguments about sex, money, or kids. Yet it always felt like his house and his things because he earned it."

SEXUAL ABUSE AND RAPE

For women in America, sexual trauma is a common experience. Many of the women had been victims of violence from men. However, few of them sought therapy. Most did not speak out about their traumatic experience, but processed the grief,

fear, and emotional reactions alone. Some of them shared their story with comforting friends. That these women could survive sexual violence, heal themselves, and develop a rewarding sexual life is a tribute to their strength and determination. Women who were as yet unable to fully and passionately experience their sexuality did not attribute it to the trauma of past violence. Most commonly, they believed that the reason for their lack of sexual fulfillment was that they had not developed the communication skills to tell their partners what they wanted sexually.

The percentage of women in this book who experienced male violence matches up with the statistics of women in other studies. Thirty-three percent of the heterosexual women, 42 percent of lesbians, and 29 percent of bisexuals were molested as children. These differences were not significant. Women of all sexual orientations are equally likely to have been molested.

Women are also equally as likely to experience rape. Forty-seven percent of heterosexual women, 43 percent of lesbians, and 49 percent of bisexuals had been raped. Forty-eight percent of heterosexuals experienced attempted rape. Fifty-five percent of lesbians, and 7 percent of bisexuals experienced attempted rape. The difference between lesbians and heterosexuals is not great enough to be significant. But bisexuals were significantly less likely to experience attempted rape. Taking into account that some women experienced multiple assaults, 57 percent of the heterosexual women experienced some form of male sexual violence.

Rape and sexual abuse are traumatic experiences that can affect women for years. The wounding from these experiences can result in a loss of interest in sex with a partner, fear of men, hostility toward men, and self-loathing. Women who suffer from these effects of post-traumatic stress syndrome should seek professional therapy to resolve these issues. Sexuality with a partner can be a deeply vulnerable and emotional experience. To wholly participate in mutual sexual activities, women need to feel self-love, self-confidence, internal strength, and immeasurable trust in the partner. Many women who have experienced sexual abuse need the guidance of a competent therapist to redevelop these qualities in themselves, especially when recovering from childhood sexual abuse.

Abuse and Sexual Orientation

Lelah, a 23-year-old heterosexual woman, vehemently said to me, "I really think that women are lesbians because something bad happened to them sexually. They were molested or raped when they were younger." At the time, she was happily married to a compassionate man. I replied, "Then by your own theory, you ought to be a lesbian!" She had just recounted to me her history of being viciously raped at the age of 5; beaten from the age of 6 to 15 by her father (who was convicted of child abuse); and married for two years to a violent and sadistic man who raped and battered her. Unwilling to concede her theory, she laughed and said, "Who knows what my future holds? Maybe I will become a lesbian!" Research-based estimates of the percentage of women who are lesbian range from 3 to 10 percent of all women. It is unknown how many women are bisexual. If being a victim of sexual assault created lesbianism, half of all women would be lesbians! Despite the facts, many people like Lelah hold on to this false theory.

When heterosexual woman are sexually injured by men, they do not automatically think of turning to women as sexual partners. Instead, they work on recovering from the trauma. They go on with their sexual journey seeking a nurturing male who is understanding and companionable. Heterosexual women see the men who perpetrated crimes against them as one sort of man. This type of man is not in the same category as men they seek for partners. Heterosexual women tend to view the personal tragedy of being a victim of male violence as an encapsulated incident. They deal with recovering from its effects, which may include a phase of mistrusting all men. Being a victim of male violence teaches the heterosexual woman to attempt to distinguish more clearly between trustworthy and untrustworthy men. But her choice of a mate and sexual partner remains male. Not one heterosexual woman mentioned thoughts of seeking women as sexual partners following sexual assault.

Most heterosexual women find relationships with men rewarding and are happy and comfortable with the lifestyle. When they are victims of male violence, they see this as a crime that is unrelated to their quest for sexual partnership. Even if they have overcome homophobia about lesbianism, they still have no interest in exploring this territory. These women believe it is their nature to be heterosexual.

Lesbians and bisexuals are no different than heterosexuals in refusing to link sexual assault to their sexual orientation. None of the lesbians mentioned sexual assault as having any connection to their choice of women as sexual partners. Lesbians and bisexuals handle the personal tragedies of sexual assault in the same manner as heterosexuals. They work on recovering from the trauma and perceive the event as a consequence of being a woman in violent America. They viewed the perpetrator as the criminal male and did not generalize this perception to all men. Like heterosexuals, bisexual women sought out male lovers who were nonviolent men.

THE SEXUAL REVOLUTION

One popularized myth about the sexual revolution is that women have developed an interest in casual sex. This is not entirely true. Since the 1970s women have begun to be sexually active at progressively younger ages. More and more women are not waiting for marriage as a prerequisite to begin exploring sex with men. In fact, unfortunately, many teenage women think of their virginity as something to "get rid of." But venturing into sexual activity without marriage does not mean that women value casual sex. Into their twenties some women look at sex as an art to be learned and practiced with different men. But this attitude has always

been one of the minority of women. Most women want their sex partner to be a man with whom they have a stable relationship. He should be monogamous, a good companion, emotionally available, and should share her values and goals. He should respect her as an equal. If the woman has a conjoint household with him, she should expect him to share the chores. Women leave men and go on to find a new partner when the man fails on these counts. Good sex takes a place of lesser importance if women find the man is a compatible companion.

After a sexual revolution, it is doubtful that women's relationships with men will be easier and more fulfilling. In relationships both women and men learn how to express their intimate emotions and how to define their goals and lifestyles. For most people, these lessons occur in a process of trial and error as they experience love and loss, trust and betrayal, union and separation. This is the human condition, and a revolution in the sexual arena may interface with these events but will not ease them.

A sexual revolution would facilitate open communication about sexuality. Possibly this openness would encourage individuals to stop using sex to manipulate one another in order to control a relationship. After a sexual revolution, sex will be about pleasuring the partner out of desire to express affection and communion. When sexual activity keeps the couple together as lovers, it can support and strengthen other aspects of the relationship.

chapter nine

RELATIONSHIPS WITH WOMEN

Lesbians and bisexuals have to find women like themselves to date, to develop relationships, and to form a community of friends. But lesbian culture is invisible to the heterosexual world. Where does a lesbian or bisexual who is newly establishing this identity find like-minded women?

Ninety-eight percent of lesbians and 89 percent of bisexuals say they meet one another through friends. A friendship network is essential to develop. Women in a friendship community are likely to share the same interests and values. They know which friends are lesbians or bisexual, and they know their histories. All this provides a safety and support when initiating a relationship. After friends, the most common situations in which lesbians meet one another are at parties (86 percent), which can be seen as extended friendship groups; school (80 percent), and work (78 percent). Gay bars, the most visible part of

the lesbian subculture, were dating places for 65 percent of lesbians. Organized women's sporting events, like softball teams and volleyball teams, are meeting grounds for 60 percent of lesbians. Eighteen percent of lesbians found one another in the military or in church.

Bisexual women identify one another in similar ways as lesbians. Bisexual women say they meet potential lovers at parties (64 percent), political meetings (61 percent), cultural events (60 percent), school (54 percent), work (23 percent), and bars (23 percent). For the most part, bisexuals enter the subculture of lesbians and bisexuals to find one another.

Women have to overcome their passivity to meet other women, and 92 percent of lesbians and 76 percent of bisexuals said they would initiate dates with women. Rudy, 44, comments on how a potential lesbian can make contacts for relationships. "I have met most of my lovers through school settings, work, or mutual friends. I had a conversation with a woman who is wondering if she is a lesbian. She doesn't want to go to a bar because she thinks she may not be a lesbian. She asked me, 'What should I do?' She is attracted to men and doesn't know if she'll make the transition to women. I said, 'Just live your life and something will happen.'"

NUMBER OF RELATIONSHIPS

Lesbians tend to have fewer relationships with women than they did with men, in part because their lesbian relationships are more fulfilling and stable. The average number of lesbian relationships with women was three. The average length of a lesbian relationship was 8 years. The bisexual women had an average of two relationships with women. For bisexuals the average relationship with a woman was two years in duration.

Lesbians and some bisexuals think of their relationships with the seriousness that heterosexual women think about marriage. They want a long-term commitment and often mark this arrangement with a commitment ceremony. Current attempts by activists to make marriage legal for gays and lesbians are evidence of the importance of these relationships.

WHAT WOMEN WANT IN A RELATIONSHIP

Monogamy

Monogamy is very important to lesbians, and 81 percent say that they practice monogamy. It is important to 50 percent of bisexuals. Nokomis, lesbian, represents a typical position regarding monogamy: "I put a lot of energy into having a loving relationship. There is only one person that I love so much that I want to be with. I don't want to lose some energy with someone else. I am naturally monogamous because when I have one partner I feel most fulfilled, and it's the kind of relationship that I'm at my best in."

Seventeen percent of lesbians and 45 percent of bisexuals admitted to having affairs with women while they were in a relationship.

Ryfka

Ryfka, 47, speaks for nonmonogamy: "I think that people are nonmonogamous because they don't get their needs met by one person. I don't think there is anything wrong with getting your needs met by more than one person. When I was in my eight-year relationship with a woman, I was not monogamous after the second year. She travelled and was not around a lot. She was more sexually conservative than I was. So I had affairs to meet my varied sexual needs. The women knew it was an affair. It was open and honest. I chose people who knew it was not going to be more than an affair. Of course, one of the affairs lasted two and one-half years. It was made more difficult when three of them fell in love with me. I fell in love with one of them, but it was not going to be a relationship. I'm friends with all of them. As long as it didn't infringe on our time and space, my lover didn't want to hear about it. I was always available to her, and she knew it. I think it was an unusual arrangement, and it worked. Most lesbians condemn nonmonogamy. They think it's bad, inappropriate, unsisterly, and patriarchal. My response is 'Different strokes for different folks.' It was never done in an underhanded kind of way. It was always up front."

Twenty percent of lesbians stated that they on occasion had a brief sexual tryst with a man after they identified as a lesbian. These flings were purely for physical pleasure. Ryfka was sexual with men after identifying as a lesbian. "I had sex with a man I met who seemed like fun, and I had an affair with a heterosexual couple. The man was about a six-month affair. The other was three months. They were fun. I told lesbian friends, and they thought it was gross. I said, 'Hey I'm having fun.' I was single, and both were clearly affairs." Like Ryfka, lesbians never let an affair with a man become serious. But few would want their lesbian friends to know about it. Being sexual with a man does not challenge their identity as a lesbian. These women say that they are innately bisexual, but that they prefer women for sexual contact, intimacy, and social bonding. Their social identity is as a lesbian. The affairs with men are regarded as a pleasant diversion to be

kept discreet. There is little emotional involvement with these men. One woman said, "I like to fuck a man about once a year. You know, just to remember what it's like. Then he's out the door."

Companionship

Companionship is a major aspect of lesbian relationships. Spring, 43, ranks companionship as important but she links it to love. "From women I get companionship, fun, and sex. Mostly it's enjoying doing things together. Someone to count on and depend on. I remember being shocked by the realization that I love this woman more than anyone else in the world!"

Different than heterosexual women, lesbians and bisexuals go far beyond an expectation for mere companionship in their partnerships with women. The most common answer as to what was important to them in an affiliation is nurturing, support, and love. This joining includes the concept of companionship, but carries the fun of camaraderie to a more significant level of intimacy. This support comes in the form of a sense of acknowledgment of their individuality. LaQuita, 29, finds she has the "freedom to be myself, not having to play a role; not to have to impress someone. I am comfortable to be however I want." Cleo, 28, also has discovered a special personal acceptance from being with a woman: "What's important to me is being able to be myself and yet be supported. I can be independent but have support no matter what I do. It's a springboard or base from which I can accomplish a lot individually. It's emotional and financial support, too."

Emotional Availability

Women want and enjoy an intense emotional sharing with other women. Most women feel that the emotional shared space with another woman is deeply fulfilling and on a higher level than what men offer. Daphne, bisexual and 29, speaks of an almost telepathic connection. "Emotional bonding seems to be more intense and more natural. I feel closer to my female partner than I have to any male partner. She seems to know more of what I want and without having it verbalized, sometimes before I even know." Patricia, 37, finds that her alliance with a woman is elevated over what she would give a man. "The intimacy and closeness we share is what is so important to me. There is a commitment to the relationship I could never make to a man." Devorah, 25, describes emotion in distinctly feminine terms. "I know my lover wants to spend time with me when she is sweet, caring, warm, sexy, and funny. She cares about my feelings and thoughts, and she acts like I matter."

Good communication is a component of the ability to give emotional support. Lesbians and bisexuals believe that the communication that heterosexual women have to work for and must demand from men is freely and easily exchanged in lesbian connections. Lakeisha, 32, says, "I get validation. I feel my opinions, what I have to say is listened to. If I was upset about something that she was doing it's not blown off with 'That is your problem.' It makes the sex great."

Being listened to and being validated as a unique person are starting points in lesbian relationships. This common language of open consideration creates an intense, emotional support that comes easily to women, who are socially conditioned to be emotionally available. A camaraderie in communication is expressed by Nancy, 34, "We have equality and understanding. I don't have to explain everything as I would to a man. There is tenderness, emotional support and nurturing, being nurtured, and play. Loving communication and trust. We are very careful with each other's feelings and always try to be gentle with each other."

Women feel most real when they can express feelings without editing themselves. This is what is special to Marion, 57. "There's nurturing, affection, closeness, dependency upon my partner. I can count on her. There's the touch of a woman; being able to share feelings with someone special. Discussing what's happening in the world. In our social activity I am able to totally be myself and not have any image."

One reason for ease of communication between lesbians is that lesbians find that being with a woman places them in an immediate position of equality. The equality that must constantly be won in relationships with men is instead a baseline with women. Anita, 50, sees this equality as the reason why all the forms of communication come more easily with women. "It's an equal balance of power. It swings, but basically it levels out. There's open and honest communication. It's not possible to have this level of communication with men. I'm not sure if it's because women think and feel differently than men or because our experiences are different." Alizon, bisexual and 31, describes her womanly connection as a result of shared experiences: "I love the emotional bonding and good sex. It's easier for one woman to know what is good for another woman because she's been there herself. The bonding doesn't seem to require as much work. It seems instinctive."

Ryfka looks at the issue of equality and communication from the fact that women as an oppressed group have a special commonality. She finds with women a "sense of intimacy and the creation of intimacy through the sexual connection, shared communication, and a shared language. There is a connection between women found through the shared experience of being a woman in this culture." Phoebe, bisexual, 46, also relates how her coupling with another woman is all-inclusive. "Women give me emotional closeness, freedom to express myself, support, and companionship. There is a greater understanding and appreciation of each other as women. We have the same female struggles so there is deep bonding."

Because gender conditioning is so powerful and because it places men and women on diametrically opposed sets of human behavior, there is always a crack in the veneer of closeness that men and women can create. Georgia, bisexual, 31, notes how being with another woman emphasizes a togetherness that is impossible with a man: "From women I get physical comfort and a special identification. Men always seems to be on the opposite pole." All of these women note that this sort of opposition does not exist between women. Their intimacy can be more immediate and deep.

Lesbians feel strongly that men cannot offer this level of intimacy, but not all bisexuals agree. Some bisexual women do not feel this polarity between men and women. When they think of a relationship, whether it be with a man or a woman, they expect and anticipate the same aspects. Star, 48, is one of these women. "I want good communication. I want someone who is playful, not taking everything too seriously. It is similar to what I said about men. I want a feminist. Someone smart and funny. She must have political savvy. She has to like me a lot. She has to think I'm the greatest thing that walks the earth. Communication is the key. She has to be able to be vulnerable, emotionally and physically. Being comfortable with safe sex. We must have hot sex!"

Shared Values

For lesbians, having shared values means that their partners support their efforts to live an individualistic and authentic lifestyle. Support includes equality, recognition of the self, good communication, mutual caring, and personal growth. Virginia describes how her relationships with lesbians provide her with a community of women that fosters her work of self-creation. "Lesbians give me support for the qualities I aspire to. These qualities are the ability to be totally honest, to be able to be real with another human being, to have good sex, to be able to share equally, to transcend the oppressive patriarchy, to transcend all the bullshit and reach a higher plane together."

"Transcendence," "reaching a higher plane together"—this language brings a spiritual dimension to the discussion of intimate relationships. None of the heterosexual women discussed a spiritual communication or transcendent element of their relationships with men. Yet this is a very common theme in lesbian and bisexual descriptions of their relationships. The spiritual sensibility is a practical one for Rosalie, 46, who sees it as one aspect of similarity to be embraced with another woman. "We have a commonality of spiritual belief and political belief. There is a willingness to work together in an egalitarian way." Practical spirituality underpins all the elements of communication and companionship for Audrey, 42. Her values include a sense of service to others, and she expects her female partner to understand this implicitly. "The difference of a relationship with women and with men is in being able to communicate our feelings. I feel strongly about serving others and getting outside myself to do something for others. I want to stay stimulated intellectually. I like romance, fun, travel. I want a friend, a best friend. I want financial independence, not feeling stressed financially together. Honesty,

nurturing, loving spirituality, too. I want my partner to be spiritually conscious about how the universe works."

Practical spirituality creates a holistic personal bond, involving all elements of the being. When she started her travels into lesbian territory, Danielle, 42, did not realize that this was possible. Today she knows that with a woman she finds "the good sex and an ability to play. There's a sexual openness and an emotional connection where it's not just body stuff. There has to be a psychic connection and an ability to make an intellectual connection. I want all four of these things in a relationship: physical, emotional, psychic, and intellectual. This is what I've come to." Once this complex form of relationship is understood and experienced, it becomes the starting point for growth and change, an impetus to a greater sense of the self. Tina, 36, finds that "it's a healthy, healing part of my process of evolution. It is spiritually and emotionally satisfying. I have the security of emotional protection, fun, enrichment. I am truly and deeply appreciated." On this level, nurturing and support become the most creative and energizing. Alana, 44, emphasizes that such mutual regard becomes "an honoring between the two partners to be the most fulfilled, growing woman that each of us can be. We allow that to happen even if it brings up conflict or hard places. There is a respect for one another and encouragement to grow. We create a safe environment to communicate. Each woman having a spiritual practice and path has been very important."

Sex

Being sexual with another woman is a large part of the definition of the word *lesbian*. Yet lesbians and bisexual women did not rate sexuality as the most important aspect of their relationships. As with heterosexual women, they place it of lesser importance than emotional availability and companionship. Lesbians and bisexuals do end relationships when there is sexual incompatibility. But a great many of them will sacrifice the sexual part of the relationship when the emotional bond is intense. A sense of loyalty and the rewards of the emotional contact apparently are worth the trade-off.

Lesbians and bisexuals find that without the struggle for equality that their relationships with men involved, their contact with women moves into a deeply emotional and typically female nurturing domain. Complex communication, the enhancement of one another's personal growth, and a psychic and transcendent experience of themselves and one another are the marks of their most satisfying relationships. These are not utopian visions. Seventy-eight percent of lesbians and 52 percent of bisexual women say that these expectations are met in their relationships. Seven percent have not yet formed their ideal relationship with a woman. Twenty-two percent of lesbians and 41 percent of bisexuals say that their relationships meet their needs "at times." Seven percent of bisexual women say that their relationships with women have not fulfilled their needs.

SEX ROLES WITHIN THE RELATIONSHIP

Most lesbians do not play a traditional feminine role with one another. Only 3.4 percent of lesbians and 3 percent of bisexuals stated that they play the feminine role with their lesbian lovers who play a masculine role. Jolene, 40, is comfortable with this role division, feeling that it reflects her personality. "I do more cooking and take care of the house. Sexually, I'm more feminine and she's masculine." Some lesbians feel that their personality is more "butch" or masculine, and they may find themselves playing the male role in certain ways. Still there is not a rigidity here. Audrey, 42, rejects the feminine role. "I see the traditional feminine role as passive. I always see myself as more aggressive. I'm attracted to more feminine women than myself. I used to be real butch, but it's not who I am, so I'm softening. I want to be somewhere in between, and I'm not attracted to the very butch."

Twelve percent of lesbians and 20 percent of bisexuals stated that they do play the feminine role at times. These women feel, as heterosexual women do, that it is a backsliding into an old pattern. Naomi, 25, says, "I work hard at not being traditionally feminine. I felt conditioned by being with a man. The woman I was with had been a lesbian all her life, so it was easy to let her do nontraditional stuff. But I struggled with doing both."

Nontraditional Roles

Eighty-five percent of lesbians and 77 percent of bisexuals answered that they reject the feminine role. LaQuita, 29, has worked to discard the feminine role she played in her marriage. "I'm independent financially. I make my own decisions. I'm me. I don't take orders." Molly, bisexual, 35, relates that "I never lived with a lover. I've been very clear on that. I never wanted to rush into something that wouldn't work out. I did not provide services for them unless I wished to." Molly's response indicates her perception that the traditional feminine role is subservient. Jody's disdain for the feminine role is evident in her definition of it. "That role is nonassertive, sacrificial, martyred, and I don't do that stuff."

Working-class women saw their mothers as surviving under a burden of labor that did not generate the traditional concept of femininity. Guadalupe, 29, is one such daughter. "I don't know what a traditional feminine role is. My mother worked at a job, and she also cooked, cleaned, and did laundry. But it wasn't as if it was a role. She did those things like someone who was at home eight hours a day. We kids took care of ourselves a lot. Mrs. Cleaver is traditional, not my mother. I work. I play sports. I don't like to cook; I don't mind laundry. I don't put a dress on and make dinner when you come home from work. I don't think I want children."

Lesbians rate equality as a major benefit of being with a woman, and this equality extends into the sharing of house-hold tasks. Most lesbians say that they share tasks by being jointly responsible. If something needs to be done, the one who notices it does it. Others say that chores even out when each woman does the jobs that she likes to do. Rene, 39, "I won't play a feminine role, and I don't play a masculine one either. I don't play roles. I do what I'm best at, and they do what they're best at." When there is conflict about household tasks, both are responsible. Maggie, "Both of us take full responsibility for the house, animals, and bills. We go with our strengths and desires." The same sensibility is echoed by Spring, 43, "We divide things up in whatever way feels natural. We do what is comfortable and fun to do."

Rudy

Rudy, 44, refuses the traditional feminine role: "I've never played a traditional feminine role. I've lived with three different women. We always divided up tasks in terms of who had time and inclination to do them. Money was pretty equal in most relationships. The last one made more money than I did. I was the sexual initiator. I prefer to be with someone who would initiate sexual behavior and emotional caretaking. I am feminine in that respect. There were times when one lover would be excessively quiet and I would say, 'Is there something wrong?' And she'd say, 'No.' And I would leave it at that. I didn't want to be the emotional caretaker, and I wouldn't do it. It's been rare that I've been with anyone who would emotionally caretake me. I spent years drawing things out of people. I remember a conversation with one woman. We were up all night talking. I pulled things out of her. I told her, 'I don't want to do this. I want to be a lover, not a counselor. I want to work on changing this behavior. Be up front and tell me what you feel.'"

Androgyny

Most lesbians see role playing as a restriction on their personalities. They actively reject roles and seek to replace them with an androgynous sense of self or the ability to behave in both feminine and masculine ways, depending on the demands of the situation. Alana, 44, understands that she keeps working on an awareness of roles. "I'm pretty conscious of roles, and I bring up the issue of roles with my partner. I try not to have a set pattern of behavior. I like being a varied individual, and I do not want to get locked into the role. I play both roles." Destroying ensconced roles sets the ground for the basis of equality that lesbians want in their relationships. Rosalie, 46, notes this fact: "I don't play a role. I don't believe in roles. I believe in an equalized relationship. Some tasks are shared." Tina, 36, feels very strongly about breaking down gender roles as a source of growth and personal development. "I can be very dominant. I'm not passive, manipulating, nonassertive, domestic, jealous, or powerless, which is

how I view the feminine role. My first ethic is in evolution. I attempt to break bad communication habits, foster positive relationship behaviors, rise above role orientation with generosity of spirit. I want to foster all these in my partner without the limit of a role."

Some lesbians want to allow for self-expression of their moods through androgynous roles. Lakeisha, 32, states: "I could go either way. I could be femmy or butch. It depends on how I wake up in the morning. I like make-up, and sometimes I like to have dinner ready when my lover comes home from work. But I'm not a traditional butch either. I won't put up walls. I have no desire to go to the hardware store!"

Since she has not had the experience of living with a lover and sharing household tasks, Ryfka thought about roles in terms of sexuality. She, too, likes the idea of being at both ends of the spectrum. "I don't play a traditional feminine role in my life. So why should I in a relationship? I'm assertive and independent. I don't take shit. I'm not afraid of confrontations. There is the traditional butch/femme thing that some lesbians do. I use that sexually in terms of using butch/femme roles. I love to dress up in fishnet stockings, push-up bras, and silk. But I also like to wear boxer shorts, a harness, and a dildo. So I play both ends of it. It's all a game. It's a big mistake to identify the femme sex role with passive or 'bottom' [powerless] and butch with 'top' [in control]. It is not correlated, although many people think it is. It is not." For Ryfka, the gender roles that some women take very seriously are nothing but games or roles to play with as sexual fantasies. As a role consciously invented for sexual titillation, it has nothing to do with the everyday habits of living.

While most lesbians and bisexuals welcome the opportunity to be themselves without rigid roles, the lack of roles or patterns of expectations of how to act can create an ambiguity that becomes a new problem. May, 30, discusses her difficulties relating to women without a role. What form is to be created that constitutes a bisexual lifestyle? She has not lived with a woman, so her concern is solely with the interpersonal dynamics.

May

"It's been difficult for me to get involved with women because the women I've gone out with have been bi and we are unclear on what the roles are, who does the asking, and how to turn it into a sexual relationship. I have a bit of unresolved sexism in me. I feel very protective to women. I'm awkward about asking women because I feel I'm pressuring them. Other bi women feel the same way. So it's a bit harder to get things moving than it is with men. In terms of a relationship, it's hard to say because I haven't been very involved with women. I've had two sexual involvements with women that were more than a one-time fling. One was with a woman who was a lot younger than I was. It only lasted a few weeks. There were no roles one way or the other. She took the initiative in making it sexual, but I didn't really feel there were any roles. We were just two women having sex with each other and talking. Any power imbalances came from the age differences. I was eight years older, and she wasn't really mature. She was more politically radical than I was. There was some tension because she felt I should give her more approval. She didn't understand that I was working so hard academically.

"I was involved for five months with another woman who had been a friend for over a year. I had been interested in getting something going sexually, and she wasn't sure. She was in a relationship with a man. In this case, I took more of a male pattern. She left it to me to be sexually aggressive in the initiation, and she was sexually passive. I got cast into a butch role, and she was being femme. I see these as a different set of categories from traditional role playing with men. The context is different. They are chosen roles. I have no desire to be a man. I see it as decision-making and taking initiative sexually. But butch/femme is a choice of power decisions. I've been out for a whole bunch of years. I come across as the person who is going to be in charge. I get put into that position. I don't want to be with a passive woman. I want to collide in the middle with another active woman. I don't want to do all the work. I think bi's have to learn social skills to get women into bed. I don't know what the game is. How to pick up a woman. One can flirt with a man, and he'll take it from there. I don't have to do much asking." May has clarified her ideal of what it should be like to relate to a woman, but she has not found it.

Housework

Do lesbians share male and female assigned household tasks equally, or do they fall into a pattern like heterosexuals where one is expected to do female tasks and the other the male tasks? Are lesbians living the androgynous lifestyle that is their utopia? Forty percent of lesbians rate their relationships as having an equal distribution of household tasks. Each of them does some female tasks and each does some male tasks. However, 60 percent of the lesbians believe that they do slightly more of the work, both female tasks and male tasks. So lesbians are sharing all the work and are not dividing it along an artificial gender line. They both pitch in for the task at hand.

Socially there is a common perception that lesbians play butch/femme or male/female roles with one another. But these lesbians believe that such roles are too simplistic and confining. Only 18 percent of the lesbians I interviewed identify as butch and 10 percent as femme. Forty-nine percent label themselves as androgynous, or able to combine within themselves the best qualities of both male and female gender assignments. It is a political statement for them to be liberated women who are free from the constraints of gender roles that usually limit women's freedom of expression.

CONFLICTS WITH WOMEN

Interpersonal conflicts are inherent in all relationships. Although lesbians and bisexual women tend to have fewer and more stable relationships with women than they did with men, they inevitably meet opposition with one another. Conflicts between women are very different than those between men and women. Power and control issues, the major complaint about relationships with men, were not mentioned. Neither were the two common complaints about men that they cannot communicate and that they are emotionally unavailable. The conflicts between women reflect their cultural conditioning to be nonassertive, nonsexual, and dependent. Women vary in their ability to overcome these self-denying traits. When women are unequally matched for these qualities, conflict arises.

No single form of conflict emerges from the discussions with bisexual women about their relationships with women. Instead, their assessments of conflict with women stem largely from individual personality differences and lifestyle goals. Conflicts between women were minimized by lesbians and bisexual women. They focused on the issues that led to the dissolution of a relationship. Bisexual women tended to have a limited number of relationships with women, so they thought in terms of their individual contentions with the few women with whom they were intimate.

Sex

Problems with sexuality were the most commonly mentioned by lesbians. And the most common problem was that women wanted sexual activity more often than their partner did. Some women were on the other side: their partner wanted sex more often. Virginia, 35, finds conflict when her partner gives her "pressure about my sexual performance and pressure if I didn't want sex. But it's not the same problem as with men. Still, I think it's a problem from when I was heterosexual. I wonder, 'Does this mean I'm not sexually adequate?' I'm very sensitive to sexual pressure, and I think it's left over from my marriage." For Penny, 49, sexual incompatibility is the subject of her self-analysis: "My sexual partner is very sexual, and I have problems seeing sex as an expression of love. I have a fear of losing control if I submit to my partner's sexual advance. I get panicky when that happens. I fear danger or harm. I don't know what it's all about." Penny has had lifelong ambivalence about sexuality. The most important aspect of her relationships is friendship. Sex is at the bottom of her list. So sexual activity is always a problematic issue for her.

When there is sexual incompatibility around frequency of sex, some lesbians want to solve it by opening up the possibility of nonmonogamy. The sexually frustrated woman wants to resolve the issue by having affairs, yet keeping the one relationship primary. This solution acknowledges the deep emotional attachment women feel for each other and the desire to preserve it while having their sexual needs met elsewhere. Unfortunately, this proposal is usually not well received. Instead, it raises another issue: commitment. Many women feel that a committed partnership must be monogamous. The conflict around this sexuality leads to a crisis in the entire relationship and often ends in complete separation.

The typical scenario of incompatible sexual drives can take a different twist when the incompatibility is due to the fact that women are similarly passive. When two women who have each learned to be sexually passive come together, another problem arises. Claire, 37, discloses that, for her, "conflicts about monogamy and nonmonogamy surfaced. And we both were passive or shy sexually, not taking the sexual initiative. And in other ways, too. I have trouble getting involved. The passivity interferes with getting started." When she felt sexual interest in a woman, Claire could not find in herself the assertiveness to move into that territory. With an equally nonassertive partner, nothing happens.

May

May, 30, discovered a more complex form of sexual incompatibility. Of her lover she says, "She was irresponsible and would wait to return my phone calls, so I had some trust issues. The open conflict was safe sex. She was not interested in playing safe as I was. The first time we had sex we didn't know we'd do it, and we were all involved, and we didn't play safe the first time. Later when we talked about it, she didn't want to use dental dams. I got upset. I have a male lover, and he is very sensitive about safety issues because he had a lover die of AIDS. So I got concerned about that. Then the issue came up again, and I did not like the way she brought up safe sex. She didn't say, 'Let's renegotiate.' But she would do this whiney, manipulative routine and said I was depriving her. I got angry, and I told her I felt she wasn't respecting what I needed. I was wound up about it. We stopped talking about the need for safe sex. We both had herpes, and she really didn't understand the seriousness of this disease. So I broke it off. I felt it wasn't clicking sexually. She was too passive and it didn't work for me."

Responsible practices around safe sex are important to everyone, but May was the only woman who mentioned explicit conflict on this issue. Since she is sexually active with bisexual men who may have homosexual contacts, she is potentially more at risk for contracting AIDS. Therefore she is consistently safe in all her sexual interactions. Safe sex negotiations become another arena for personality differences to surface about the level of personal accountability.

Priorities

Conflict about priorities is a reflection of different values about how to spend time and money; which relation-ships are important to develop; how to keep the house clean. Like heterosexuals, lesbians can find themselves living together before they discover these basic differences. For Naomi, 25, priorities were how to spend time. "I did not want to accompany her visit to her mother. I did not want to go to every single softball game. She didn't give me space to write." Nokomis, 28, found her arguments revolved around "If I wanted to do some-thing, she wanted to do something differ-ent." Never the housekeeper, Nokomis also had conflict with her lover over "when I don't clean up enough or at all." Living in this five-year relationship she adds, "These are not major fights. They're intense, but short."

Anita, 50, found that as two busy women the biggest problem is "prioritiz-ing time. My lover works, takes classes, and has separate activities with her friends. I would be content to spend extra time with the two of us. When I worked and went to school full-time, it was hard. We quit talking to each other. We were separated for three weeks and both rethought the investment of the relation-ship. We like our social life and saw the investment of the relationship was impor-tant enough to make it work."

Tina, 36, has found that conflicts differ with each woman and cover a range of issues. "Monogamy and nonmonogamy; frequency of sexual activity; levels of clean-liness for our shared spaces; quality time together, friendship loyalties, hating each other's friends; personal finances."

Josie, 58, found her 17-year relation-ship suffered constant problems. "We had arguments over laundry; she didn't sort. I needed more time to myself. She expected me to do certain activities that I didn't want to do and might not enjoy. I wanted sex, and then she didn't. We argued over money. I earned and she stayed at home. She was spending too much. But I made no objections, and then suddenly I would. Her kids were in financial difficulties, and she bailed them out."

Rudy

Rudy, 44, also found that various relationships created a range of problems. She attributes the cause to priorities, personality differences, values, and needs. "We had conflicts over sex. Just trying to work it out. Do you want to do it as often or not as often as the other person? I also had time conflicts. I tend to be a night person, and there aren't that many of us. My natural time is go to bed at 5 A.M. and get up at noon. I've had conflicts over money, though I'm easygoing about money as long as there's enough. Power struggles is probably the biggest conflict with women. I'm a funny kind of person. I have little desire to have any kind of control over what people do, but I don't want them to have control over what I do. I don't want to struggle over little stuff, but if something is important to me, I don't want someone telling me what to do or how to do it. Ninety-five percent of the time I don't care what we do. But every once in a while I get it in my head, and I get cranky if someone tries to stop me. Once we had a fight about who got up first to

leave someone's house. I'm so easy in some ways. Not because I'm a pushover but because I see the majority of things people get their shorts in a bundle over are so insignificant. That it's not worth making a 'to do' about. I've had conflict about animals. I've had many women say I'm too permissive with pets. My view of animals is that we share this space. What they want to do is fine with me as long as it doesn't infringe on what I want to do. I would never tell an animal it can't get on the furniture."

Star, bisexual, 48, has experienced two levels of conflict: one, her personality, the other her bisexual lifestyle. "I process too much. I like to keep things really clear. They think it's already worked out, and I need to talk longer. The bisexual movement is my career. My relationships are with lesbians, and many of them have never been with a man. Sometimes my passion for the movement and the amount of energy I put into it is a complaint for their desire for time."

Dependency

Women are conditioned to be dependent on men. When lesbians do not form intimate relationships with men, they can transfer these dependency needs to their relationships with women. Lesbians want to be with a woman who is self-sufficient. Women can be self-sufficient in one area and not in others. A woman may be independent regarding her work, but in an intimate relationship she may feel that the two should be totally devoted to each other and retreat from the world. When the world is hostile, as it often is to lesbians, the tendency to withdraw into one another is strengthened. Women who are more independent find this trend is a burden and source of conflict. LaQuita is always aware of cultivating her independence and says, "Sometimes I feel smothered by my partner. Due to her insecurity she would want to do more for me, but I don't want it. She needs to feel needed. I don't want to be dependent on her." For Cleo, 28, the trend toward dependency can take several forms. "There's a kind of dependency with money. They may want a joint checking account and no independent money. I don't go for that. Growth can be an issue of dependency, too. Some women don't want to change. I need stimulation and to learn. Couple-itis is another form. They want to be together constantly. They do not want to let me do things by myself. I need to have my own personal life and friends."

Peggy

Peggy, bisexual and 48, revealed that her unconventional personality and her desires for independence were the source of the termination of her relationships. "I am extremely independent, and I'm not monogamous. I know about myself that if I am sexually interested in someone, I'll explore it regardless of whether or not I have another lover. I always tell potential lovers this from the start. I don't want to live with a lover. I need excessive amounts of time alone, compared to everyone else I know. I have had successful relationships that have lasted years. But eventually, whether it was a man or a woman, they left me because they wanted a marriage. Every woman I was with went away saying that our situation was too free. She wanted to live with her lover in a marriage-type situation. She wanted monogamy. The men said the same thing. They saw me as too independent. I have no hard feelings about it. It was clear and honest. We wanted different things.

"Marriage is not for me. I see it as a patriarchal remnant of man's ownership of women. As such, there will always be an element in it of an attempt to control a woman. I have lived with a man and with a woman. I saw both situations as experiments in communal living. Unfortunately they saw it as some kind of marriage. The conflict became too great. I perceived them as trying to restrict and manipulate me. 'For the sake of the relationship' I was supposed to do things that I didn't want to do. I tried acquiescing, and it made me unhappy. This life is fleeting, and I must follow my own spirit. No one else hears my inner voice."

The issues of independence and interdependence are a constant challenge in the lives of bisexuals and lesbians who have been trained as women to expect to live in a dependent relationship.

Personality Differences

Lesbians and bisexuals can fall in love and not discover the other's true personality until they are already emotionally involved. When they eventually uncover personality dislikes, the clashes are problematic. Spring, 43, found that "I am more open, and she is very controlled and keeps her professional persona, so she is embarrassed by my familiarity. I get embarrassed by her remoteness." Cleo sees the conflicts as requiring modification of her own level of tolerance. "My partner wants much more of an emotional relationship than any I've experienced before. I expect more emotional needs to be met and so does she. It bothered me that my partner was so strong, too rigid in opinions. I've also had to adjust to her moodiness." Polly, 34, finds that her personality differences with her partner create conflict about "sex and money. We both assume defensive posturing. We argue about who gives more, who's going to do what. We're both jealous. We want different things. We have insecurities around whether it will last or not." These women are working on developing a relationship despite dissimilarities in personality. While these are sources of conflict, they are not sufficient causes to end the relationship.

Many lesbians and bisexual women find large women attractive. So when Devorah, 25, became involved with a woman, she expected that her lover would not make this an issue. Devorah spent her teenage years as an asexual woman because of her huge size. When she lost over 100 pounds, she decided to become sexually active. But she is still a big, tall woman. Though afraid to place herself in a vulnerable situation, she forced herself to take the risk. "One woman rejected me on a physical level. After we became lovers she said she wasn't physically attracted to me. She was the one who made a pass at me and initiated the relationship. She put herself on my lap in a hot tub and started kissing me. I thought I had broken through a barrier in terms of accepting my body, and I was very vulnerable. She felt other people were judging her because she was walking down the street with me and I'm so big. I fell in love with her and she did that. I lost feeling healthy in that relationship. The conflict was that she was shallow, looks-oriented. She did not think the relationship was in a place where she could hurt me. But she did." Devorah was devastated by this series of events. She thought that she had come to terms with her body and that her lover accepted her as she was. This rejection temporarily threw her back to her teenage self of alienation from her physical being. Conscious work at self-acceptance and continued effort to maintain a healthy body constitute her path to recovery from this rejection.

Molly, 35, had two unsuccessful relationships with women before she met and married her husband. She feels that she was not able to create what she wanted with a woman but attributes the cause entirely to personalities. "I initiated and broke up both relationships. I had a tendency to think, 'You've got great breasts, you must be a wonderful person!' One woman always held up my habit of marking up books. She hated that I lectured and patronized her. It made me realize our conflict styles were so different. She was four years younger, and my personality may have been overpowering. With my second lover, I had to take time to write. I worked full-time and I was devoted to karate. I gave up karate for her, and I pined. I felt I was parenting her. She had temper tantrums. I felt I was being made to pay for her rotten childhood. She expected mean treatment. She became emotionally abusive. I have a lot of bitterness about it. I told her I didn't have enough time for her." Emotional immaturity and lack of skills to manage a relationship led to termination of these unfulfilling connections for Molly.

Ryfka has never lived with a female partner. She likes this arrangement because "there are no big arguments. I don't like to fight, so I just don't fight. When you don't live with someone, it's a lot easier not to fight about things. I ended my longest relationship of eight years because I wasn't getting what I wanted from the relationship. I wanted things that she didn't want. Conflict with other women was more around my constant movement, my hyperactivity, my inability to relax." Like most lesbians, Ryfka minimizes the experience of conflict with her partners. When break-ups occur, it is without a major upheaval. Instead there is an amicable parting of the ways.

Some women listed a range of issues that amounted to differences in personality, values, and interests. When Phoebe, bisexual, 46, takes into consideration all of her relationships with women, she has a list of issues: "There were issues about how to be close, developing our individuality, and keeping an intact sense of self. There were arguments about time spent together or away from each other, communication struggles. There is a question of honesty and having different expectations of each other. It's hard allowing for differences in each other." Phoebe is caught up in the problems that can beset many woman-to-woman relationships. Because she is with another woman there is an expectation and even a demand of sameness. Up against this edge comes the urge for individuality and separation. This friction does not reach the same intensity with a man. His gender creates the assumption of difference and separation from the outset.

Rebecca, 25, unearthed a separate complex of issues with her lover. "We had boundary issues—problems of defining what is private from each other. The levels of commitment may be different. Sometimes there were monogamy issues. It was a problem not having our relationship acknowledged publicly. She kept the relationship a secret. I wanted there to be more public validation. With other women, there was a fear of combining love and sexuality. Women who cared about me could not be sexual. They were terrified of being sexual with me, but they were great emotional lovers."

Being "Out" as a Lesbian

Lesbians have a unique problem regarding their relationships—how public to be about the fact that they are lesbians.

Every lesbian has decisions to make about her public representation of herself. To whom should she disclose her sexual identity in a world where she can be discriminated against and even suffer physical assault? Where is it safe to be "out"? Lesbians carefully consider whether and how to tell their family members about their sexual identity. Usually the longer a woman has identified as a lesbian, the more she has disclosed this side of herself to family, friends, and co-workers. Women with differences of how "out" they are can form couples. If one is more comfortable with this public identity than the other, conflict can arise. Lesbians who have been public for a while feel more safe in the public sphere. Or, they are willing to risk any possible threat for the cost of maintaining their personal integrity. These lesbians want their partner to be as open as they are and sometimes they meet resistance. Alice, 33, found that her partner did not want to be completely out due to fear that her children would suffer discrimination. Younger lesbians more often suffer the problem of breaking the news to their parents. Kameko, 21, has problems with her lover: "We're playing the denial game. We're acting straight, and my partner is my 'roommate.' No one talks about it. I think it's very dysfunctional. But at the same time my family wants to include her in family gatherings. But since she's antisocial she'd rather not go."

Personal Problems

Lesbians readily acknowledged that their own personal problems or immatu-

rity created conflicts in relationships and eventual break-ups. Guadalupe looks at her first relationships as a time when she was learning about herself and how to communicate. "I had conflicts about stupid things when I was young. Emotional misunderstandings that came out like 'You didn't clean the litter box!' I came home with anger and let it out. One little comment could get me off. I hadn't addressed my own emotions, and I didn't know how to handle them. They came out in the form of anger. My mate couldn't figure out what was wrong with me. What went wrong in my relationship was my inability to look at myself and address my emotions. I failed to recognize what the good one was—that this person would have stayed with me to get through some things. That kind of thing happened in all but my present relationship. I'm changing out of love. I look at myself before I go looking at them. I start with me first, not my mate." Maybelle, 50, sees that her issues created problems for each of her lovers. "I'm jealous out of insecurity. I'm possessive. I wanted to do everything with my partner. They weren't like that. They would want time without me."

Most lesbians minimize the experience of conflict in their relationships. Yet anger and physical aggression can be critical problems in some lesbian relationships, but to a lesser extent than in relationships with men. Heterosexual relationships are more likely to be violent than lesbian ones. Women are conditioned to be passive, but some women explode in inappropriate and abusive ways. Twenty-two percent of lesbians and 5 percent of bisexuals stated that they were at one time physically battered by another woman with whom they had a relationship. Ten percent of lesbians and 7 percent of bisexuals admitted to battering their partners. Fifty-seven percent of lesbians and 20 percent of bisexuals stated that they suffered emotional battery from a woman. And 31 percent of lesbians and 11 percent of bisexuals did emotional battery to a woman.

LESBIAN POLITICS

While most heterosexuals think of the term *lesbian* as meaning a woman who wants sex with other women, for lesbians the term has a much wider definition. Many lesbians and bisexual women see their choice of women as love objects as a political position. Their lives as lesbians are not circumscribed solely by their relationship with a lover. For them, lesbianism is political in that it means taking a stand on social change. It is a personally lived ethic of raising the esteem of women by prizing them more than men. In a culture that devalues women, they choose to love women above men. Thirty percent of the lesbians therefore call themselves "androgynous feminist lesbians."

Political lesbians hold a set of social activist beliefs that are progressive and liberal. They live outside the mainstream culture by living with and loving women. They examine mainstream culture as outsiders in other ways, too. Lesbians organize themselves into activist groups and social clubs along the lines of their leftist political beliefs. While they may also be a part of broader, primarily heterosexual organizations, their lesbian groups see the world with a specifically female and feminist eye. For 26 percent of the lesbians, a connection with the earth and environmental concerns is uniquely bonded in their perception of their lesbianism. These women are activists in environmental campaigns, such as Greenpeace and the anti–nuclear power movement. Their lesbianism is part of their "eco-feminism."

Some lesbians see the development of their full womanly personalities as a radical response to the conformity impressed on heterosexual women. Twenty-six percent of the lesbians perceive themselves as strong, independent, and self-defined, and chose the label "amazon" to define themselves. Finally, women's spirituality was very important to 15 percent of the lesbians, who identified with a revival of pagan or earth-based spirituality. These women call themselves witches, and affirm the title as representative of the pre-Christian female shamans of Europe. They are claiming the archetypal right of women to be spiritually strong and to recognize the feminine in the divinity. These lesbians who have created roles for themselves as feminist, androgynous women, "green" lesbians, amazons, and witches are one aspect of the development of a lesbian identity that moves far beyond the culturally inspired gender roles. These evolving labels express values, beliefs, and styles of living that reflect an individualistic complexity joined to social concerns. They take lesbianism beyond the sexual realm to a generalized personal perception.

THE SEXUAL REVOLUTION

The sexual revolution for lesbians and bisexuals will only come when their relationships can be widely accepted on the same grounds as heterosexual relationships. Gay political activists have done a great deal to make the heterosexual public aware of their presence. Yet for the most part, if lesbians choose to be open about their relationships with one another, they still fear for their physical safety, the security of their jobs, and the possible loss of custody of their children. This situation makes it difficult for lesbians to meet one another unless they are friends of lesbians and bisexuals who disclose their identities. Their opportunities to interact are restricted until they discover the subculture of lesbian organizations.

Within their relationships, lesbians and bisexual women build on the skills that they have learned in their gender conditioning as women. They are mutually nurturing, emotionally available, openly communicative, and motivated to bond. Their sexual interactions are satisfying and orgasmic. When they create a household, they usually share the tasks of maintaining it. The negative aspect of their conditioning appears as the need for too much dependency, too much togetherness and its resultant isolation. A sexual revolution would not necessarily affect these broad issues.

After the sexual revolution, lesbians and bisexual women will continue to experience the same elements of companionship and sexuality that they do today. The difficulties of exploring intimacy and resolving conflicts will also remain. However, when their sexual orientation is seen by heterosexuals as but another human variation, they will have access to greater emotional support from their families and heterosexual friends. Their integration into the dominant culture will mean that less personal stress will be brought into their relationships with one another. Heterosexual couples, too, will profit when lesbians can openly share the relationship skills that they develop in woman-to-woman communications.

Lesbian and bisexual women form relationships with women on the basis of emotional intimacy, shared values, and companionship. They believe that there is an inherent equality in a relationship with a woman that does not occur in liaisons with men. Although sex is important, they, like their heterosexual counterparts, tend to minimize it as a less than central feature of their connection. Most lesbians and bisexual women refuse to play stereotyped sex roles with one another, and they share their household tasks. They tend to minimize their conflicts, but describe break-ups as due to a lack of shared values or personality struggles. Lesbians and bisexual women do not regard their sexual orientation as simply a desire to establish sexual relationships with women. Many of them define their sexual identity as a political act of placing women as the first priority in a world that ranks women as secondary to men.

chapter ten

CREATING A PERSONAL SEXUAL REVOLUTION

UNLEARNING OUR PAST

A woman's first awareness of sexuality happens in childhood. Early experiences set the tone of how she will think about her sexuality and her femaleness. Remembering and thinking about childhood messages around sexuality is important. Those messages are the ground of her sexual travels. If she is one of the few fortunate girls whose parents nurtured and honored her sexuality, she finds that she is secure and steady as she moves along her sexual trek. If she was severely injured by child sexual abuse, she needs to seek individual psychotherapy to heal herself and to continue on the journey.

Most girls were set on a sexual ground somewhere between these extremes. Thus, there are a number of messages they must discard before achieving a personal sexual transformation. Since these messages are still part of the woman's psyche, it takes conscious effort to alter them. The first set of messages has to do with what it means to be female. A woman needs to replace her negative associations of women as passive, controlled by men, and victims of the environment and instead reinforce the new outlook of women as autonomous, independent, and active creators of their lives.

The second set of messages is about female sexuality. Girls are taught not to look at bodies and that bodies are shameful. They learn that sexuality is secret, performed clandestinely, and never discussed. They are told that sex is wrong and that they are bad if they do anything sexual. Many girls have the strength of personality to set up their own countermessage, even as children. They decide that adults think it is wrong, but it is okay for themselves. These messages must be replaced with a love, respect, and honoring of one's body. A woman needs to experience a sense of joy that she inhabits a female body. She must learn to enjoy her size, her shape, and all the mysteries and changes of her hormonal cycle. A woman needs to replace the idea that sexuality is secret with the knowledge that it is healthy and essential to talk about her sexuality. She can learn from her women friends about sexual experiences that they have in common. And it is absolutely essential that she discuss sex with her lovers. Finally, a woman must replace the ideas that sex is immoral and that she is nasty if she does it, with the knowledge that sexual experiences are one of the great joys and mysteries of life. She needs to know that sexuality is an intense pleasure that she has a right to enjoy and that sexual sharing can be the most exquisite and amazing bond that can happen between two people.

In adolescence, young women learn another set of messages about their sexuality that they need to discard before they can joyously move on through their sexual trek. The teenager is carrying the childhood message that sex means sexual intercourse and that it is something that men do to women. Teenage women learn a mixed message that their sexuality is in service to men but that they can get something out of it. They believe that performing sexual intercourse is something they must do to become women. They mistakenly think that sexual intercourse is the

route to their orgasm. Teenagers also become aware that women can be sexual with one another. Unfortunately, the message they usually hear is that lesbianism is sick, immoral, and unnatural.

If the teenage woman is to move forward into a happy and guilt-free experience of her sexuality, she must examine and discard this harmful set of ideas. She needs to learn about her sexual response cycle and to understand that female sexuality is centered on the clitoris and not the vagina. She needs to learn how to produce her orgasm through masturbation. The teenager must come to understand that sexual intercourse is one of the sexual activities that she can enjoy, but that intercourse alone will probably not produce an orgasm.

As the adolescent begins to develop sexual affiliations with men, it is essential that she see herself as an active participant who can determine the course of the relationship. She needs to drop the concept that he is in charge and that she must service his sexual needs. She needs to learn how to develop a partnership that takes into consideration both his goals and her desires. When they begin sexual activity, she must make a conscious decision to participate after selecting birth control and agreeing to practice safe sex. She can also negotiate the extent of the sexual activity. She has all the options of outercourse. She and her partner can share fulfilling sex without engaging in intercourse.

Teenage girls must also come to terms with the homophobia that they have been taught. Lesbianism is but another form of sexuality that is as fulfilling to its participants as is heterosexuality. (In fact, lesbians report greater sexual satisfaction than do heterosexuals.) Teenage women need to become comfortable with their own sexual interest. They may be feeling the first stirrings of interest in other women. They need to know that moving in that direction may bring them more happiness than anything they might discover in heterosexual lands.

DISCOVERING OUR SELVES

When a woman sets forth toward the goal of creating a personal sexual revolution, she must learn to discard the negative and sexually repressive messages that she has heard throughout her life. It is difficult to abandon the familiar, however distasteful it is. She is leaving behind what she's been taught and is heading toward a new place of physical, mental, and emotional pleasure. Like pioneers who left the desert strewn with the nonessential possessions that weighed them down, she will need to abandon all the sexual habits that burden her. Her compass on her travels is her own body, intuition, emotions, and values. Her reactions to her experiences will tell her which ones to pursue and which ones to take as a lesson that does not bear repeating.

BECOMING AWARE OF THE BODY

Many women live in their bodies without really knowing them. They feel their bodies only when they are ill and in pain. In these circumstances, the body is a burden. Once health is regained, they return to their head and the place of watching their life experiences. Taking charge of creating a healthy body is one means to change this mental stance. Embracing a regular exercise program is essential. In exercise, the woman brings focus to her breathing, her perception of her physical balance, the strength or weakness of her limbs, and her sense of being invigorated or tired. Exercise forces a woman into her body. She knows what her body can do. She can play with pushing the edge of exertion or slowing down her pace. This play comes with being aware of the physical changes in the body and learning how to heighten a sensation or to diminish it. Sexual activity in its most thrilling form is exercise. All these elements of focus—breath, flexibility, strength, and stamina—come into play in the sexual exchange. A woman can learn to live in and through every square inch of her body so its entirety is a sensual, sexual organism.

A woman must have a complete awareness of her body and all the sensations it offers. When the body is exercised and in good health it is a pleasant, sexy place in which to reside. A woman exploring her sexual consciousness learns that by retreating into her head, the thinking processes, and away from her body, she is removing herself from understanding the feedback that her body offers. Full sexual expression is full sensual and physical residence in the body. The sexual woman cherishes all the nuances of physical information from her body—the odors and the slipperiness of her perspiration; the altered patterns of breathing that sponta-neously accompany her sexual build-up; the muscle tension that precedes the release of orgasm, and the relaxation that follows.

Knowing the Inner Experience of Sexual Arousal

Some women do not know when they are sexually aroused. If they are trained to passivity, they hold the false-hood that the presence of an available man is the essential ingredient to their sexual excitement. This places the source of their sexual fire outside themselves. These women are watching their partner for cues of sexual interest. They look to the outer world and not to the inner world for sexual signs. The right moment, the right setting, the proper mood are certainly important aspects of the context of the sexual interaction. But before these are attended to, the primary necessity for gratifying sexual activity is the woman's interest and early stage of arousal. The women in this study who engaged in sexuality solely for reasons of the man's pleasure all acknowledged that they were ultimately disappointed and felt used. This sexual sacrifice is an inju-rious sexual habit that women find they must leave behind as they wend their way to a fulfilled sexuality.

Living in the physicality of the body is essential to creating a good sex life. Annie is a woman who loves the sensuous-ness of her body. As an adolescent, she spent hours combing Florida beaches and reveling in the sensations of the sun on her skin, the slickness of her perspiration, and the exhaustion of a full day's activity in the semitropics. Her physical cycles are intensely involved in her erotic experi-ence. Here she describes what a sexual encounter feels like inside her body: "Sometimes it would seem as if I was in heat. I would have sex with a man and it would be out of this world. But if I had sex with him on another occasion, it could be totally unsatisfying. It would make a big difference if I was ready, if I was in this state of being in heat. It seemed cycli-cal. There wasn't anything different about the sex act; it was more of what was going on inside me. I think I'm in heat just before my menstruation. If that coincides with the full moon, look out!"

It is important for women to pay attention to their own particular phases of arousal. Some women are especially in tune with the lunar cycle. Internal sexy feelings and thoughts about sex may vary in intensity with hormonal cycles. Some women are especially interested in sex during menstruation, others feel increased desire while ovulating. Many people engage in sexual activity in the evening or night, but some women discover that they are more easily aroused in the morning with the new light of day and after a restful sleep. A good first step to understanding your sexual preferences is to start attend-ing to your own sexual cycle. Keep a note-book recording days of increased sexual interest or periods of less interest. Such a record can help plan for exciting sexual trysts when you know all the internal elements are working to make you active and enthusiastic in the sexual encounter.

Knowing the Clitoris and How It Gives Pleasure

It is amazing that women who obsess over smooth skin, good hair, pretty eyes, and any other body assets they can detect do not explore the wonders and beauty of their sexual organs. To truly be in the sexual body, a woman should examine with loving interest this physical location capable of producing exquisite pleasure. We live in a culture where nicknames of the vulva include such negative appellations as "stench trench," "tuna boat," and "oil pan." These are all labels that connote ugliness, dirt, and disgust. If a woman carries even the slightest attitude of revulsion toward her genitals, she will be unable to fully engage with a partner who loves and admires her sexuality. Negative attitudes about the appearance and smell of the vulva should be replaced by admiration and wonder at the beauty of this hidden jewel of the body. (Self-examination of the genitals is described in Chapter 4.)

Practicing masturbation is essential to understanding and experiencing how the clitoris must be stimulated to create orgasm. Here is another area where women need to eradicate from the recesses of their minds any established, societal admonitions such as "don't touch!" These thoughts need to be replaced with the willingness to enjoy, love, and derive sexual satisfaction from your body as only you can. Taking the time to masturbate is allowing yourself to experience exquisite self-pleasuring. It is when you are able to abandon both stress and obligations and are able to indulge in the quiet erotica of internal sensuous worlds. In masturbation a woman learns how her body functions optimally. She can bring this knowledge to her partners so that the sexual experience with them is free, open, and confident.

Psychological Self-Awareness

The journey of psychological awareness is an adventure of continual change and transformation. To know who you are and what you want as a sexual woman means to be always confronting this process of unfolding consciousness. As a teenager you will want different things than when you are middle-aged. Change happens as your goals and needs for a full life evolve. There is never a point of completion and resolution here. Rather, there is an openness to the novelty of the new you, familiar yet unknown, the pushing outward of your developing self.

Every woman has the prerogative to express herself sexually. Just as she has the right to express her opinions, so she has the privilege to determine her sexual preferences. It is every woman's choice to contain her sexuality in celibacy, to express it with a particular partner of either gender, and to immerse herself in the kinds of activities that give her pleasure. A woman's sexual life is one that should be pursued out of a drive felt within herself.

Some women are so steeped in sexual passivity that they have no sense of what their body feels like when they are sexually aroused. They count on cues from the environment to assess their arousal. If their partner is turned on and initiates sexual activity, they will join him or her and get into it. They expect their partner to define when the moment is a sexual one. Some women are so crippled by repressive sexual training that it is difficult for them to acknowledge when they are sexually interested. These women need to first overcome any faulty training that sexual expression is wrong for women to do. Female sexuality is a natural and healthy emanation of the self. As free adults, women can determine the extent of their sexual activities. It is important to do this and exorcise from the mind the guilty recriminations from parents that "nice girls don't." Responsible sexuality brings a deserved and exquisite joy to a woman.

When women open themselves up to their bodies, they learn to know and enjoy the sensations of feeling sexy. These can be a range of feelings. There can be a change in the perceptions from the skin, an erection in the nipples, spontaneous tensing of the vaginal walls, increased vaginal secretions, weak feelings in the legs or knees, an increase in perspiration, sensations in the clitoris. These physical sensations can be accompanied by sexual fantasies or memory recall, or plans for the next sexual encounter. Women should learn recognition of all of these sensations as a delicious banquet of their sexual bodies. Each feeling brings its own form of pleasure as well as anticipation.

FEELINGS OF SEXUAL ATTRACTION

There is a mystery in the experience of being sexually attracted to someone, but this mystery can be unfolded. Sexual attraction is often an instantaneous experience when a heterosexual woman feels an attraction to a man. Occasionally, there is a slow progression into attraction as friendship deepens. In either case, the attraction is not questioned. The heterosexual woman's problem is in calculating how to create the personal connection that will lead to a sexual exchange.

The mystery of sexual attraction is more problematic when the desired one is a woman. Some women are able to conceal these attractions from themselves for years. They simply close the door to a new form of sexuality that is ajar before them. It is disconcerting and strange to think that one could be sexually attracted to someone and not know it. Yet many women say that they have experienced this with other women. When an automatic repression of sensations of attraction to women occurs, it seems impossible to challenge it. Most women are reared to disavow attractions to women as the "wrong" sort of liaisons, and it takes courage to face inward and understand that their desire for women is both normal and natural. Most lesbians and bisexual women have had to develop this boldness. A woman must cross these mental barriers before she can take the next step and approach the woman of her interest.

SEXUAL VALUES

As young girls, most women are given one directive about sexual values: "Wait until you are married." This offers no advice to the woman who is determined to experience the mystery of partnered sexuality before the nuptials. More enlightened or realistic parents may advise: "Use birth control." And now, with the presence of AIDS, a lethal sexually transmitted disease, some women are told: "Always use a condom." Each of these sets of advice is an example of a sexual value. Values are an individual matter. Each woman needs to determine what are the conditions that must be present for her to have an enjoyable and safe sexual interlude with a partner.

The use of effective birth control and practicing safe sexual activities are essential values to creating a good sexual transaction. But there are more conditions that must be considered. Most women find that casual sex or one-night stands are ultimately not sexually rewarding. Men who engage in casual sex are often the least interested in her pleasure. As one 24-year-old man said, "One-night stands are a game. The goal is to win. And when the game is over, it's out of mind—except to brag to your buddies a couple of times." Women need to teach their sexual partners how to please them. This training is not part of the game of a one-night stand. Rarely does a man want to bother with this communication if the sexual interlude will only be one time.

So women discover that the sexual transaction must be with a partner who has an interest in communication about sexuality. Most specifically, he must have an interest in giving her pleasure. Beyond this, women vary as to their requirements for a sexual partner. Some women desire to explore sexual flings with men who are casual acquaintances. Others demand different levels of intimacy before they will feel safe moving into the sexual territory. A woman's level of confidence in approaching the sexual sphere can only be gained through practice and experience with sexual partners. It is developed through intuition, knowledge of the partner's personality, and the intensity of physical attraction.

After the conditions of responsible sex and the appropriate sexual partner are met, a woman must take into consideration the particular needs she has for the timing of the sexual event. Deciding to be sexual should be made in a sober frame of mind. Many women regret the periods of their lives when they were drunk or using drugs and thoughtlessly threw themselves into a sexual interaction. These moments were usually sexually unrewarding, hastily forgotten, self-alienating, and followed by embarrassing awakenings in the morning with a stranger. Women look back at these moments as misguided and lost periods of their lives.

It is best to engage in sex when rested and energized and when other responsibilities will not intrude in the form of worries. Some women find it exotic and exciting to do sex in the outdoors or in various rooms of a house. Others want the privacy and comfort of a bedroom and a good bed. While some women enjoy "quickies," most want the hour or more necessary for leisurely outercourse and extended intercourse or oral sex. Time to relax afterwards and for a prolonged parting are also considerations. When a woman determines what she needs in terms of these conditions, she is refining her sexual values. After a woman has defined her sexual values for herself, communicating these sexual values to her partner is the next move in creating a good sexual event.

LEARNING TO BE A SEXUAL PARTNER

Communicating Needs and Desires

Discussions of sexual values and needs should happen before the sexual interaction has begun and before passion has had the opportunity to rise. Sharing one's sexual values and needs is also a way to determine how concerned the prospective partner will be about meeting those needs. It is another way to evaluate the partner before initiating sexual contact.

A woman often finds herself tongue-tied when asked what she desires. Her partner may be interested and open, willing to cooperate with a woman's needs. He or she asks the woman to tell him or her what pleasure she would like. Sometimes the woman finds herself looking at her lover speechless. She knows what she would like, she hopes it will

happen, but she cannot say the words. The rule of silence around sexuality is so strong that even when she is in an intimate situation, she is unable to talk. The only thing to do is to blurt out something. It may be tactless. It may be even crude, but it is the beginning of sexual expression. Women sometimes find themselves searching for the perfect phrase, unable to find a "ladylike" way to talk about sexuality. There is no ladylike way to discuss sexuality. "Ladies" are not sexual. Therefore, just say whatever you like with a spirit of play and affection.

Many women feel vulnerable when they begin to talk about sex. It is odd that talking about sex makes women feel more vulnerable than doing it. Women need to free their voices and learn to speak about sexual interests and activities well before they begin sexual activities with a partner. The deep cultural conditioning about silencing sexual talk must be turned around by each woman in her own personal sexual revolution. It is no longer safe to be sexual in an unconscious and submissive manner. If a woman wants to maintain her health, she must learn to talk about sexuality.

Women need to communicate their sexual values to their partners. This seems easy and simple enough. But women are not yet doing this. Few young women discuss pregnancy control methods with their male partners. If they did and were responsible, there would not be an epidemic of teenage pregnancies. Women are now at the greatest risk for contracting AIDS and many other sexually transmitted diseases because they do not insist that their male partners wear condoms. This is a serious problem. Diseases like chlamydia can make a woman infertile. Herpes can be a lifelong, recurring, and painful disease that can make her an undesirable sex partner when partners are afraid she will transmit it to them. If women are not clearly expressing and demanding their basic sexual values, it is unlikely that they are taking the lead in all the other aspects of the sexual exchange that they need to define. Women need to take the initiative to create the sexual experiences they desire.

Instead of approaching sexual activities from a place of feeling their internal arousal and sexual attraction, some women engage in sexual relations to appease or to please their partners. This is a bad idea. Sexual activity should always be associated with internal interest. Engaging in sexual activity when one is not aroused or interested can change the woman's sexual experience in a very detrimental way. Women who are highly sexually satisfied see themselves as an active participant in the sexual exchange. They are part of the sexual conversation.

This way of being sexual takes practice and assertiveness. It is best pursued as a steady course of complete involvement with the partner. It is a wayward pitfall to engage in disinterested sex. This sort of sexual experience is ultimately a personal loss of the woman's sexual balance. It casts a shadow of alienation over the sexual energy of the woman's self. Women who find themselves engaging in sexual activities for any reason other than their own interest should stop and talk to

their partner about what conditions must be present to awaken their true sexual interest. If these prerequisites cannot be created at the moment, it is best to find another activity and to save the sexual activity for the moment when the woman's interest is there.

It is best never to involve yourself in sexual activities solely out of a need to appease your partner. To engage in sex only because your partner is interested is to alienate yourself from your own sexual energy. It is ultimately a tourniquet on your sexuality. You will associate your sexual life with a passive acquiescence instead of a passionate reach for engagement.

Listening to Your Partner's Messages

When you begin to talk about sexuality with a prospective partner, you can think about the situation as interviewing him or her for the position of lover. This means that when you find some information that concerns you, you have the option to end the opportunity for a sexual interaction to happen. You can gauge his reaction to the type of birth control you are using. You should also find out if he refuses to wear a condom. When these discussions are carried on well in advance of sexual contact, it becomes easier to disengage. Women give up on these demands when they are already undressed, aroused, and ready to move into a more intimate involvement. It is difficult to change direction in the middle of sexual activities when conflicts about sexual values surface. Many women simply concede and hope for the best. When you know that your partner shares your attitudes, the sexual interaction is more likely to proceed along your erotic agenda.

Talking about sexuality with a prospective partner does not have to be treated like an ordeal. In a time when phone sex is one form of safe sex, many people are enjoying the erotic stimulation that can happen in talking about sexuality. When you talk about sexuality and elicit someone's sexual history, you can also find out what is sexual exciting to your partner, what turns him or her on. Ask about previous sexual partners and favorite sexual activities. How does he or she like to touch and kiss a woman? Does the person enjoy intercourse and in what positions? Does she enjoy cunnilingus? Does he want fellatio?

Talk about sexual health. Ask your partner if he or she has had any sexually transmitted diseases and how they were medically treated. If your partner does admit to having had diseases, it may mean that he or she was irresponsible. It could be a red flag for problems. It is best to take a step back from the feelings of passion and find out how the person handled this health problem. It is better to discuss this before any sex. If you don't, you may later regret the sexual encounter when your doctor tells you that you have an STD. Ask your prospective partner, How did (s)he contract the illness? Were they not practicing safe sex? How long ago did this happen? Ask how having these diseases affected him or her and how

(s)he protects himself from disease now. Has (s)he ever transmitted a disease to a partner? What happened after (s)he found out? How has (s)he changed the sexual practices to be sure this does not happen again? On the other hand, if you are the one who has an STD that is still contagious, like herpes, you owe it to your partner to reveal this and to talk about how to keep sex safe for both of you. If you and the person can talk about these issues in a forthright and trustworthy manner, you can be reassured that your sexual health will be maintained.

These interactions can give you a sense of how interested the partner is in you and consequently how interested in your pleasure. If you begin a string of questions and he or she does not ask you for your answers to the same items, it may be that (s)he will not be interested in anything else about you, including your sexual satisfaction. This means that you must be open to answering any questions that you might ask and any more intimate questions that the partner might pose. It is a time to shed all embarrassment about your sexual history. It is important to acknowledge that you and every future partner have been on a sexual journey. That trek has had its high points and its lows, its mistakes and its lessons. Frank acceptance of your own story and the willingness to hear the other's is the attitude that must underlie your stance as an open listener. If your partner is unwilling to talk about her or his sexual history, you can expect that this closure to you will extend into the sexual arena. Someone who is open and willing to share his/her experiences will carry this attitude into making the sexual interlude equally shared. For example, ask about what birth control your partner prefers to use. If a man says, "That is the woman's problem," start giving him points for being sexist. Make clear that you are concerned about safe sex and that condoms are imperative. Note whether his reaction is matter-of-fact or if he is angry or irritated by this demand. Your potential partner's emotional reactions can set the tenor for the sexual tryst. His or her responses will be a sign to you that you are going to have a joyous, cooperative sexual play or that he or she is inconsiderate and using you only as a sex object.

When you move the discussion to specific sexual activities, it is good to have a sense of how experienced your partner is. Ask how many sexual partners (s)he has had and of what gender. Do not assume that anyone is heterosexual. Some people are afraid to talk about their bisexuality. But if you have established a nonjudgmental attitude, you may unearth a deeper level of the other's sexual life.

If you want a sense of the person's sexual values, ask "What was your best sexual exchange? Who was your best lover? Why? What was it that made this person the best? How did that relationship end?" Be willing to answer these questions yourself. These descriptions provide a context for what is necessary for a good sexual experience. If, for example, you need a relationship to feel secure enough to be sexually free, you may not find it a good match to be with someone whose best scenario is an affair.

The personal revolution means that a woman must set aside any false mental guilt about being sexually experienced, or inexperienced for that matter. Women fear that they will be judged promiscuous, labelled as "sluts," "easy," or lacking judgment if they have been sexually active with a number of partners. A woman may especially feel awkward about a gender role reversal if she has had more partners than her new prospective lover. Self-acceptance as a woman who has made her sexual choices is an essential foothold for these discussions. It is not necessary to give all the details of one's sexual history. But when one moves into the specific talk about sexual activities, it can be assumed one knows what feels good from having experienced it.

Practicing the Art of Sexual Exchange

Being sexual with a partner is an art that can only be developed with practice and interest. The list of sexual activities—outercourse, positions for intercourse, and massage techniques—can be learned easily enough. It takes time, knowing one's partner, and communicating changing sexual needs to become more comfortable with one another. Once this comfort level is attained, the couple can be more experimental. Tell one another your sexual fantasies. Find a catalogue of sex toys to look at and purchase one. Read erotica to each other. Watch erotic videos and talk about whether they are arousing and why. Read sex manuals. Be open to new ideas about how to share your sexuality.

CONTINUOUSLY TRANSFORMING YOUR SEXUALITY

Whatever your age, whatever your sexual orientation, whatever your past experiences, your sexuality is a creative mystery that is ever ready to change. How can you identify the mystery of your sexuality within yourself? Think of the physical sensations and the feelings you have when you gasp in awe at a beautiful sunset, when you are touched by the smiling innocence of a child's trusting face, when you are carried away by some beautiful music. Something spontaneous rises up in you to meet these experiences given to you by the world. The wonder and joy you feel is all yours; it reflects something of your nature.

So it is with your sexuality. It is an expression of your unique nature. It arises in you and brings a sense of pleasure and joy. Your sexuality comes from within you, not from the external world. You carry within yourself the ability to enhance your sexuality. Your sexuality is an expression of your life energy.

You can shape and revitalize your sexuality, just as you can determine other aspects of your life such as your career, your living space, and favorite hobbies and entertainment. Whether you are masturbating, practicing your sexual activities with a partner, or both, you have the ability to create more pleasure, more satisfaction, and more peace with your sexual self. The basis for creating this change is by claiming the awareness that it is both possible and important to grow sexually. Know that your sexual growth in physical pleasure is your right. Your body is capable of giving you exquisite pleasure once you are open to the reality of it.

RESEARCH INFORMATION

This book is the result of 13 years of systematic research with 213 women in Northern California. I interviewed the women in private using a structured interview of 150 questions. The length of the interview varied from 15 minutes to eight hours. The lengthier interviews were conducted in several sessions. The shortest interview was with a Fatima, a 25-year-old virgin from the Middle East who had no history of sex play, had never masturbated, and had never dated. Consequently, she had little to say. Longer interviews were with older women who shared many experiences and analyses of their sex lives, like Barbara, Sanura, Ryfka, Cheryl Jean, and Leah.

The interviews were confidential. All the names used here are aliases. I gave women from minority groups names that are identifiable as names from a particular ethnic group. For example, Kameko and Lily are Asian-American; Leotie and Nokomis are Native American; Sanura and Lakeisha are African-American; Ryfka, Mitzi, and Barbara are Jewish; Conception and Carmen are Latinas; Star and Aloha are Hawaiian. Names also fit the popular names for each age group.

It is impossible to find a sample of people to participate in sex research who reflect an average distribution of the population. The average woman in America would refuse to participate in sex research. The women who participated in this study are representative of sexually open women who want to discuss sexuality. While most of the interviews were conducted in Sacramento, California, many of the women had emigrated from other states as well as other regions of California. States that are represented are

Alaska, Connecticut, Florida, Hawaii, Idaho, Illinois, Iowa, Missouri, Montana, New Jersey, New York, Nevada, North Carolina, Oregon, South Dakota, Texas, Utah, Virginia, Washington, and Wisconsin. In addition, some women originated in Canada, Chile, Iran, Mexico, and Singapore.

I found women to interview by using a networking technique. I began with some students and friends. I asked women at every social function I attended, and I asked interviewees if they could recommend anyone who might be willing to be interviewed. Although I asked women over the age of 60 to be interviewed, all declined. The age range of the women is 18 to 58. I specifically sought women of color, and 15% are minority women. In addition, 29% of the women are lesbians, and 21% are bisexual. Most sex researchers do not work with these groups, so it noteworthy that these women are represented here.

The women who contributed to this book are primarily white, nonreligious, middle-class, politically liberal, and educated. The demographics of the groups are as follows:

Ethnicity: 85% Caucasian, 6% African-American, 3% Latina, 2% Native American; 2% Asian-American; 2% Hawaiian.

Religion: none 40%, Catholic 12%, Protestant 9%, Jewish 9%, pagan 30%.

Political affiliation: none 27%, Democrat 43%, Republican 8%, socialist 2%, feminist 20%.

Occupation: professional 35%, white collar 22%, student 29%, blue collar 5%, self-employed 7%, unemployed 2%.

Education: The range of schooling was from sixth grade to completion of a Ph.D. The average education was completion of a B.A.

As found in the text and appendix, most of the results are summarized in percentages, averages, and ranges. Many analyses of variance (ANOVAs) were run on combinations of variables. The significant differences are reported in the text. Most of the analyses showed no differences across sexual orientation, age, and ethnicity.

Using a phenomenological approach, narratives were examined for themes and repetitions of events. In this way the structure of the analyses evolved. What is noteworthy is the similarity of experiences of women across ethnic boundaries, across age groups, and across sexual orientation. The background of sexual repression appears to be universal, and the experience of surfacing to reclaim the sexual self is also one that crosses all these differences. There is no event or experience that is unique to any group of women.

PARTICIPANTS IN RESEARCH

Name	Ethnic Background	Age	Is a mother?	Orientation
Abigail	Caucasian	36	no	lesbian
Adrianne	Caucasian	34	yes	bisexual
Alana	Caucasian	44	no	lesbian
Alexa	Caucasian	33	no	bisexual
Alice	Caucasian	33	yes	lesbian
Alizon	Caucasian	31	yes	bisexual
Aloha	Hawaiian American	37	no	heterosexual
Amanda	Caucasian	24	no	heterosexual
Amber	Caucasian	37	no	bisexual
Amelia	Caucasian	24	yes	bisexual
Amity	Caucasian	18	no	bisexual
Amy	Caucasian	25	no	bisexual
Angela	Caucasian	24	no	heterosexual
Anita	Caucasian	50	yes	lesbian
Annie	Caucasian	42	no	heterosexual
Artemis	Caucasian	53	no	heterosexual
Ashley	Caucasian	29	no	heterosexual
Barbara	Jewish	51	yes	heterosexual
Bea	Caucasian	43	yes	heterosexual
Bernice	Caucasian	46	no	bisexual
Beth	Caucasian	38	no	heterosexual
Betty	Caucasian	22	no	heterosexual

Name	Ethnic Background	Age	Is a mother?	Orientation
Beverly	Caucasian	47	yes	heterosexual
Bianca	Caucasian	20	no	bisexual
Blythe	Caucasian	34	no	heterosexual
Bobbie	Caucasian	43	yes	heterosexual
Bonnie	Caucasian	52	yes	heterosexual
Brandy	Caucasian	24	no	bisexual
Brandy	Caucasian	26	no	heterosexual
Brenda	Caucasian	36	no	lesbian
Brittany	Caucasian	20	yes	heterosexual
Camille	Caucasian	40	yes	heterosexual
Candy	Caucasian	34	yes	heterosexual
Carla	Caucasian	24	no	heterosexual
Carmen	Chicana	42	yes	heterosexual
Carol Ann	Caucasian	43	yes	heterosexual
Carolyn	Caucasian	29	no	bisexual
Cath	Caucasian	45	no	lesbian
Catherine	Caucasian	43	yes	bisexual
Celeste	Caucasian	30	yes	lesbian
Charlene	Caucasian	48	yes	heterosexual
Cheryl Jean	Caucasian	42	yes	heterosexual
Chloe	Caucasian	22	no	heterosexual
Cindy	Caucasian	21	no	heterosexual
Claire	Caucasian	37	no	bisexual
Claudia	Caucasian	40	yes	heterosexual
Cleo	Caucasian	28	no	lesbian
Colleen	Caucasian	34	no	lesbian
Conception	Chicana	28	no	lesbian
Concha	Chicana	19	no	heterosexual
Crystal	Caucasian	20	no	heterosexual
Cynthia	Caucasian	21	no	heterosexual
Dale	Caucasian	21	no	heterosexual
Danielle	Caucasian	42	no	lesbian
Daphne	Caucasian	29	no	bisexual
Dawn	Caucasian	22	no	heterosexual
Delphine	Caucasian	35	no	lesbian
Denise	Caucasian	39	yes	bisexual
Devorah	Jewish	25	no	bisexual
Dixie	Caucasian	50	yes	lesbian
Donna	Caucasian	46	yes	heterosexual
Doris	Caucasian	50	yes	heterosexual
Edie	Caucasian	36	no	heterosexual
Eileen	Caucasian	30	no	heterosexual
Elaine	Caucasian	45	no	bisexual

Name	Ethnic Background	Age	Is a mother?	Orientation
Elizabeth	Caucasian	58	no	lesbian
Ella	Caucasian	25	no	lesbian
Ellen	Caucasian	57	yes	bisexual
Emily	Caucasian	32	yes	heterosexual
Erica	Caucasian	38	yes	heterosexual
Eve	Caucasian	33	no	lesbian
Evie	Caucasian	21	no	heterosexual
Faith	Caucasian	28	no	bisexual
Fatima	Iranian American	23	no	heterosexual
Fawn	Caucasian	22	no	heterosexual
Faye	Caucasian	23	no	heterosexual
Fran	Caucasian	42	yes	heterosexual
Gayle	Caucasian	25	no	heterosexual
Georgia	Caucasian	31	no	bisexual
Gina	Caucasian	38	yes	lesbian
Ginger	Caucasian	33	no	lesbian
Giselle	Caucasian	44	yes	bisexual
Glenda	Caucasian	37	yes	heterosexual
Gloria	Caucasian	44	yes	heterosexual
Glynis	Caucasian	37	yes	heterosexual
Guadalupe	Chicana	29	no	lesbian
Harmony	Caucasian	28	no	lesbian
Heather	Caucasian	26	no	bisexual
Heidi	Caucasian	30	no	heterosexual
Helen	Caucasian	38	no	lesbian
Holly	Caucasian	33	no	heterosexual
Hope	Caucasian	40	yes	heterosexual
Hoshi	Japanese American	37	yes	heterosexual
Ivy	Caucasian	27	no	bisexual
Jade	Caucasian	22	no	bisexual
Jane	Caucasian	55	no	lesbian
Janelle	Caucasian	30	yes	heterosexual
Janet	Caucasian	43	yes	heterosexual
Jennifer	Caucasian	21	no	heterosexual
Jessica	Caucasian	38	no	lesbian
Jill	Caucasian	39	no	heterosexual
Jo Marie	Caucasian	37	no	lesbian
Jody	Caucasian	25	no	bisexual
Jolene	Caucasian	40	no	lesbian
Josie	Caucasian	58	no	lesbian
Joy	Caucasian	33	no	heterosexual
Julia	Caucasian	38	no	heterosexual
Julie	Caucasian	58	yes	heterosexual

Name	Ethnic Background	Age	Is a mother?	Orientation
June	Caucasian	28	no	bisexual
Justine	Caucasian	24	no	heterosexual
Kameko	Japanese American	21	no	lesbian
Kara	Caucasian	34	yes	bisexual
Karen	Caucasian	28	yes	heterosexual
Kate	Caucasian	31	no	heterosexual
Kelly	Caucasian	35	yes	lesbian
Kenya	African American	25	no	heterosexual
Kim	Caucasian	37	no	heterosexual
Kirsten	Caucasian	24	no	heterosexual
Koren	Caucasian	28	no	heterosexual
Kristie	Caucasian	23	no	heterosexual
Kyoko	Japanese American	36	no	heterosexual
Lakeisha	Black/Chicana	32	no	lesbian
LaQuita	African American	29	yes	lesbian
Larissa	Caucasian	31	no	lesbian
Laura	Caucasian	35	no	heterosexual
Leah	Jewish	45	no	bisexual
Leanna	Caucasian	20	no	heterosexual
Leanne	Caucasian	41	yes	bisexual
Lelah	Iranian	22	no	heterosexual
Leotie	Native American	40	yes	lesbian
Leslie	Caucasian	23	no	heterosexual
Leza	Caucasian	24	no	heterosexual
Lily	Japanese American	20	no	heterosexual
Linda	Caucasian	41	no	heterosexual
Lindsay	Caucasian	22	no	lesbian
Lucy	Caucasian	30	no	lesbian
Lynette	Caucasian	21	no	heterosexual
Maggie	Caucasian	35	no	lesbian
Mandy	Caucasian	29	no	bisexual
Marcia	Caucasian	49	no	bisexual
Margot	Caucasian	29	no	heterosexual
Margret	Caucasian	43	no	bisexual
Marion	Caucasian	57	no	lesbian
Marla	Caucasian	44	no	heterosexual
Martha	Caucasian	42	yes	heterosexual
Mary	Caucasian	23	no	heterosexual
Maureen	Caucasian	38	yes	heterosexual
May	Caucasian	30	no	bisexual
Maybelle	Caucasian	50	yes	lesbian
Melanie	Caucasian	34	no	heterosexual
Melissa	Caucasian	27	no	lesbian

Name	Ethnic Background	Age	Is a mother?	Orientation
Merry	Caucasian	37	no	lesbian
Minette	Caucasian	38	yes	lesbian
Mitzi	Jewish	32	no	heterosexual
Molly	Caucasian	35	no	bisexual
Nadia	Caucasian	38	yes	heterosexual
Nancy	Caucasian	34	yes	lesbian
Naomi	Caucasian	25	no	lesbian
Nicole	Caucasian	42	yes	heterosexual
Nokomis	Native American	28	no	lesbian
Olivia	Caucasian	30	no	lesbian
Paige	Caucasian	48	no	heterosexual
Pam	Caucasian	31	yes	heterosexual
Patricia	Caucasian	37	yes	bisexual
Paula	Caucasian	41	yes	heterosexual
Peggy	Caucasian	48	no	bisexual
Penny	Caucasian	49	no	lesbian
Phoebe	Caucasian	46	yes	bisexual
Phyllis	Caucasian	35	yes	lesbian
Piper	Caucasian	22	no	heterosexual
Polly	Caucasian	34	no	lesbian
Rachel	Jewish	35	yes	bisexual
Reanna	Caucasian	30	no	bisexual
Rebecca	Jewish	25	no	bisexual
Reed	Caucasian	27	no	lesbian
Rene	Caucasian	39	no	lesbian
Rita	Caucasian	48	yes	lesbian
Robin	Caucasian	33	no	heterosexual
Rochelle	Caucasian	26	no	bisexual
Rosalie	Caucasian	46	no	lesbian
Roseann	Caucasian	22	no	heterosexual
Roselle	Caucasian	32	no	lesbain
Rosie	Caucasian	38	yes	heterosexual
Rudy	Caucasian	44	no	lesbian
Ruth	Jewish	25	no	lesbian
Ryfka	Jewish	47	no	lesbian
Sandy	Caucasian	41	no	lesbian
Sanura	African American/Caucasian	31	no	heterosexual
Sara	Caucasian	30	no	lesbian
Shaniqua	African American	24	no	heterosexual
Shannon	Caucasian	29	no	heterosexual
Sharisse	Caucasian	23	no	heterosexual
Sharon	Caucasian	34	yes	heterosexual
Shawna	Caucasian	36	yes	heterosexual

Name	Ethnic Background	Age	Is a mother?	Orientation
Shelley	Caucasian	34	yes	heterosexual
Skye	Caucasian	35	no	bisexual
Spring	Caucasian	43	yes	lesbian
Star	Hawaiian American	48	yes	bisexual
Susie	Caucasian	33	no	heterosexual
Tamika	Japanese American	29	no	heterosexual
Taneisha	African American	23	no	heterosexual
Tina	Caucasian	36	no	lesbian
Toni	Caucasian	50	no	bisexual
Trina	Caucasian	24	no	heterosexual
Trudy	Caucasian	49	yes	heterosexual
Tsuruko	Japanese Amercian	33	no	heterosexual
Vanessa	Caucasian	21	no	heterosexual
Vicki	Caucasian	35	no	heterosexual
Violet	Caucasian	37	yes	heterosexual
Virginia	Caucasian	35	yes	lesbian
Wendy	Caucasian	37	no	heterosexual
Willa	Caucasian	37	yes	lesbian
Yvette	Caucasian	25	no	heterosexual

STATISTICS

CHAPTER 1 CHILDHOOD

Number of women   213

Issue	All women
Never looked at the bodies of other children	29%
Explored the bodies of other children when they were younger than eight years old	71%
Studied the bodies of both girls and boys	44%
Looked at other girls only	11%
Looked at boys only	16%

Heterosexuals, bisexuals, and lesbians were equally as likely to explore both boys and girls as children.

Parents did not punish for looking at other children	17%
Parents told them looking at bodies was wrong	64%
Parents said nothing, but they got the idea it was wrong	19%

Issue	All women
Age learned about sexual intercourse	age 7: 24%
	age 10: 64%
	age 14: 90%
	age 15 to 18: 10%
Average age learned about sexual intercourse	10
Mother explained the fact of sexual intercourse	14%
Range of the ages of girls when parent told about intercourse	4 to 13
Average age when were girls told	7
First learned about sexual intercourse from classes in school	6%
Average age for girls in school sexual education classes	11
Learned about sexual intercourse from other children	80%
Learned about sexual intercourse from reading pornography	4%
Average age for reading pornography	$10^{1}/_{2}$
Range of ages for reading pornography	8 to 13

CHAPTER 2 ADOLESCENCE: PROGRESSING WITHOUT A MAP

Issue	All women
By age 16 said that they had changed their attitude about sexual intercourse	47%
By age 20 said that they had changed their attitude about sexual intercourse	88%
Changed their attitude about sexual intercourse between the ages of 20 and 40	12%
By age 20 had a more positive attitude about intercourse	88%
By age 13 had voluntarily experienced intercourse	7%
By age 16 had voluntarily experienced intercourse	40%
By age 20 had voluntarily experienced intercourse	92%

There is a significant difference of age at first intercourse among the age groups of women. Women in the age group of 18 to 25 experienced first intercourse on the average at the age of 16. For the age group of 26 to 35 it was age 17. And for the group of women over age 35 it was 18 years. There is a significant difference between the youngest group and the oldest group. The historical trend in recent years is toward an earlier age at first intercourse.

Average age learned about lesbianism	14

CHAPTER 3 ADULTHOOD: WHO WE BECOME

Issue	Heterosexuals	Lesbians	Bisexuals
Number of women	108	61	44
Was a tomboy	60%	93%	20%
Was once exclusively heterosexual	82%	80%	65%
Never exclusively heterosexual	18%	20%	35%
Chose to be heterosexual	43%	21%	26%
Did not choose to be heterosexual	57%	73%	74%
Innately heterosexual	61%	0	0
Had been married	60%	39%	46%
Confused about their sexual orientation	13%	0	0
Labelled self bisexual	0	49%	100%
Chose to be bisexual	—	76%	67%
Did not chose to be bisexual	—	24%	33%
Age labelled self bisexual	—	23	25
Innately bisexual	26%	30%	82%
Do not believe in innate traits			10%
Sexual fantasies about both men and women	44%	33%	100%
Chose to be lesbian	—	70%	—
Did not choose to be lesbian	—	30%	—
Innately lesbian	0	68%	0
Experienced sexual attraction to a female	51%	100%	100%
Average age of sexual attraction to a female	21	17	18

Issue	Heterosexuals	Lesbians	Bisexuals
Range of ages of sexual attraction to a female		6 to 39 years	5 to 40 years
Labelled self lesbian	none	100%	30%
Average age labelled self lesbian		28 years	25 years
Range of age labelled self lesbian		18 to 47 years	18 to 40 years
Range of length of time as a lesbian		1 month to 46 years	1 to 20 20 years
Average time as a lesbian		11 years	6 years
Average age labelled self bisexual		28 years	25 years
Range of age at labelling self bisexual		10 to 33 years	11 to 40 years
Length of time as a bisexual		3.5 years	8 years
Range of time labelled self bisexual		one month to 12 years	two weeks to 37 years
Had sex with a woman	10%	100%	100%
Average age of first sex with a woman	19	20	20
Range of age of first sex with a woman	8 to 40 years	5 to 47 years	7 to 50 years
Had sex with a man	98%	87%	100%
Average age of first sex with a man	17 years	18 years	17 years

CHAPTER 4 MASTURBATION: THE COMFORT ZONE

Issue	All women
Discovered masturbation before the age of 10	40%
Discovered masturbation after the age of 13	50%
Discovered masturbation during the teenage years	28%
Discovered masturbation after the age of 20	20%
Began to masturbate after their first experience of sexual intercourse	24%
Say that they never masturbate	age 18 to 25: 24% age 26 to 35: 15% age 36 to 58: 7%
Average times of masturbation per month	age 18 to 25: 4.2 age 26 to 35: 5.5 age 36 to 58: 7.7

Women over the age of 35 masturbate more often than women aged 18 to 25. This is a significant difference.

CHAPTER 5 SEX WITH MEN

Issue	Heterosexuals	Lesbians	Bisexuals
Never had sex with a man	2%	13%	0
Average number of male sex partners	Overall: 16 age 18–25: 16 age 26–35: 20 age 35+: 25	15	27
Range of number of male sex partners	1 to 300 age 18–25: 0 to 30 age 26–35: 2 to 200 age 35+: 1 to 300	1 to 75 one woman, 200; one woman, 500	1 to 100

Issue	Heterosexuals	Lesbians	Bisexuals
Never orgasmic with a man	overall: 7% age18–25: 16% age 26–35: n=1 age 35+: n=3	33%	7%
Percent of times orgasmic, considering all sexual contacts	53% age 18–25: 42% age 26–35: 60% age 35+: 56%	32%	51%
Range of percent of times orgasmic	0 to 100%	0 to 100%	0 to 100%
Are you sexually satisfied with men? *Yes.*	47%	22%	30%
Are you sexually satisfied with men? *At times.*	40%	39%	55%
Are you sexually satisfied with men? *No.*	8%	39%	16%
Percent of satisfaction considering all sexual contacts	63%	31%	60%
Range of percent of satisfaction	0 to 100%	0 to 98%	0 to 100%

Lesbians are significantly less sexually satisfied with men than both heterosexual women and bisexuals.

Is sexually passive	8%	18%	10%
Is sexually active	30%	22%	37%
Is both sexually active and passive	62%	60%	52%

CHAPTER 6 SEX WITH WOMEN

Issue	Lesbians	Bisexuals
Age labelled self lesbian	27	25
Range of age labelled self lesbian	12 to 40	18 to 40
Average length of time as a lesbian	11 years	6 years
Average range of time as a lesbian	6 months to 46	1 to 20 years
Range of age labelled self bisexual	10 to 33	11 to 40
Average length of time as a bisexual	3.5 years	8 years
Range of length of time as a bisexual	1 month to 12 years	2 weeks to 37 years
Average number of female partners	8	5
Range of the number of female partners	1 to 30; one woman, 100	1 to 50 one woman, 200
Never orgasmic with a female partner	one	none
Percent of orgasm considering all sexual contacts	75%	62%
Range of percent of orgasm considering all sexual contacts	1% to 100%	1% to100%
Are you sexually satisfied with women? *Yes.*	80%	72%
Are you sexually satisfied with women? *At times.*	17%	28%
Are you sexually satisfied with women? *No.*	one woman	none
Percent of sexual satisfaction considering all contacts	85%	77%
Range of percent of sexual satisfaction considering all contacts	5% to 100%	8% to 100%
Is sexually passive	one woman	6%
Is sexually active	28%	25%
Is both sexually active and passive	69%	69%

CHAPTER 7 MEN AND WOMEN AS SEXUAL PARTNERS

Issue	Lesbians	Bisexuals
Agree: sexually men are better lovers	0%	22%
Agree: sexually women are better lovers	55%	28%
Agree: women and men are equally good lovers	10%	39%
Agree: men are better emotionally	0%	17%
Agree: women are better emotionally	82%	64%
Agree: women and men are the same emotionally	18%	14%

CHAPTER 8 RELATIONSHIPS WITH MEN

Issue	Heterosexuals	Lesbians	Bisexuals
Had been married	60%	39%	46%
Had children	58%	28%	14%
Average number of relationships	overall: 8 age 18–25: 4 age 26–35: 9 age 35+: 9	5	6
Range of number of relationships	1 to 50	1 to 30	0 to 25

Heterosexual women age 18 to 25 had significantly fewer relationships than heterosexual women aged 26 to 35 and those over the age of 35.

Average length of sexual relationships	age 18–25: 2.5 years age 26–35: 8 years age 35+: 12 years	3 years	5 years
Range of length of sexual relationships	age 18-25: one month to 6 years age 26–35: 4.5 years to 12 years age 35+: 4 years to 27 years	1 month to 20 years	8 months to 16 years

Issue	Heterosexuals	Lesbians	Bisexuals

The average length of the relationship for younger heterosexual women is significantly different (shorter duration) from heterosexual women aged 26 to 35 and over 35.

Issue	Heterosexuals	Lesbians	Bisexuals
Practice serial monogamy	58%	47%	50%
Practice serial monogamy at times	40%	23%	38%

(This 38% of bisexuals state that they are nonmonogamous by nature, but would agree to monogamy when in a relationship.)

Issue	Heterosexuals	Lesbians	Bisexuals
Nonmonogamous	2%	30%	50%
Had affairs with men while in relationship with a man	40%	8%	50%
Had affairs with women while in a relationship with a man	0%	21%	50%
Relationship gave them what they wanted	44%	63%	43%
Relationship gave them what they wanted at times	53%	31%	55%
Relationships never gave them what they wanted	3%	6%	2%

Seventy-five percent of the heterosexual women did not mention sexual intimacy or sexual compatibility as essential to a relationship with a man.

Issue	Heterosexuals	Lesbians	Bisexuals
Play a traditional female role	30%	43%	35%
Play a traditional female role at times	26%	28%	28%
Never play a traditional female role	44%	30%	37%
Think of themselves as nontraditional with men	70%	58%	65%

Issue	Heterosexuals	Lesbians	Bisexuals
Does all female household chores	35%	——	——
He does all the housework	1.5%	——	——
She does all the housework	1.5%	——	——
Household work is equally shared	55%	——	——
He does more work than she	10%	——	——
Physically battered by a man	36%	22%	32%
She physically battered him	23%	8%	23%
Emotionally battered by a man	72%	52%	55%
She emotionally battered a man	40%	46%	30%
Victims of child sexual abuse	33%	42%	29%
Victims of rape	47%	43%	49%
Victims of attempted rape	48%	55%	7%

CHAPTER 9 RELATIONSHIPS WITH WOMEN

Issue	Lesbians	Bisexuals
Average number of sexual relationships	3	2
Range of number of relationships	1 to 9	1 to 7
Average length of sexual relationships	8 years	2 years
Range of length of sexual relationships	1 month to 20 years	1 month to 10 years
Practice serial monogamy	81%	50%
Practice serial monogamy at times	17%	50%

Issue	Lesbians	Bisexuals
Play a traditional feminine role	4%	3%
Play a traditional feminine role at times	12%	20%
Never play a traditional feminine role	85%	77%
Physically battered by a woman	22%	5%
She physically battered a woman	10%	7%
Emotionally battered by a woman	57%	20%
She emotionally battered a woman	31%	11%

INDEX